CW00797270

STEVE BUNCE

AROUND THE WORLD IN 80 FIGHTS

A LIFETIME'S JOURNEY TO THE HEART OF BOXING

HEADLINE

First published in 2024 by
HEADLINE PUBLISHING GROUP

1

Cataloguing in Publication Data is available from the British Library.

Hardback ISBN 978 1 0354 1398 0

Designed and typeset by EM&EN
Printed and bound in Great Britain by Clays Ltd, Elcograf S.p.A.

HEADLINE PUBLISHING GROUP
An Hachette UK Company
Carmelite House
50 Victoria Embankment
London EC4Y 0DZ

www.headline.co.uk
www.hachette.co.uk

For Jacqueline, my wife.

And for Dad.

And the men we lost along the way:
Mick Carney, Billy Webster, Dean Powell, Gary Mason,
Reg Gutteridge, Wally Bartleman, Keith Bunker, Phil Martin,
Bradley Stone, Jimmy Murphy, Micky May, Glyn Leach,
Len Woodhall, Roy Francis, Errol Christie, Ron Peck,
Oliver Harrison, Brendan Ingle, Alan Murray,
Mickey Mullins, Enzo Calzaghe, Tony Burns,
Akay Isola, Steve Hiser, Ken Buchanan
and Frankie Lucas.

CONTENTS

CONTENTS

CONTENTS

CONTENTS

FIRST BELL

Watching boxing from ringside is unforgettable and I have been watching boxing from ringside for over 40 years and in nearly 30 countries. There is no sport quite like it.

I have seen the greatest fighters from six decades in the ring. I saw George Foreman's last fight and Naseem Hamed when he was just 12. I have found the best fighters in private moments. I have sat with the broken and the brilliant, the richest and the poorest, the damaged and the saints. I have taken their testimony. It's all part of a shared journey. My personal tour of the world of boxing and 80 incredible stories from within, if you like.

I have been detained by armed security and sat with presidents. That sounds a bit grand, but one time it was the President of Yemen. And the other president, Donald Trump, was not yet 'the President'. He was just one of a thousand hustlers I have met on the road to the rings. And he was not even the best hustler.

Some of the journeys I have been on with fighters lasted for years and years: from the amateurs to a world title. Some are friends now for life. There are others who still ignore me because I picked against them in the paper before a fight. Fighters have a tremendous ability to absorb punishment, but often have the thinnest skin. It has not always been a love-in; I have been sued and had to sue. I have won and lost in the courts.

It is a business that sucks you in. When you are up that close every punch, moan and cry is loud. You can feel it, smell it and when the blood is flowing, you can touch it. I have had blood on dozens of shirts, my face, my writing hand and notepads over the years. It's like evidence of a mad addiction.

Since 1984, I have written for just about every British news-paper, magazines, appeared on radio, on a dozen television channels, made a thousand podcasts, penned a couple of books and contributed in some way to so many other outlets that I have forgotten most of their names. When I started, I would get paid as little as £10 for a report in a paper. I was in the industry 35 years before I had a business class flight to a fight. I was known as Steve Ready, Steve Royce, Frank Ward, Mark Hilton and James Reed in different national newspapers in the Nineties.

It's been a long journey to a lot of unknown rings in forgotten cities, outdoor markets, car parks, on beaches and down back alleys. It has also been a long journey to Madison Square Garden and the MGM in Las Vegas to witness the best and worst of nights. I have sat under the stars in Italy and Saudi Arabia and stood behind police lines at warehouses in London's lost boroughs.

Being in a dressing room with a beaten fighter is still humbling at any level. It's a sport of extremes. And the people running it, and those run by it, are extreme.

I have my seat at ringside as a professional journalist and before that I was in the same halls, leisure centres and gyms as a fan. It's a thin line and even now I still pay to watch amateur boxing. I can go from 90,000 at Wembley Stadium to a room above a pub in south London in seven days. I believe that making that journey between rings is essential; it's part of what I need to do.

This is the journey in 80 stories with the men and women from both sides of the ropes. Their glories and failures. Their deaths, their struggles and their desire to win. I have been lied to, threat-ened, sickened, shocked, hit with a handbag, marvelled at, cried with, humbled by and laughed with the boxers and their people on that journey. Here is a collection of those days and nights in the world's rings. It's my truth and I was at every event I write about.

1

JOHNNY GREAVES:
KING OF THE LOSERS

YORK HALL, BETHNAL GREEN, 2013

'Is that your bird in the white? She can't stop looking at me.'

Greavsey loved a snout. He is one of an old breed of fighting men.

Before and after every single fight, he would have a cigarette. He would have smoked in the 60 seconds between rounds if he could have. No need for water. There was a British champion from the Seventies called Pat McCormack, and he did have a puff between rounds.

In September 2013, it was the end for Johnny Greaves: snouter, fighter, father.

He was at York Hall in Bethnal Green, not far from where he lived, and where he had fought a lot. It was a Sunday afternoon show and it was, for the first time, all about Johnny.

It was his 100th fight and that was causing him some grief. That's why I knew he would be out the back, in the drizzle, in a doorway having a cigarette. Out the back at York Hall is strange: there is the old town hall, now a restaurant with a Michelin star and a hotel with rooms at about a grand each night. There is also a shabby block of flats on the other side. York Hall's back entrance is obscured by giant bins and an ambulance on fight night. There is never much of a delay watching fleeing rats. And that is where I found him that afternoon, his bandages loosely attached to his fists, his worn boots damp from the rain and Johnny in a philo-sophical mood.

Greaves had just turned 34, he had lost 96 of his previous 99 fights, but that afternoon he was booked to win. It's not fixed, but he was fighting another man with a similar record and, well, gentlemen are gentlemen in the boxing business, and there was no way Dan Carr was going to ruin the retirement fight of Johnny Greaves. That would be very bad behaviour.

'Fuck me, it's murder having to sell tickets,' Greaves told me between long, loving puffs. 'I know now why I never sold tickets. I've moved about 200 for this fight and I've got people calling me up all the time, driving me fucking mad.'

He shook his head, threw away a dead cigarette, nodded at somebody and cadged a fresh cigarette from a man called Ralph. He was fighting in about 15 minutes so was having a prolonged last cigarette before his final fight. It was ceremonial, close to a superstition with him.

'In my business, Steve, I get matched against all these unbeaten fighters, and they have all their loved ones there. They have to sell all the tickets and they have all the pressure: their girlfriend is there, their mum, their nan, the lot. I love that and I will tell you why.'

He moved back an inch in his doorway, took a long suck on the cigarette and continued. 'You see, it's simple: If they are all there, the kid will try like a nutter and then I know it is going to be an easy night. He will start swinging and I will be saying to him: "Is that your bird in the white? She can't stop looking at me. Good sort, her, mate." Now, the kid with all the fans will start throwing wild punches and I can avoid those easily. No problem. The problems start when the kid ignores me – then I gotta fight a little bit.'

It is, I admit, confusing to understand the way some fighters think. Greaves talks about making fights easy, but he had lost 96 times before getting in with Dan Carr. He had also met over 70 men who had never lost a fight. He had also been robbed a dozen or more times on shows where the opponent had sold hundreds of tickets. He never complained, just smiled and climbed out of the ring, stepping down from the lights at the Magna Centre, Rotherham, the Winter Gardens, Blackpool, or the Pyramids Centre, Portsmouth. No shower, in a car and home; possibly, no shower and in the bar.

Johnny was given a nudge and finally had to quit the sanctuary of the doorway and go and get his gloves on. It was nearly time.

The walk to the ring at the old East End venue was emotional that afternoon. Johnny Greaves got a standing ovation and Carr was booed – pantomime boos.

It was not much of a fight, but he did enough and got the nod after four rounds; he came close to being carried from the ring on the shoulders of his fans. It was Johnny's first win in 43 fights and three years of craft. Carr lost for the 43rd time in 47 fights; Carr won just once in his next 42 fights before leaving the ring four years later.

'It went to plan,' said Greaves from his now familiar plot outside the back door at York Hall. 'I was a bit disappointed that I never threw in an Ali shuffle but, to tell you the truth, it was hard because he (Carr) was trying to out-Greaves Johnny Greaves. That was a liberty.'

Greaves now works as the house-second on shows. That means he washes the gumshield and lifts the stool in and out of the ring. He picks up a few quid for being in the corner. He told me a few years after his last fight that he wanted to come back. He never did; there were rumours that he had made a few quid on the unlicensed circuit, which is where he started. He is still out the back on fight night at York Hall, holding court and smoking.

Johnny Greaves: *King of the Journeymen – 100 fights: four wins and 96 defeats. He fought four world champions and over a dozen British champions.*

2

AUDLEY HARRISON

— v —

MIKE MIDDLETON

WEMBLEY ARENA, LONDON, 2001

'Mom, it's getting a bit crazy over here.'

Warning: the story you are about to read is a five-star, ocean-going, fur-lined farce. It's ludicrous and comical – and true.

Johnny Bos made the match and that should tell you all that you need to know about the debut of Audley Harrison.

Bos, sadly, was not ringside at Wembley in his trademark white fur coat. The international matchmaker and fixer was already a recluse back in New York. Don't worry, there were enough panto-mime acts on a night at the end of a week of wonderful comedy. I'm not sure where to start.

The story so far: Audley Harrison won the super-heavyweight gold medal at the 2000 Sydney Olympics, the first gold won by a British boxer since 1968.

Harrison secured a £1 million deal to fight live on the BBC, Wembley was a sell-out and Big Aud was the boxing, talking, danc-ing, smiling, baby-head-kissing darling of the British public. What could go wrong?

It turns out, just about every single thing.

Harrison was determined to do it his way and that was a brave move. And a bit stupid, to tell the truth. He had a manager, Colin

McMillan, the former WBO featherweight champion and he had a promoter, Jess Harding, the pallet king of Potters Bar. But it was Harrison's show, and he was not afraid to tell people about the boxer revolution he was leading.

Mike Middleton was found as the opponent by Bos. It was Bos who had helped Mickey Duff build Frank Bruno. It was Bos who had famously talked about the requirements for any opponent that he found: 'A pulse, but not much of one.' Bruno removed toupees and false teeth from the men that Bos supplied. Bos chuckled at ringside; nobody found bodies like Bos.

Middleton worked in Florida at Walt Disney World. He was often an undercover agent, dressing as Mickey Mouse to trap thieves and other undesirables inside the Kingdom of Disney. It is hard to invent this stuff. So, Harrison fights a man in a Mickey Mouse costume. You can pick your headlines for that one. Harrison was fast undoing all the great publicity from Sydney; he was proving tetchy and distant with the media. There was an ugly impasse brewing.

Middleton arrived in London and what a lovely fella he was. Silly as a sack, but adorable. And then, Middleton was - ahem - 'kidnapped' from his hotel room. There was no sign of a struggle, thankfully. It was the week of the fight, and the big lump was gone. What a mystery.

Harrison, his promoter, manager and legal team of Jonathan Crystal and Robert Davis were left to solve the disappearance. They were kids in the boxing game back then. Davis is now one of the most powerful lawyers in the boxing business.

There were some clues. Middleton had called his mom - his spelling - the night of the vanishing and told her: 'Mom, it's getting a bit crazy over here.' It certainly was.

The fight, live on BBC television and in front of a capacity audience of over 8,000, was just days away and Middleton was gone. Slowly, the story began to emerge.

Middleton was being paid $5,000, but he would end up with less than $1,500 dollars after deductions and payments. However, the contract he had signed entitled him to a higher percentage of the television money. The tiny clause was traditionally marked with a giant X, meaning that it was not valid. However, McMillan and Harding had overlooked a small error and failed to cross out the box. When they realised their potentially costly error, they went to visit Middleton in his hotel room. It was not a threatening visit, but Mike was alone, it was late, it was a tiny, cheap hotel room and Harding is a considerable lump. And the lighting in those poxy two-bob hotels is always bad; Harding might have cast a giant shadow from the door. Harding is big enough to have been the door.

The purpose of the visit was to offer Middleton a new contract, one with the small box pertaining to the television rights crossed out – there was also an offer of an additional $500 dollars for his troubles. He never signed, they left, and he called his mom.

He made a couple of other calls and then he finally spoke to a man called Andy Ayling. Then, Mike Middleton, Gulf War veteran, Mickey Mouse detective and journeyman boxer from Florida, was – how shall I put this? – sort of 'kidnapped'.

'We sent a lovely car to his crap hotel near Wembley and then put him in a luxury hotel in Hertfordshire. We kidnapped him, basically,' said Ayling, who works for Frank Warren but was acting independently. Harrison and Warren had fallen out. It was said that Kellie Maloney was the one in the back of the limo, driving with Middleton away from Wembley, but he cannot remember being there.

'It's an outrage what they are trying to do to my fighter,' said Ayling, who had become Middleton's agent overnight. Ayling and Middleton had known each other for about ten hours.

A few nights later at Wembley, there was another tense standoff when Middleton, represented by his new mentor, Ayling, started to get ready to fight. Team Harrison had two other fighters preparing to fight, warming up in adjacent dressing rooms, and they were coming in cheap: Middleton was there and ready to honour his original contract, and he was now entitled to somewhere in the region of $65,000. He would become the highest paid six-round journeyman in history.

There were desperate scenes in one of the dressing rooms just minutes before the first bell. I was invited in as an official observer to the very final negotiations. I could hear heavyweight journeymen, Gary Williams and Derek McCafferty warming up, both hopeful of a late, late call-up. If Williams or McCafferty had fought, Team Harrison would have been about $60,000 richer. However, Middleton was also getting ready, hitting pads and dreaming of $65,000; he knew that he had to walk to the ring to get his bumper purse and not be in breach of his contract. It was a fabulous game of chicken. Ayling, a representative from the British Boxing Board of Control and Harrison's trusted men got their heads together for a last whispering session. It was out of my earshot. The fight was salvaged, Middleton walked, Harrison the idol walked, the place went crazy and over eight million watched live boxing on the BBC on a Saturday night. That little double has not been repeated since then.

Harrison stopped Middleton in the opening round. Middleton went down swinging, defiant and smiling. It was a bad, comical and perfect debut; the rest of Big Aud's career would be the same. But never forget he could fight, and that gold was exceptional.

Audley Harrison: *There was the European title, a defeat in a world title fight and a lot of highs and lows in the career of Audley Harrison. The gold changed the course of British amateur boxing when it led to massive funding; that is a truly glorious legacy. Middleton got his $65,000. 'It was justice for our man,' said Ayling. It was certainly something. No charges were ever filed for the 'kidnapping' of Mike Middleton. When he died in 2019, Harrison led the praise. 'It was dramarama for real. Rest easy, Mike.'*

3

JANE COUCH:
TRAILBLAZER

THE CAT'S WHISKERS, STREATHAM, LONDON, 1998

There were tales of distinctly lively nights out in Blackpool . . .

Jane Couch had to prove that she was rougher, tougher and cruder than any other fighter. She did a decent job, to be fair.

Couch challenged the British Boxing Board of Control in 1998 and was given a licence to fight. The Board had a nightmare. The amateur boxing authorities in England had already decided in late 1996 to allow women and girls to compete from 1 October 1997. Meantime the Board built a case against women entering a boxing ring that would not have been out of place in 1860: according to them women were weak, they had periods, and they were pretty. It was poor. Couch triumphed at the industrial tribunal in April of that year, and by October she was in the ring.

Nobody should ever doubt that Couch was a pioneer, but she was in the Jane Couch business. She had to raise her profile first and not pull anybody with her. There were tales of distinctly lively nights out in Blackpool. They all helped establish Couch as a character, which she was.

She had fought nine times when she finally made her legal British debut one cold Wednesday night at the old Cat's Whiskers in Streatham. The main event that night was Peckham's Lester Jacobs and Jason Hart for the vacant WBF Pan European middleweight title. Jacobs won in the sixth. Couch was the real attraction though, and I'm sure she was paid more than the men. The place was packed to capacity, there were queues down the high street. I remember going in search of the promoter, Roy Cameron, who I think also had a second-hand car front. I found Roy in a room near the box office and the room was filled with people counting the takings. It was old-school that night in Streatham.

Couch had told the Board she had offers, good offers. She was alleging restraint of trade, and she was right. One offer was from American promoter, fixer and manager, Stan Hoffman, for $50,000. That was proper money in 1998. At that time, there were perhaps 800 male boxers, and it is doubtful more than 25 made that much money for a fight. Perhaps Kellie Maloney, then operating as Frank Maloney, who was the manager of Lennox Lewis, summed up the mood best.

'I'm against women's boxing, but I've got a few welterweights who could have a sex change for the money – for $50,000 I might even have a change.' Maloney was not against Couch, just shocked at the money she was being offered.

So, Wednesday night in south London and Couch, known as the Fleetwood Assassin, made her way to the ring to fight German teenager, Simona Lukic, who was known as Demona. The atmosphere was fantastic, people hanging off the walls, howling, drinking, shouting. Lukic looked like she had seen a ghost; the kid was petrified. Couch entered the ring like she was ready to fight a monster. Couch feared nobody, that should be her memory.

Poor Lukic had lost four times and won just once. Couch was fresh from losing a world title fight in Atlantic City. It was a horrible mismatch, and the crowd loved every second of it. It finished after 64 seconds of round two. History had been made. Lukic never fought again, she walked away for good. Couch was going nowhere; she was just starting.

Couch gets upset if she is reminded about her legal debut and the quality of Lukic. Couch, it is fair to say, is a bit angry that she missed the real money, the money in the fights now. She is critical of the modern fighters, convinced that the women she met and lost to were better. She got beaten by some great women like Lucia Rijker, Holly Holm and Anne Sophie Mathis. They could live in any era and so could Couch. The Rijker fight was at the Staples Centre in Los Angeles on the undercard of Lennox Lewis against Vitali Klitschko.

Make no mistake, Couch was a player and pioneer, but she would need two Sherpa guides to find Lauren Price in a ring. There is one thing that growing old in this business has taught me, and that is never to believe the fighters from your youth were better. Living in the past is a boxing sin. I should add that Price would need a sledgehammer to hurt Couch.

As a quick footnote, there is a woman called Sue Atkins (who is mentioned again in a later chapter), a gardener from Mitcham, and she is another pioneer. She never gets the credit. She formed the British Ladies Boxing Association in 1993; her first shows were hijacked by soft-porn magazines and a genuine dirty-mac brigade – I saw them, an outrageous gang of Benny Hill extras. She once showed up for a fight at a hotel near Watford and her German opponent was oiled and topless. That, my friend, is pioneer country: the real wild west of women's boxing.

Jane Couch: *After 39 fights, including 16 world title fights for belts from five different sanctioning bodies, it was time in 2007 for Couch to walk away. A year later, women's boxing would receive Olympic blessing. Then came the revolution. Couch is part of that. In 2024, Couch was inducted into the International Boxing Hall of Fame. She deserved it.*

DAVID HAYE
— v —
NIKOLAI VALUEV

WBA HEAVYWEIGHT TITLE: NUREMBURG, GERMANY, 2009

'Nobody cared about me, only about my size.'

The Beast from the East loved Agatha Christie novels, his ballerina wife and he hated violence.

On the night Nikolai Valuev lost his world heavyweight title to David Haye, he was just over seven feet tall, weighed close to 23 stone and had lost just once in 52 fights. Don King was involved with the promotion.

It is not certain that Valuev had ever had a normal life, a life away from being called a freak. He was placed in a sports academy in St Petersburg when he was 13; it was one of the last Soviet traditions. He was big, he was tall, he was there to be used. He played basketball and he was the Under-19 Soviet discus champion. A pot-bellied boxing trainer called Oleg Shalaev discovered the towering boy/man when he was 20. He had just a handful of fights and then he turned professional in the West. He made peanuts and they treated him like a performing ape at the start. He was a one-man touring attraction, the great hairy man-beast of the ring.

His granny claimed that her father was eight feet tall and an assassin. His parents were both under six foot. His father repaired radios, his mother cooked pancakes for her beloved little giant. His management called him the Russian Giant and then the Russian Bear. His boxing career had no path, and he was taken all over the world; he fought in six countries in his first ten fights. He was the boxing freak, part bear, part killer. He was said to have wrestled wild bears, slaughtered wild boar with his bare hands. The reality was that he was a gentle soul, preferring quiet nights in with a good Agatha Christie mystery. He was painted for violence but loved his Poirot.

He was with Kellie Maloney briefly, fighting at Battersea Town Hall. There were gasps as he walked out and biffed his way to an easy win. It was October 1996 and then six weeks later, he was out at York Hall. He was fighting normal men: Neil Kirkwood was a mere six-foot four and Darren Fearn a tiny six-foot one; they lasted about seven minutes combined. It was a success, but Valuev had baggage, men making demands. Maloney walked away. 'There were too many managers and people with a share in him – too many scary people, fuck that,' said Maloney, who now lives with a dozen different animals on a small farm in the Algarve. It was Maloney who gave Valuev the Beast from the East nickname.

In 2003, after 32 wins and no defeats, Valuev started to work with Kalle Sauerland, a young German promoter, who had a home in Wembley and had followed Spurs all over the country in a former life. 'I told him that the circus is over,' Kalle said. At the time, Valuev was in danger of joining Primo Carnera, an Italian giant from the Thirties who won the heavyweight world title with the help of mobsters, and the tragic literary creation, Toro Moreno, an abused heavyweight in Budd Schulberg's *The Harder They Fall*. The Beast from the East was a circus act.

'Nobody cared about me, only about my size,' Valuev told me. 'People always looked to see what I could do for them.'

Valuev won the heavyweight world title in 2005, lost it in 2007, won it back in 2008 and met Haye in 2009. The Haye fight was his 53rd. The World Boxing Association heavyweight title was the prize – the Klitschko brothers, Vitali and Wladimir, held the other three titles. Haye had withdrawn from a Wlad fight a few months earlier when 60,000 tickets had been sold and, the day he announced the Valuev fight, he was due to sign for a Vitali fight.

Haye called him slow, stupid and smelly to sell the fight and then praised him in private. 'He's more than just a clueless giant,' he said the night before their fight. 'Haye is another idiot in boxing,' countered Valuev.

In the days and hours before the fight, he looked so forlorn in Nuremburg, a man with deep troubles on his vast, hairy shoulders. Standing near the pair after the weigh-in it was hard to see how Haye could survive getting hit. That was easy; it turns out, he never got hit – not once. He performed a masterclass in survival and the Beast followed him like a slow shadow. If the Beast had connected, it would have been all over.

It was not a pleasant watch. 'Don't you dare go looking for the knockout,' Adam Booth told Haye at the end of each round. They had spent three months preparing and Booth had worn six-inch tall Spice Girl boots to simulate the height. Haye listened to Booth until the last round: 'In the end, as the final seconds faded, Haye wobbled the sad-faced Russian for the first time in his 53 fights and he looked a shot or two away from coming to rest in a 23 stone heap.' He stayed upright, Haye won on a majority decision, that is two judges to him, and one returned a drawn score.

Valuev left that ring on that night with his dignity. He never fought again and talked of opening a carvery in Nuremberg, his adopted home town. He liked to go off hunting for wild boar, armed with just a bow and his own thoughts. That is a fine way to exit the boxing game.

•

David Haye: *In 2011, Haye finally met a Klitschko and lost his world title to Wladimir. He tried to retire and just kept on unretiring. Adam Booth still looks after fighters and still has the crazy platform boots. Valuev is rarely sighted, which is odd considering that he is probably the same size now as a small caravan.*

5

AVTANDIL KHURTSIDZE: CHOCOLATE THIEF

LEICESTER, 2017

'I'm crazy Georgian man.'

Not all funny boxing stories are very funny. But this is one of them, and it is hard not to chuckle.

In April 2017, Tommy Langford, the British middleweight champion, was looking at the sport's best fighters and planning a million-dollar career.

Langford was matched that month in Leicester against a man who was an important part of a multi-billion-dollar criminal gang. Nobody knew at the time; poor Tommy never stood a chance.

On the night, Avtandil Khurtsidze walked through Langford, dropping him three times and stopping him in the fifth. An interim belt for the WBO was the prize. It was too easy. Back in New York, Khurtsidze's real boss, Razhden Shulaya, who was the *vor v zakone*, the thief-in-law, as they say in Russian criminal circles, was happy with his number-one enforcer.

Meanwhile, back in Leicester, Langford was nursing his bruises when Khurtsidze was confronted at ringside by Billy Joe Saunders, the full WBO champion at middleweight. It was the start of the fight's publicity, a nice pantomime interlude on a long night of domestic boxing.

Saunders was up for a scrap, but soon started laughing; Khurtsidze, you see, was tiny. He claimed to be five-foot six and he would have been if he had been in stiletto heels. He was closer to five-foot one and Saunders simply could not get agitated. I guess he looked different when he was doing his day job back in New York as an armed and dangerous man of menace for Shulaya's gang. The Tracksuit Man, as he was known, certainly had a face for threatening.

'I come break bones,' Khurtsidze promised when it was announced that he would fight Saunders for the full title on 8 July. The FBI had proof that he did indeed break bones, but with the help of a baseball bat.

'I'm crazy man. I'm crazy Georgian man. I'm crazy Russian man. I'm very beautiful man, man,' Khurtsidze said at ringside in Leicester.

'I just couldn't take him seriously,' Saunders said.

I was close to the exchange that night and Khurtsidze never took his eyes off Saunders. He was fixed on his prey, calm. He looked dangerous and fearless. His height never bothered me, it was clear he was nasty.

Khurtsidze had won 32 of his fights at that point; he would never fight again. He returned to New York and started to prepare for the Saunders fight. He also took control of a container or two of contraband cigarettes, 10,000 lbs of chocolate bars, ran a few errands, cracked a few skulls. The usual day-to-day jobs of a baseball-bat wielding criminal thug.

On 8 June, he was arrested with 32 other members of Shulaya's gang. His boxing life was over and he was looking at 20 years behind bars. Shulaya, incidentally, had been involved on the fringes with Nikolai Valuev ten years earlier.

The charges were complex and violent: robbery, hacking casino machines, theft of sea containers of chocolate, extortion, kidnap. Khurtsidze was Shulaya's personal enforcer, a very ugly man capable of immense violence. He was not the comic figure we loved at ringside.

Khurtsidze was attacked and stabbed in the face before he was sentenced to ten years in 2018. 'It's a very serious misunderstanding,' Khurtsidze said. I bet it was.

Avtandil Khurtsidze: *In June 2023, after his early release, Khurtsidze had a message for Saunders: 'Hey, Billy, I wait for you.' Saunders is still thinking about fighting. Langford had six more fights and vanished.*

6

LARRY HOLMES
— v —
BRIAN NIELSEN

IBO HEAVYWEIGHT TITLE: COPENHAGEN, DENMARK, 1997

'It's the money, ain't nothing but the money.'

Larry Holmes was back in his dressing room, smiling and shaking his head in the middle of his 32-member travelling entourage.

'They done robbed Larry again,' somebody said. Nobody laughed.

An hour earlier, the first bell of his 71st fight had tolled in a grand hall on the outskirts of Copenhagen. The capacity crowd had chanted his name out of respect. Just a few minutes earlier, they had sung the theme from *Monty Python's Life of Brian* in perfect English as their hero, Brian Neilsen, entered the arena and then the ring. If it was a big night for the Danish fighter, it was another night for the great Larry Holmes.

An 11-year-old girl stood in centre ring and sang the American anthem; Holmes looked on like a proud grandfather. He was old, 47 at the time, and a veteran of dozens and dozens of big fights. The long debate about his greatness had started.

The fight had a pattern; Larry covered up, standing mostly in a corner and Big Brian tried to find a way through for his punches. It was a decent fight. Holmes collapsed heavily onto his stool at the end of each round and his cornermen, as I said at the time, 'poured gallons of water over him. The canvas at his feet was sodden and heavy'. That is the detail you need.

During the last four rounds, Holmes barely moved from his soaking wet corner. The referee, Marty Deakin, told him to get out of the corner. Holmes stopped and clearly replied: 'Damn, that is where I do my work, give me a break.' He was right, even Deakin smiled.

Holmes was fighting strictly for the money. He was getting £310,000 for the fight. He even had a line in a song about his boxing philosophy: 'It's the money, ain't nothing but the money.' Holmes still toured with Marmalade, his band.

'I'm here because I'm overweight and old,' he said. 'That is why they picked me.' Nielsen was managed and promoted by a gentleman called Mogens Palle. He had the Danish boxing monopoly and had controlled boxing in Scandinavia for a long, long time. Big Brian had some big fights left in him.

In the end, Holmes gave Nielsen a good test. I scored it a draw, but then I had a soft spot for Holmes, who had been known as Black Cloud back in the Seventies when he was a sparring partner for Muhammad Ali.

At the final bell, Holmes never even bothered lifting his arms. He stood passive as the scores were read. One for him, one for Nielsen; Holmes then climbed through the ropes – the final score was from the Danish judge and obviously it was for Nielsen. Some eyebrows were raised. I followed Holmes as he left the ringside area.

The dressing room was not glum, it had been strictly business. Nielsen came in to thank Holmes. In 1980, Holmes, in tears, had done the same when he beat his idol, Muhammad Ali.

Some talked of appeals and Holmes mostly ignored them. He had been there before, and it had mattered back then. Larry at 47, carrying the weight, seasoned, wealthy and wise was not bothered by events on a Danish winter night.

And then Larry Holmes came up with a lovely line: 'Brian Nielsen can kiss me where the sun don't shine.' I was on the blower within minutes, copy sorted, pay-off a beauty. Thanks, Larry.

It was gone midnight when I left that place. We traipsed away, hopefully in the direction of Copenhagen on a snow-lit night, shivering, blowing out steam, shuffling mostly in silence like European refugees at the end of the Second World War. I never saw Black Cloud box again, but I did tour with him and Gerry Cooney a couple of times. Royalty on the road.

Larry Holmes: *In his last-ever fight in 2002, Holmes beat Butterbean, a man with a 70-inch waist. His first fight had been in 1973. He left the sport with 69 wins. Nielsen quit the ring in 2011, lost to Mike Tyson in 2001 and always looks on the bright side of life.*

7

GARY MASON:
A SPECIAL TEN GRAND

FUNERAL: LONDON, 2011

'It's for Michael [Watson], he needs the money more than me.'

'He would have loved this,' said Kellie Maloney.

We stood together, looking out at over a thousand people in All Saints Church in Carshalton. The streets outside were also packed. It was the funeral of Gary Mason, one of the best British boxers in the last 50 years to never fight for a world title.

Mason had been riding his bike and he was hit by a van at a dangerous junction early one morning. He died at the scene. Mason had bad eyes. It was his eyes that damned him in the end in the ring.

The funeral was filled with equal parts laughter and tears. I made my way to the raised pulpit for my celebration and one of his aunties collapsed two rows in front of me, fell off the bench, big drama, people fanning her and me getting the 'hurry up'. The great Lennox Lewis was in the row behind her, the place was hot. It was an easy job, a crowd in love with the man I was serenading. 'And then, there were the women . . .' They loved that bit.

The real story that day was one that had never been told. It was about Gary Mason's heart, not in the ring, but in life. I told it for the first time, but it was from 20 years earlier. It was from a dark, dark time in the old game. It was late September in 1991, Michael

Watson had been in a coma for a week or so. His fight with Chris Eubank had finished in the 12th round, Watson somehow had escaped with his life, Eubank was left drained. 'I thought I was going to die,' Eubank told me in 2023. Over 17 million watched it on ITV. It was front- and back-page news. In the middle of the storm, I met Mason. He wanted to talk to me. He cried.

Mason had been forced to quit the British ring because of retina damage. His last fight in Britain was in March of 1991 against Lennox Lewis. It was savage, Mason finished with a fully closed right eye, still swinging, still believing, still hoping. At the end of the sixth, Mason had lost all the vision in his right eye. His corner begged the referee to let him continue. He lasted just 44 more seconds; Lewis won in the seventh and Mason lost for the first time in 36 fights. Mason tried the pirate and dangerous circuit in the USA and then returned to London and started his post-fight life.

He tried a lot of things. He managed a white rapper from Stockwell. The British Eminem, he told me. He launched the arm-wrestling world championship. He drove a taxi. He did security shifts at a hospital. He worked, he always worked. He needed the money. He was involved with a drumming therapy group when he was killed.

Anyway, back to 1991 and the meeting in late September. Mason's last real fight had been just six months earlier. The dread that night after losing to Lewis was that the eye was badly damaged. He had already had surgery on the right eye. The injury was detected straightaway; his boxing career was over. And so was the dream.

Mason had friends at the Circus Tavern, and they organised a fundraiser for him. They raised ten grand, Mason left with ten grand that night, and that is why we had a late, late meeting. It was about his ten grand.

Mason wanted to give the money to Michael Watson. They had been friends; they had fought on the same bills. They shared the same boxing dreams. I arranged for Gary to come and see Mrs Watson, Michael's mother, with me at Barts, the hospital where the neurosurgeon, Peter Hamlyn, had performed his miracles to save Michael's life a few days earlier.

Mrs Watson had a room next to intensive care and always had a sister or two from the church with her. It was a heartbreaking scene: stepping into that small room was overpowering, an attack on the senses. It was utter devotion inside that temporary home of hope. Mason and I made our way there and it was late, but time in the intensive care unit is not measured the same way as it is in life; in the ICU, every second of life is sacred and days blur. I have been in too many with fighters.

It took about three seconds before people were crying. Then Gary produced a plastic shopping bag from somewhere. He placed the bag on the tiny bed. 'It's for Michael, he needs the money more than me,' he said. It was a piece of loving magic. It was all there, every penny. Gary Mason's ten grand. 'It was my security,' he had told me. He had never touched it, never. He was saving it for the darkest of days; instead, he gave it all to Michael Watson and that is the story I told at the funeral.

Before we left the hospital, we went in and saw Michael. He was connected to a dozen tubes, full six-pack, bare chest and looking so serene and happy. Mason sobbed, ducking his head, his tears falling on the blanket. The bandage on Watson's head had the deathless message, scrawled in black pen: No bone flap. That is about as real as the boxing business ever gets.

'You better not tell anybody about this,' Mason had said as we left Barts that night. 'I will if you die first,' I replied. I told the story from the pulpit to that captive audience and, according to *Boxing News*, 'the church roared with tear-coated laughter.' I will take that. I just cried.

•

Gary Mason: *His smile will never die. Lennox Lewis won his first world title a couple of years after beating Mason. He is now recognised as one of the best heavyweights in history. At Wembley that night, he had the fight of his life to beat Mason. That is testimony enough.*

8

DENNIS ANDRIES
— v —
AKIM TAFER

EUROPEAN CRUISERWEIGHT TITLE: MENTON, FRANCE, 1992

'I saw old age in the ring, and I did not like it . . .'

The Hackney Rock was on the French Riviera, and it was a boxing marriage made in heaven.

Dennis Andries was 38 when he travelled to France to fight Akim Tafer for the vacant European title. Andries had been in the boxing game for so long that his first title fights were over the 15-round distance. He had also won and lost the world light-heavyweight title three times. He would not go away.

He had travelled to Menton with Manny Steward, the man behind the Kronk gym in Detroit. The pair were odd souls, a strange fit.

At the time, Andries said he was 35, the record books said 38 and his previous manager said he was 40. 'It's just a number,' Andries told us one morning in Menton. Sure, but it was a very important number. It was bright and sunny on the Cote d'Azur that day. One or two of the boys even undid their ties. I do remember that there were very early drinks arranged once the sit-down with Steward and Andries was over. A ritual is a ritual, after all.

It was an old-fashioned travelling press pack. Neil Allen of the *Evening Standard* had his portable typewriter. The others had their suits and ties and preferences for French wines. And one or two had memories of fights in Monte Carlo, just down the road, and San Remo, just down the road the other way. We were a travelling pack of national newspaper writers that had not changed very much in 50 years. I had bought a terrible tweed jacket that belonged on the back of a door. It was an attempt to look like an ancient hack. I still had loads of hair – it was an odd mix. I was on duty for about three papers. It was a good earner.

Tafer was inexperienced but he was big, young and fresh. He knew enough to not get involved, just to box sensibly. Andries struggled at times. It was not much of a fight. One judge scored it a draw, which was generous to Andries.

'I saw old age in the ring, and I did not like it. It is time for Dennis to stop,' Steward told us after the fight. He never did, he fought 12 more times and won and lost the British cruiserweight title. He won the belt at 41 and lost his last fight at 43 and then he vanished.

Andries once told me his version of a boxing fable, a story that many believe is fake. It is not, it is mostly true. One morning at Heathrow, two boxers returned from big fights in America. Dennis had his world title belt in a plastic bag and Frank Bruno had his bruised face from his latest defeat hidden behind giant shades. Bruno was met and swamped, Andries slipped through, got on the tube and went home. A smile on his face and the belt in a bag on his lap.

'I wouldn't want that pressure, the pressure Frank has,' Andries said, and he was not bothered about going under the radar. 'I never worried about what the press said. I took all the criticism; I was never going to cry over a few words. No way.'

Meanwhile, in Menton, pre-cocktails were served in Neil's room; he had ordered a dozen tiny bottles of gin from the plane – miniatures, as they were called. It was an old trick by one of the oldest and finest trickers. There was a glorious view of the Mediterranean and the talk was of simple things like the boat passage to the Melbourne Olympics and the best house on the street outside the boxing stadium in Dublin to file copy from. There was only one public phone inside the stadium and Tom Cryan of the *Irish Independent*, known as the Squire, had been given exclusive use of that by the Pope. Hey, that's the story. So, if you needed to file copy, you went outside and knocked on doors. How mad is that? And it's true – I did it after an England v Ireland clash. Sweet and innocent days.

Dennis Andries: *He turned 70 in late 2023 and he is still invisible, no book, no fanfare. He had a foot in both camps: the black and white days of silent fights and the excesses of the Nineties when British boxing changed. I went back to Menton the year after the Andries fight. I went with a woman I had just met, and it was a disaster: we ran out of money, got ripped off in a fish restaurant, threatened with arrest and we were kicked out of the hotel. We then spent 28 years married – Menton is a special place on my boxing map.*

9

RUBIN CARTER:
THE HURRICANE

TORONTO, 1997

'I started to get a bad feeling. It was like a lynching.'

The Hurricane kept me waiting two days in a frozen Toronto. He had met me briefly on the first morning; I was shattered from the red-eye flight from Las Vegas. He sat me down with a couple of his friends. It was a vetting breakfast and I thought I had failed. A day went by in silence. I knew he was capable of vanishing, but on the second morning the call came. It was on, he gave me directions.

I was off to interview Rubin 'Hurricane' Carter. I think it was the first one-to-one interview he had done with a British boxing writer since his release from a prison cell. I could be wrong, but that is my spiel. He had been discharged 12 years earlier and had then moved to Toronto. The team of friends and lawyers behind his release were there, and he was very protective of his story. I had been trying to set the interview up for many years, maybe four.

He had been convicted in 1967 of triple murder and sentenced to three life terms in prison. He was innocent; Bob Dylan in his song 'Hurricane' told us that. And so did Carter. Eventually, the world agreed, and he was made a fully free man in February 1988 when a judge in New Jersey formally dismissed all charges against Carter. That was real freedom.

At the time of the conviction, he was a leading contender for the middleweight championship of the world. Carter could fight and was vicious. He finished his boxing career with 27 wins in 40 fights. He lost a fight for the middleweight world title, won and lost against some of the very best. He left behind a lot of images.

His story is known from the movie, a few books and the glorious Dylan tune. This is a short version: in June 1966, Carter was driving around in his white Dodge car and at some point, after midnight, three people were gunned down in the Lafayette Bar and Grill in Paterson, New Jersey. Carter was driving between another club and his house when the killings happened. He was out driving again and was stopped at 3 a.m. by the police. And that is it really; he was fitted up for the murder, arrested, his career finished, and he went to trial and was sentenced. His freedom was a long way off.

I got to his house. He invited me in and made me tea. The Hurricane drank English breakfast tea. I placed my worn Dictaphone on the table, and we started. It was the early afternoon, but the dark was close. Carter spoke. We went straight back to that night. It was three in the morning; the police pulled him over.

'They told us to follow them, we did. There were several cars and the police were leaning out through the windows with shotguns pointing at us. We drove to a bar I'd never even heard of. They told us to get out. There were a lot of people crying and standing around. I started to get a bad feeling. It was like a lynching.' He was held for 17 hours, then released. It was only the start; the police wanted Carter for the killings, and they would get him.

He had one more fight and then he was arrested. A second world title fight was scrapped forever. He never stood a chance.

'When I was convicted, they wanted the electric chair. The amazing thing is that the white jury came back guilty with a recommendation for mercy. If they just for one second believed that I killed those people, they would have burnt me to death.'

That is what we work for, quotes ('nanny goats', as we once said) like that from somebody like the Hurricane. Thank you.

In prison, Carter was known as the Lord. He was private, revered, worshipped. Untouchable. In 1999, I met one of his prison counsellors, a man called Brian Raditz. It was Raditz who fought for the release of an enigmatic and violent boxer called Tony Ayala Jr. Raditz, who was head of psychology at the Trenton State Prison, told me that Ayala Jr and Carter would often talk in the corridor outside his office. Ayala Jr was damaged, very damaged. Carter recognised the man's pain and tried to help him.

The meeting with Carter was epic. He talked, my Dictaphone whirred, and I filled two tapes. At one point, we had a break, and he took me upstairs to show me the sauna he had built next to his bedroom. It overlooked the city; it was Carter's silent retreat. He was a gentle soul on that afternoon he gave me; he was small, quiet, just turned 60 that day. But prison had slowed the Lord; the man feared and hated by the police in the Sixties in New Jersey was regal in his decline.

He told me that he would not even fly over New Jersey.

The bald Carter from his fearsome fighting days had mellowed. He had ridden white horses, built a safe retreat and was fighting for the wrongfully convicted. He had some hair. In the ring he had blitzed the great Emile Griffith in just one round. He had beaten Jimmy Ellis on points in the main event at Madison Square Garden in 1964 – four years later, Ellis won the vacant heavyweight championship of the world. Muhammad Ali was banned at the time, and Carter-victim Ellis took the title; Carter was in prison, his living hell barely a year old when Ellis ruled the world. It is hard to invent.

I wrote that at the end the streetlights were the only thing keeping the room from total darkness. In that blackness, the shadow moved, and Carter got up and left me sitting there. I saw the great Hurricane, once again, bald headed and vicious, one of the boxing icons, leave that room. That was the man I had gone in search of. He was back, but he was gone. Five minutes of silence later, I let myself out and walked the few miles in a daze back to my hotel. I never saw Rubin 'Hurricane' Carter again.

Rubin 'Hurricane' Carter: *The Hurricane remains an enigma in the boxing world. He died in 2014, the same year as Ellis. The Tony Ayala Jr story is even more disturbing. In early January 2024, I went with Lennox Lewis to look for Carter's house in Toronto. No chance, but it was a good way to stay out of that savage cold.*

10

JULIO CESAR CHAVEZ
— v —
GREG HAUGEN

AZTECA STADIUM, MEXICO CITY, 1993

'They covered me in shit and piss on the way to the ring . . .'

The record books will show that 132,247 souls paid to watch a massacre at the Azteca Stadium on a cool February night. The cheapest ticket was only a few pesos more than the cheapest beer sold in the highest seat in this glorious cauldron. It is a living monster of a stadium, seemingly moving with the life of thousands that work and possibly even live there.

It was the Julio Cesar Chavez show, and he was there to butcher an American.

Dogs patrolled the moat, their handlers had machine guns, fat-bellied cops ruled backstage and against a backdrop of ugly intimidation, poor Greg Haugen was fighting for his very life. That is what it felt like. It was heavy.

It had been a fun week in Mexico City. I had been sent to the opening of a new sewage farm by the *Daily Telegraph*, and filed a column on then-Prince Charles, the guest at the opening. I had also sat next to Don King in an Argentinian steak house, watched him eat the cow equivalent of a light-flyweight and listened to his mind talking. He had left behind his scholarly guidebooks, packed with his quotes and philosophy. It was all pure King that night.

He taught me one of boxing's most important and sacred maxims. He had his beefy arm across my shoulder, and he fixed me with his blurred eyes and told me: 'In boxing, you don't get what you deserve, you get what you negotiate.' That is the truth, the whole truth.

To King, the signing of the contract was just the start of the negotiations. I sat with him 29 years later in Miami and he was still able to spin the truth his way. On that occasion, he was praising Frank Warren's fighter, Daniel Dubois, who would beat King's man, Trevor Bryan. It would soon emerge that there was a problem with payment for the fight. King was not paying; it took Warren a long time to get the money King owed Dubois for the fight that week in Miami. 'That's business,' King always said. There was some legal action after that fight. It seems the more praise, the more chance there is of a bit of trickeration.

I went to the Azteca early that afternoon in 1993. The place is big, the concourses were packed with people selling food, beer, hats, flags and just about every trinket known. I paid my pesos to pose next to a cardboard cut-out of Julio Cesar Chavez. I looked about 15, trying hard for a cool look in a lightweight jacket and the final days of my old and trusted mop of hair. I nearly pulled it off, trust me.

The terraces, when empty, slope away to the highest point. It is hazy up there and a long, long hike. It's a beast. A few hours later, the place was packed, and the fights had started. King had stacked the card with truly great fighters: Michael Nunn, Azumah Nelson, Terry Norris, Felix Trinidad and Gerald McClellan. They were all sideshow attractions for the Chavez fight.

Chavez, unbeaten that night in 84 fights and the pride of Mexico, was defending his WBC light-welterweight title against Haugen. A few days earlier, Haugen insisted that Chavez's record was compiled in fights against 'Mexican taxi drivers'. Well, that was never going to end well. Haugen knew why he was hired.

My seat was in the centre of the front row of the press section, but that meant I had to stand to see the action on the far side of the ring. It was a small price to pay. Behind me, the giants of American boxing writing were banging away on their very early versions of laptops. Some still had typewriters, others had phones. There was a massive turnout of scribes.

Nunn stopped Irish Danny Morgan in just 179 seconds. It was expected. The moment it was called off, I heard Pat Putnam, the iconic *Sports Illustrated* writer, start to file his copy. I was blown away by a beautiful intro: 'Over 132,000 showed up for Irish Danny Morgan's wake in Mexico on Saturday night . . .' I looked round. He was kidding. Funny man. It was later discovered that Putnam's impressive Korean war record was not totally true. Hey, the man could write on deadline and under pressure like an angel. What is a small fib about fighting and winning wars when you are the deadline king of the press row?

It was at about this point that the seat next to me was finally filled. I had sensed a commotion a few minutes earlier, but there was no way of seeing. And then the commotion was sitting down. The commotion was Mr T. Yep, that Mr T. He was wearing gold chains, lots of gold chains and speedo trunks and flipflops. That was it, that was Mr T's Azteca clobber. He shook my hand; he shook a thousand hands that night as pilgrim after pilgrim came over for a chat. In 2004 at the Mike Tyson and Danny Williams fight in Louisville, I was drinking coffee with Gene Kilroy and Rahman Ali, Muhammad's brother, when Mr T joined us. Bless him, he pretended to remember me from our night at the Azteca. Top man.

With Morgan's wake filed, Mr T in his kecks, it was time for the show. The lights went down, the howls went up and a zillion lighters set that vast building twinkling and then Chavez and Haugen were in the ring. The Mariachi band had played their idol in, tears streaming down their chubby cheeks as they worshipped him in song. It was before the narrative ballads were written for the drug lords. Those narcocorridos praise the illegal; the Chavez corridos were all about pride. I had heard them all week and they come with action from the lead singer: he throws punches, sits and has his bandages taped, is reunited with his mother, his proud father. The singer cries; it is remarkable stuff. I'm not kidding, these songs are for life.

Haugen was smashed to bits. The referee ignored the slaughter, the crowd screamed for more blood and suffering. They got it. The two tiny flags that Don King waved were stained with blood at the end. It finished in the fifth, but Haugen still had plenty more to take.

At the post-fight conference in front of 300 blood-thirsty fuckers, Haugen was abused some more. 'This American dog had no chance to beat me,' said Chavez to his flock. They roared and I swear they all moved forward; they had paid their pesos and it looked like they wanted a slow lynching. The next morning at the Hilton, Haugen stopped and talked. 'They covered me in shit and piss on the way to the ring and on the way from the ring.' He was badly marked and a bit scarred by his night in fighting hell.

And then it was over. Somehow, 132,247 people and all my colleagues from the press area had vanished. It was deathly still and vast on the concourses outside. In the car parks, fire bins were warming huddles of people. It seemed like it would be a good idea to get lost. I found a three-seater, two-door Volkswagen and got out of Dodge a bit sharpish.

Azteca fallout: *Chavez fought on too long on both sides of the ropes; Nunn served 16 years in prison; Norris has been ruined by boxing; McClellan remains in need of constant care following surgery to remove a blood clot from the surface of his brain after a fight in London; Morgan volunteers at a gym; the great Putnam died in 2005 and in 2008 his military record was attacked. I had listened to his tales in The Flame, the last watering hole in the world of Las*

Vegas boxing. Putnam, when he wrote for the Miami paper, had a world exclusive when the kid, Cassius Clay, changed his name to Muhammad Ali in 1964. That was true – so what if he was not a war hero?

11

KIRKLAND LAING:
THE GIFTED ONE

PARK BENCH, HACKNEY, 2003

'The older you get, the harder life gets. I'm a man of my own destiny.'

Sweet Kirk finally died in 2021. He was, amazingly, 66 at the time and it was peaceful. It seems that he had defied the odds again and again and again.

In 2003, he was pushed off a building in Hackney late one night and his life was trapped in a hospital, soft-blue lit twilight zone. 'He's dead,' I was told at midnight. 'He's survived,' I was told at dawn.

Two weeks before he was shoved, I had worn a stab vest – a requirement – and spent 48 hours searching the flats, boozers, shops and parks of Hackney Downs looking for Kirkland Laing. I had three useless phone numbers, a dozen hopeless tipoffs. 'He looks like a black Santa,' one of the dossers outside a shop told me. I stood with them, buying lager and snout and getting no closer. I called Ian Napa, a local fighter, former British and European champion, and he told me which corners to look at. I came close, according to another dosser. 'He looks bad, he's in a bad way,' a 9 a.m. drinker told me. 'He's gone downhill, man.' He's gone downhill? It's 9 a.m., you are on your third can of Special Brew, you are standing outside a shop, shuffling your feet, asking for spare change, but Kirk is the one that has gone downhill. And they say irony is dead in Hackney since the sourdough gang arrived.

After a long, long day, I had a break. I was – and this is true – standing at the edge of the park and there was one of those signs that are in every park. The one with the park rules and regulations. There was the usual stuff about dogs on leads, no camping, no harvesting of marijuana. And there, right at the bottom, was the contact name and number for the man to call if you had a complaint or a question, John Zeraschi. How many John Zeraschis could there be? I knew John, he was my idol in the Seventies when I was six stone and ten years old in the Fitzroy Lodge gym. He was an ABA champion, a king in my world. I had not seen him for decades. I called the number; it was him and at about 6 p.m. we met in a chicken shop. Not a good one.

'I know where he is,' John told me after a long round of hugs and old-fashioned bollocks. 'It's going to cost a few quid.' We settled on £250, I gave John my number and we went back to the flats, back to Kirk's landing. I shouted through his letterbox: 'Kirk, I've just spoken to John, he's going to call you.' We stayed out until midnight, knowing that troublesome hour is a good time for a man with addictions. And Kirk had his addictions. We never saw him.

In 1972, when Kirk was just 17, he won the British amateur title, we call it the ABA title, but he was not picked for the Olympics. He was just a kid from Nottingham, he had no pull and the selectors ignored him. He was brilliant. He turned professional and won the British title in 1979. In 1982, he travelled to Detroit to meet the great Roberto Duran. It was a terrific fight and Laing won. It was a massive shock; Duran was in top shape, closing in on another world title. Kirk was paid ten grand, and he was gone, lost somewhere. His people couldn't find him.

Duran went back to the gym; nine months later he won the world title at a sold-out Madison Square Garden in New York. Kirk was still missing. Then, Duran made over $10 million for fighting

Marvin Hagler. Kirk had surfaced and lost a fight for peanuts. He regained the British and added the European welterweight title. His last fight was in 1994, he was 40 and fighting from memory. Then Kirkland Laing, arguably the best British boxer to never even fight for a world title, vanished. That is where I come in, hidden microphone, hat, stab vest and a mission.

In Hackney, Zeraschi worked his magic. At about 3 a.m. I was left a message on my phone. It was Kirk, he wanted to meet at 10 a.m. opposite the school in the park and he wanted the money. We had found him; the Gifted One, as he was known, was on his way. Well, that never quite worked out. We gave up after an hour or so and drove in our van to look for him and then I spotted him, the black Santa of Hackney, swaggering through the park, his girlfriend and dog in his slipstream. I jumped from the van, called him and he stopped. We bought beers and cigarettes, and I gave him the agreed fee; he gave me over an hour of unforgettable stuff. Full emotions: despair, joy, brilliance, dribble, confusion and a pledge to get clean. He was exceptional, his memory of his best nights in the ring crystal clear.

He had his European belt with him in a shopping bag and that belt remains a wonderful piece of art in the sport of shameless baubles. He also had a picture of him fighting and he had thousands of memories to share. That bag was his connection with his former glory, the last two items from those lost days. No money, no riches, just the belt and a picture in a Tesco bag. 'I had the talent, I did, didn't I? Imagine if I was disciplined,' he said, his voice and eyes and head off somewhere, and that can easily happen after four or five extra strengths before noon.

I had seen Kirk box over 20 times; I had seen the good, the bad and the awful. I had interviewed him a dozen or so years earlier in the flat where he lived on that estate. He was long past his best then, but there was still something there. He had a giant spliff as a permanent prop that day. In the park there was a point when he put down his beer, stood and shadow-boxed with style. Real style. Man, he was good. He talked of comebacks and, just a week or so before he was pushed off the fourth floor of the building, he showed up at the Peacock Gym in Canning Town to train. It was a solitary visit. They said he looked incredible for about three minutes, and I can believe it. Fighters from all parts of the gym got close to look.

'I wasn't mature enough back then,' Kirk told me that day. 'The older you get, the harder life gets. I'm a man of my own destiny.' There was a long silence, his girlfriend came closer, Kirk sparked and told me that he had to go and see somebody. We hugged and he swaggered off, his giant overcoat flapping. I watched him walk to the edges and vanish from my view and that park. I never saw him again. The ten-minute film was extraordinary. I had a brilliant producer and cameraman. It should have won awards, cleaned up.

The attempt on his life was just a few days away. 'Keep your pity hidden,' I wrote when he died. 'Laing is not interested in that; he lived, make no mistake. And, man, could he fight.'

Kirkland Laing: *After a stay in the intensive care unit at Whitechapel's Royal London Hospital, he moved back to Nottingham. There were pictures of Kirk and grandchildren, Kirk at a function with a lopsided bowtie. Kirk relaxed, smiling. The Gifted One was home and happy. There was a slightly bitter footnote to the short film. Somebody in his family, when he was in a coma, accused me of making 'hundreds of thousands of pounds off Kirk.' Nice idea, but my BBC fee was £250 per day and I was paid for two days.*

12

BERNARD HOPKINS
— v —
FELIX TRINIDAD

WORLD MIDDLEWEIGHT TITLE: MADISON SQUARE GARDEN, NEW YORK, 2001

The ones next to me had come straight from the wreckage of the Twin Towers . . .

It would be hard to invent a night like this.

It was the night they fought for all the versions of the world middleweight title and for something called the Sugar Ray Robinson trophy in boxing's most adored venue, the Garden.

The night Bernard Hopkins and Felix Trinidad fought for something that is hard to describe, something that was out of their hands. They fought that night in a city that was thick with death.

After 78 seconds of the 12th and last round, Trinidad was rescued from his burden and Hopkins was the man. It had been one of the great fights and one of the most emotional nights to have ever taken place at the old venue. This fight, you see, was meant to have taken place two Saturdays earlier, but the attack known now as 9/11 forced a delay. Outside the Garden, the city was still stunned, still covered in a light dust of ruined buildings.

Don King, the promoter, was desperate to honour the dead and celebrate New York's ability to fight back. There were offers from Atlantic City and Las Vegas, but King was determined. 'New York City deserved it,' he insisted. He visited fire stations all week.

King and Trinidad bought a fire truck and opened the doors to all firefighters in the damaged city. They came in their dusty and dirty outfits and hugged and cried. The ones next to me had come straight from the wreckage of the Twin Towers, the dust still thick on their faces. They placed each other in fierce grips, cried and howled. It was a release for the pain. All the firefighters and police had filed in to the Garden for the fight at 9:45 p.m. and the standing ovation was and will remain the loudest I have ever heard. That was all before any of the ring entrances. The Garden had never seen a night like it.

The Garden greats were then introduced: Emile Griffith, Roberto Duran and Jake LaMotta. Don King was waving his flags, and I wrote that 'his flags are so faded they look like relics from a battle. Flags displayed in a museum.' It's funny, but New York felt like a museum that week, a living museum with the scent of tragedy hanging in the air. I had been due to fly out for the original fight on Wednesday 12 September.

Hopkins entered the Garden – the official capacity was 19,075, but there were thousands more – wearing his red leather face mask; Trinidad had a New York City policeman's hat on; Hopkins entered to Ray Charles singing 'America the Beautiful.' Trinidad was unbeaten in 40 fights, the crowd were his and Hopkins was 36, the man who started to fight in prison. He loved playing the pantomime villain.

I wrote that what Hopkins had achieved 'was the right to declare with certainty that in the manipulative complexities of modern boxing he had done it his way.' He was the first unified middleweight world champion since Marvin Hagler in 1987. At that time when Hagler ruled, Hopkins was a bad petty criminal, just months away from sentencing. He had done it all his way.

In the ring on the night, Hopkins was masterful and by round nine it was a lost cause for Trinidad, who had started as a strong favourite with the bookies. Hopkins broke Trinidad down, dropped him in the last round and when Trinidad's father, who was his coach, touched the referee, Steve Smoger, on the shoulder, the fight was over. It was a small moment of mercy in a city of blood.

Hopkins was the perfect winner on a night the city, the Garden and boxing will never forget.

Bernard Hopkins: *In 2013, Hopkins was 48 when he won the light-heavyweight world title. He is a freak.*

13

AKAY ISOLA: BOXING PIONEER

ALL STARS GYM, LONDON, 1973

'I had no choice back then. So, I started my own boxing club.'

There are no herons on sandy beaches at Hermes Point on the Harrow Road in north London. It sounds lovely. It's not.

It is a council block of flats, a mile or so from Paddington, and it is where a little man called Akay Isola started a boxing club one winter in the early Seventies.

Isola had once been a boxer in Ghana, but by 1973 he was a father in London. His big boy, TeeJay, went to a local and established boxing gym one night. TeeJay was about 11 at the time. The gym was five minutes from his home on the sixth floor at Hermes Point. He was refused entry and told, well, take your pick: 'No spades here, son.' 'No n*g-nogs here, son.' 'Fuck off back to your own country.' Hey, it was 1973 and any of the above could be true.

Akay took the news well. 'I had no choice back then,' he said. 'So, I started my own boxing club.' It started in his flat and on his landing. No herons on the beach at Hermes Point, just kids in plimsolls hitting the pads on the landing.

'When it was cold, we did the groundwork in the flat,' he told me. 'Sometimes when the lift opened, we had to stop it and let people get into their flats. Soon about 12 boys were regulars and we realised it wasn't a joke.' A dozen boys skipping and hitting the pads on the landing of a block of flats – it is a Seventies vision, a natural film. Where is Idris Elba when you need him?

Within a year, Westminster Council had found him a space inside a local youth club for just one night each week. It was a start. In 1980, the club, known as All Stars, moved into a derelict church; pigeons were still flying about when the first sessions started. It has been a long, costly, litigious, heartbreaking and glorious road, but the club is still in that church on the corner of Harrow Road and First Avenue. The walls are filled with faded pictures, cuttings and posters to record the gym's history and the role of Mr Akay, which is how everybody in boxing addressed him. It is a time capsule: in 2020 I found something I had written over 25 years earlier. It left me speechless.

A boy called Everton Holmes became the first boxer from All Stars to have a bout under the rules and regulations of the English Amateur Boxing Association. It was 1975 and I like to think that Everton had been one of the original landing boys.

There was success and lots of it. The club that had refused TeeJay never had anything like the same number of winners. A local kid, saved by Mr Akay, called Tyrone Forbes won the ABA middle-weight title in 1983. That is an astounding achievement for a new club at that time.

In 1984, TeeJay boxed for Ghana at the Los Angeles Olympics; he lost to Evander Holyfield. As a pro, TeeJay won the British title. He died young and was just 44 when we gathered at the Regent's Park Mosque for his service in 2006. I stood with Mr Akay that day and when his son's casket arrived, even he had a chuckle; it remains the biggest coffin I have ever seen. TeeJay still worked out and worked hard. It was like they were burying a small car that afternoon.

In 1986 and 1987, Michael Ayers and 'Big Bad James' Oyebola won three more ABA titles for the club; they went on and had successful professional careers. Both won the British title. After the

ABA finals in 1987, which took place at Wembley Arena, hundreds drove the few miles back to the gym for an open-house party. The doors were unlocked at about midnight and people came in, walked up the stone stairs, followed their noses and ears to the food and sounds.

Ayers and Oyebola were honoured, loved by their friends and family that night. It was a proper mix of locals, boxing people and old-fashioned scoundrels. Anybody passing that church door was welcome, there were no exclusions in the house that Mr Akay built. It was close to dawn when I left and got a bus home. I had filed my copy late the night before at Wembley. It was one of about three after-fight parties that I have ever attended. I have never been to one in Las Vegas, I hate the poxy place. OK, I also love it for every $15 glass of craft beer.

There are no herons at Hermes Point, but no shortage of heroes.

Akay Isola: *The All Stars just rumbles on. Mr Akay died in 2019. I had last seen him a few years earlier at the Haringey Box Cup. He was full of smiles and memories. Everton Holmes is still at large. Sadly, in 2007, Big Bad James was shot in the head at point-blank range when, working as a bouncer at a club, he asked a man to put a cigarette out.*

14

GEORGE FOREMAN
— v —
CRAWFORD GRIMSLEY

WBU HEAVYWEIGHT TITLE: TOKYO, 1996

**There was still enough of that iconic slugger in
Reverend Foreman, the punching preacher.**

There was no sunset for Big George Foreman to use as the perfect exit after his fight in Tokyo. The fight finished at noon and the setting sun was a long way off.

Foreman was 47 at the time, and it was his 79th fight. His status as a legend of the ring was secure. It was not the end, but it should have been.

I sat with him three days before the fight and he chuckled that deep, deep laugh when asked about the fights with Joe Frazier and the Rumble in the Jungle. The last of those fights had been over 20 years earlier.

Before he answered, he looked over at Angelo Dundee. The pair were together in Tokyo, each carrying an unforgettable life of boxing history inside their heads. A couple of relics, men with a role in the most famous of nights and fights. They were living and breathing boxing history.

'It's tough for me to remember the Seventies,' Foreman told me. 'If I try and look back, it is like an old man looking back on his childhood.'

A little later, Dundee told me how their trainer-fighter relationship worked. 'I remind him about the things he has forgotten.'
They both laughed. In the Rumble in the Jungle, the pair had
been in opposite corners: Foreman convinced that he would kill
Muhammad Ali and Dundee concerned that Foreman might just
kill Muhammad Ali. When they talked about those distant days it
was captivating. They tried to put names to faces, faces to names.
The events of the Rumble were still fresh, if a bit blurred in their
heads.

'Sure, my guy wanted to leave. You wanted to leave,' Dundee
pointed out. 'You are damn right, I wanted to leave,' Foreman
replied. The Rumble had nearly fallen through when Foreman was
cut in sparring and then asked to leave Africa. Ali also wanted out;
Dundee was just following orders. It was Gene Kilroy, the facilitator in Ali's inner circle, who went to work and kept the fight active.
Both boxers and camps wanted to leave. Had either of the fighters
left, they would never have come back, and we would not have had
the Rumble. It was close to collapse.

Each day I met and sat and ate with Dundee in the Tokyo hotel's
coffee shop. He had told me a few years earlier, when I was at a fight
in Mexico City, that the fight cities around the world reminded
him of his beloved wife, Helen. 'She's not here, so I don't like to
go out much.' He sat and talked. He always ordered a club sandwich. I ate club sandwiches with Angelo Dundee in four countries.
Lovely, stick that on my headstone.

'That Inoki fight was bad for my guy, real bad. My guy had
blood clots all up his legs,' said Dundee. In 1976, Ali fought the
wrestler Antonio Inoki in Tokyo. It had been a crossover fight and
a disaster. It was a dreadful 15-round spectacle: Inoki never once
stood up, he just wiggled all over the ring canvas on his arse, kicking out at Ali's legs. It was given as a draw. Ali needed a hospital
stay to get rid of clots in his legs.

And yes, Dundee did talk about the Rumble, the Thrilla, the end of Ali's boxing life. I can't look at a club sandwich now without getting a lump in my throat.

In Tokyo, the Seventies roadshow continued. Foreman was defending his WBU heavyweight belt. It stands for World Boxing Union, and it was founded above a flower shop in Hackney Road, east London. Trust me, I don't invent this stuff. And the man that started it, Big Jon Robinson, was once the heaviest man in Britain. Jon also wrote for the *Hackney Gazette*, and he was my original sponsor at the NUJ. That is ancient history.

The opponent was Crawford Grimsley, and he was just 24, unbeaten in 20 fights with 18 knockouts. It was part of a classic early morning show and I had to be there. It was worth the hassle to get to the Bay NK Hall, near Tokyo's Disneyland for the fights – it was a carnival, make no mistake. There were a lot of problems before the echo of the first bell sounded; it seems that it is never easy in this boxing caper, especially at 9 a.m. in Tokyo.

Tommy Morrison was also there. He was the former heavyweight world champion with a blood connection to John Wayne. He had also failed a routine HIV test. He maintained his innocence, screamed conspiracy and arrived in Tokyo to fight. The local commission agreed. His first opponent was held up by authorities at the airport in Oklahoma; a replacement, Marcus Rhode, arrived in Tokyo less than 24 hours before the first bell. Tommy was a broken man that week. I had interviewed him before when he was Tommy the Man; the champ, the blonde kid from the *Rocky* movie and the great nephew, or some such nonsense, to John Wayne. He was the top banana.

In Tokyo, he looked like he was frightened of shitting his pants. The fight lasted 98 seconds, Rhode kept falling over from taps and no blood was spilled. The local commission never said a word; Rhode was having his 17th fight, he made $25,000 and that was more than his combined earnings. That is why Marcus Rhode fought a man with HIV in the ring in Tokyo. 'How could I say no?' he said. Tommy tapped him three times, never broke a sweat or had the tiniest of nicks; Morrison cleared $400,000 in blood money for the farce. He had lost millions and millions when he failed the test – he had a fight with Mike Tyson in the pipeline at the time.

There was a savage women's fight when RTL weather girl, Valerie Wien and Mary Ann Almager shared a broken jaw, cuts, bruises, exhaustion and a pint of lost blood. In 1996, the women's game was in a dark place: bad matches, no defensive skills, just raw slugfests.

At the other end of suffering, Mark Gastineau, who played American football for the NY Jets and had shacked up with Rocky's former wife, Brigitte Nielsen, turned his back and quit in round two against Alonzo Highsmith, who had played for the Houston Oilers. They both came in towering in the six-foot seven and 19-stone region. Gastineau quit in tears and never fought again. He was married to Nielsen briefly. His life since Tokyo is hard to believe. It was the type of novelty fight that would be enormous in modern boxing.

It was then time for Foreman to get in the ring. I wrote that the 'crowd went mild' on his arrival. I thought it was very clever. I missed the cultural significance of silence. Idiot. Foreman, no matter how old, will always be Big George. There was still enough of that iconic slugger in Reverend Foreman, the punching preacher. In Tokyo he had performed a marriage ceremony for a friend, and Foreman's bible was worn and used like a giant woolly sock. It was the same trusted bible that he had held in his giant fist when he had quit the ring back in the late Seventies and gone on the road to spread God's word.

The Reverend Foreman in the pulpit, was a contrast to the man in the ring in his soaking wet shorts, with his sweat-glistening, bald head rocking as he bullied Grimsley for 12 rounds. George then was like a soap opera – you had seen every episode a zillion times, but he remained the central character, the aged hero.

'I never had timing, I never had footwork even when I could move,' Foreman had told me that week. He was possibly right, but he had rich memories of those fights. In the Tokyo ring, there were flashes of old glory and that was good enough for me. Nobody has ever and will ever clobber people like Big George Foreman. That is why I went to Tokyo: I went for history.

Grimsley lost by a wide, wide margin and Foreman never liked him. They never shook hands. 'He ran all the time,' Foreman said. Grimsley replied: 'George, you are wearing sunglasses, so I wasn't running all the time.' Show some respect, Grimsley looked great until he moved.

George Foreman: *Big George would fight two more times and quit the ring for good a year later. Morrison was a kid of 27 in Tokyo; he was 44 when he died in 2013. He maintained until the bitter end that he never had the HIV virus. Grimsley is now a successful, wealthy and legitimate marijuana farmer in Florida.*

15

FANELLI'S CAFÉ: BARMAN BOB

NEW YORK CITY, 2023

'That's me, yep, I remember that night.'

This is a story about an ancient boxing bar and a geezer called Bob.

In 1991, a New York boxing writer called Mike Marley told me about a bar called Fanelli's. It was all the way down somewhere distant in SoHo. I was in New York for the Sugar Ray Leonard fight with Terry Norris, I was in the Garden area, but I wanted to drink at a boxing bar. Marley gave me the name, and I took off for the 50-block stroll after Sugar's loss.

It was gone midnight when I arrived. The walls at Fanelli's are covered with prints of ancient and modern fighters and fights and there are a few black and white photographs. One picture was hard to ignore, it stood out against the framed prints of 19th-century prizefighters and the best from the Fifties and Seventies. It was in a black and gold frame, but it was not neatly framed. It was not a great picture, but I was about to find out it was a decent story.

In the picture two boxers are in the middle of the ring and in the middle of a fight; one guy has his hands up and is looking intently at Big George Foreman, who is winding up to unleash a giant left hook. In the picture you can only see Foreman's back. It is a stark image, raw, my kind of boxing picture. I guessed it was the Seventies.

'That's me, yep, I remember that night,' said a hulking man, who had moved in close behind me. He was the barman. His name was Bob – that was all I knew. I could tell by his face that he had been in the ring. And he was in the photograph with Foreman, and it was the Garden. It was also gone midnight; in 1991 in boxing bars, if you heard something about a fight or a fighter there was no way or need to check it. It was fact, and anyway, there was the picture. There was no phone to use to verify, no boxing record sites. That stuff is all new. I took a boxing record book that weighed about five pounds with me to all fights in America for most of the Nineties. But nobody carried a record book out at night with them and nobody would dare lie about fighting Big George at the Garden. The picture on the wall was fact.

I went back to Fanelli's a dozen times over the years. I always looked at the picture and spoke to Bob if ever he was there. I told people about it. Anyway, in 2019, when Amir Khan fought at the Garden, I took Barry Jones to the bar; Bob had not been around for a few years, but the picture remained on the wall. I knew one of the women behind the bar, a boxing nut called Claire. We looked at the photo. 'Yeah, that's Bob, he used to run the bar and that's the night he lost to Foreman at the Garden,' I told Jones. It was my bar, I knew Bob, Claire was my friend. Jones was not convinced. 'That is not Foreman,' he said. And he was right. It turns out, wait for it, Bob never boxed Foreman. Never. Jones was on BoxRec in a second checking Foreman's record: 'No, no, there is a Don, a Chuck, a Jack and a Boone, not a Bob in sight.'

His name was Bob Bozic and the picture is from his six-round points loss to Larry Holmes in 1973 and it was at the Garden. I had never looked up Bozic in the record books, never bothered. It was definitely Bob, the barman, and it could have been Foreman.

Looking at it now, it is obviously Larry Holmes. In 1991, I had assumed it was Foreman. Bob never told me it was Foreman, he never had to – I looked at the photograph, I was an expert. I still look at the picture and for a second, I see Big George's back.

Bob Bozic: *Fanelli's lives on, Bob is no longer there, Claire still serves and goes all over the world to watch boxing. The picture still hangs in 2023.*

16

JOE FRAZIER:
SMOKIN'

BOXING FINALS: ATLANTA OLYMPICS, 1996

'All I ever wanted that man [Ali] to do was apologise to me.'

Joe Frazier won his gold medal in Tokyo in 1964 and he sold his autobiography on the pavement outside the Olympic boxing finals in 1996.

It was, in many ways, the perfect ending to a bad Olympic boxing tournament. The highlights had been the lows: the two British boxers exited without a win and a teenage Floyd Mayweather filed a complaint when he lost to Bulgaria's Serafim Todorov. I was there for that fight and there was nothing in it. The fake outrage has continued since Todorov went back to Sofia and his cigarette stand in the main square, and Mayweather made his millions. It was a tight and messy fight and there was no great scandal.

I thought that Joe Frazier sitting on a crate and signing copies of his book, was a scandal. This was the great Smokin' Joe – I walked past and had to go back and check. I recognised Marvis, his devoted son, taking the money and organising the queue. They were planted right in the middle of the pavement. Joe, Marvis, a crate to sit on and a dozen boxes of books. He deserved better than that, surely.

It was Frazier, so I joined the queue. It was $100 for the book and an autograph. Marvis took the money, and he did have a fist full of dollars. There were no pictures, it was 1996 and nobody had a camera phone. Instead, Smokin' Joe signed it and made a small dedication. I made it personal: I had Frazier dedicate it to my dad. It was worth every cent of the 100 bucks. The queue was growing.

Two months later, I went to the Philadelphia gym where Frazier trained and lived. It is the wonderful North Broad Street gym, a place made famous by Joe Frazier and where Frazier and Ali were photographed before their Fight of the Century. I knew that gym, it was fresh in my mind. I had seen pictures of it for decades before I walked through the door. A 'Philly fighter' meant something long before Sly Stallone gave birth to Rocky Balboa. That gym, Frazier's gym, was rich in my history.

The trip was arranged with Marvis. I had my signed copy of the book from the streets of Atlanta. Frazier was just 52 that day, the Thrilla in Manilla had been only 21 years earlier. At the time, I missed just how young he was and just how fresh those memories were. He seemed so old, so ancient, so iconic. He was all three in many ways.

There was a problem: 'My father needs some love,' Marvis explained to me. Frazier was in his offices, looking down at me. I got it and got it quick: Smokin' Joe needed some money. That was a problem. Marvis and I talked; it was great. I knew what had happened in that gym, I knew that Ali and Frazier had met there in private, not for cameras and show. Ali had been skint and they discussed their fight; Ali had only just been allowed to return to action after his exile. Frazier helped him, I knew that. I was standing where the two legends had stood and talked and done deals.

After a couple of hours, Smokin' Joe came down. He sat on the ring, and I got a few minutes. He never said much, he pointed to a picture on the wall, reminded me that he had been good to Ali, but that he had not forgiven Ali. 'All I ever wanted that man to do was apologise to me. Just me and him in a room, man-to-man. He told my son Marvis that he never meant what he had said about me, but he never told me.'

I was taping it on the faithful Dictaphone, but I was struggling to concentrate because I was transfixed by his face, his scars and the sadness in his eyes. He looked so old up close, and yet he was so young. Those fights took his soul, they really did.

The damage was a reminder of every blow that hurt him, cut him, dropped him, dazed him and made him the man and the extraordinary fighter that he was. Every single one. Apologies to Simon and Garfunkel, by the way.

And then my time was done. It was time to leave, and I did. I'm not sure about Smokin' Joe, but I got some love from that visit.

Joe Frazier: *In many ways Frazier has never had enough respect for what he achieved in the ring. Ali called him a gorilla and it seems like it was a lot of fun at the time. He beat Ali in the Garden in the Fight of the Century, dropping the Greatest in the 15th round. You see now why 'gorilla' was never funny.*

17

CARL FRAMPTON
— v —
KIKO MARTINEZ

IBF SUPER-BANTAMWEIGHT TITLE: BELFAST, 2014

'That is the fight you never forget.'

There is a picture of Carl Frampton in bed the morning after he won the world title. It is the type of picture that Jake LaMotta had taken when he was in bed after a fight. Frampton and LaMotta shared the damage of a bruising night in the ring, their sacrifice and pain is obvious. I'm a big fan of the morning-after-in-bed picture.

Frampton holds up his thumb, he tries to smile, but he is exhausted, flat and heavy on his back. A dozen hours earlier he had gone the full 12 with Kiko Martinez; in bed that triumphant morning, both his hands were damaged, his cheeks swollen with bruises, his right eye nearly closed, his cuts were stitched above both eyes and he ached so much he walked like he was fresh from an operation on his delicate parts. That morning, every part of Frampton was delicate. A few picture-grabbers outside the Europa tenderly hovered their hands above his shoulders and posed. He had nothing left to give, that's for sure.

Martinez had slipped back to his horse ranch near Benidorm; he speaks only Spanish. He is, arguably, Spain's greatest fighter.

Frampton could barely talk: at the end I wrote, 'his exhaustion was suspended as his hand was raised and his future secured'. In the week before the fight, Frampton was officially declared a tourist attraction in Belfast. Barry McGuigan, part of the management and promotional team behind Frampton at the time, was close to tears after midnight. By then it was Arctic at ringside. Barry's last world title fight in Belfast had been 29 years earlier. It was, incidentally, indoors in the warm. 'He's better than I ever was,' said McGuigan. The pair would end up in court nine years later and that was very ugly. It turned out that Carl's future was not quite 'secured' in victory.

They had fought the year before and Frampton had stopped Martinez but wins and losses can be deceptive. After losing to Frampton, Martinez won the world title in America, then defended in Spain and Japan. I'm not sure he was the favourite in any of the three world title fights. The fight at the Titanic was never going to be easy.

There was a ringside of the finest at the makeshift outdoor arena inside the Titanic Quarter. One woman had a fur coat on. 'Stevie Boy, she looks like she is ready to get on the Titanic, son,' said Ralph, the floor manager. Only Don King and John Gotti – both Teflon Dons – wear fur coats to boxing. The fight was raw and savage, it was bitterly cold and hard at times to watch. It was brutal, the air was freezing, and the punches boomed. Martinez kept smiling, the little fucker. Martinez is fearsome and was defending his world title for the third time. It was the type of fight that takes a long and hard and inevitable toll on both men.

It took a toll on me; I was presenting the BoxNation coverage – it lasted about eight hours and I only felt my toes about three days later – with the brilliant Andy Lee. It was so cold that we could barely talk when I closed the show at about 12.30 a.m. Cruel people praised the eloquence.

'That is the fight you never forget,' Frampton told me. He is right and as many as 18,000 on the night in the Titanic Quarter will never forget it. The crowd has swollen to about 50,000 in the retelling.

Carl Frampton: *After the Martinez fight, Frampton moved up and won the featherweight title in New York, lost it in Las Vegas and walked away from boxing in 2021. He is the face of boxing on TNT. And Martinez? It's hard to explain what the little Spaniard is all about. By the end of 2023, he had fought 22 more times, a total of 58 fights; he had also won and lost a world title again. He still speaks no English and him and Frampton need to get a room whenever they meet. The respect is wonderful to watch. Barry McGuigan is still in boxing.*

18

TONY AYALA JR: A FREE MAN

NEW JERSEY, 1999

'There are no angels on this earth, I know that.'

Tony Ayala Jr died alone and desperate from a heroin overdose one day in 2015 – it put an end to the life, fights and crimes of one of boxing's most infamous men.

Very few mourned his death and that is understandable. He was 52 at the end and he was just 19 when it started to go wrong. His fall was one of the greatest in the sport. Some in the Ayala Jr world might argue he was younger than 19 when it started to go wrong. The damage was deep.

In December 1982, he was in New York to sign for a world title fight at Madison Square Garden against Davey Moore. The fight was scheduled for May of 1993 and Ayala Jr would receive $700,000. He was unbeaten in 22 fights, with 19 knockouts; he would have won, and the Four Kings would have had a troublesome prince to fight.

Two weeks after signing the deal, he left his girlfriend, Lisa Paez, in bed and at 3 a.m. broke into a neighbour's apartment and sexually assaulted the young teacher who lived there. It was brutal, Ayala Jr was an animal that night. He was also out of his head on crack and was found topless and shadow boxing in the street after the crime.

Ayala Jr was sentenced to 35 years. He had to serve a minimum of 15. And that is where I come in, that is where I join this sordid party. I remembered Ayala Jr and I remember the crime and the arrest. He was brilliant and his VHS tapes were dynamite in the early Eighties.

A homecoming party in 1998 was cancelled at 24 hours' notice and he had to serve another year. Ayala Jr had been a model prisoner; his counsellor had been Dr Brian Raditz, who also met each week with Rubin 'Hurricane' Carter. Ayala Jr and Carter became friends. Ayala Jr became a rage counsellor. He was paid, and he did this for the last seven years of his life in prison.

In 1999, he was released, and I was the last person to arrive at Raditz's home that day in the Philadelphia suburbs. There was Ayala Jr, 36 that day, balding but only 20 lbs above his fighting weight. He had offers from every top promoter in America. The comeback was on. The reformed man was free. It was an intense afternoon.

I sat by the pool with Ayala Jr. There was a vein on his head that was throbbing. In the background, Raditz took up position, close enough to hear. On the other side of the pool, Lisa Paez was clearing away dishes and glasses. Paez had married and divorced Ayala Jr during his incarceration. She was back now. She looked drained and scared. It was a disturbing interview; the vein was hard to ignore.

Two days earlier, 11 people in a limo had collected him from prison. He was living with Raditz. There was a punch bag in the garage.

'I'm surprised how easy I'm adjusting to being free,' Ayala Jr told me that day at Raditz's lovely house in the affluent Huntingdon suburb of Philadelphia. 'I was in prison for a horrible crime. I never forgot that, but if I had gone on and won a world title, I would be dead now. It would have been an overdose.' He looked over, his head throbbing and introduced a tick. Fuck me, he was dangerous.

Ayala Jr admitted to fighting high, winning big fights after scoring and using in the dressing room. He was out of control and the people in charge of him must have known. They have always denied it. It makes no difference now.

That day in the fading sunshine, Ayala Jr smiled at memories of his post-fight outrages. He hit his beaten opponents, the trainers and even an angry girlfriend if one got in the way. His cornerman, Lou Duva, was always involved in the carnage in the ring at the end and during some fights. Ayala Jr would fight them in the ring or at ringside or behind the scenes. He was wild and that was part of his attraction.

'I hated my opponents, and the big question now is whether I've lost that through the therapeutic process,' Ayala Jr said to me.

'The boxing dream was there, but I had to lose it,' Ayala Jr added. 'Rubin (Carter) and I would speak each week and he gave me great advice. He told me: "Forget you are a fighter, forget about boxing and your previous life." I did that to survive.'

He walked me over to the side of the house where my taxi was waiting. He stopped at the garage and stripped off his shirt and hit that bag, hit it with hate and venom.

Ayala Jr never denied his history, he was just fighting it.

After the party, I wrote this in the *Independent*: 'Ayala was a menace and there can never be a truly happy ending to his story.' It is, in many ways, amazing that he lived another 16 years. He fought demons every single day until he lost. He was never looking for pity, just searching for something like peace.

Four months later, 12,000 watched Ayala Jr's return to the ring in his San Antonio home. He won, was paid $200,000 and looked decent. In the dressing room there were tears of joy and relief. I stood in silence and watched. It was temporary joy, and I knew that. I reckon Ayala Jr also knew. 'There are no angels on this earth, I know that,' he had told me by the pool. Ayala Jr knew the miracle was never coming; just more hell.

Tony Ayala Jr: *The end for Ayala Jr started in 2000 when he lost for the first time. He had remarried Lisa and in December they were in Babe's strip club; he left with a stripper, but soon ended up at the home of a teenage girl he knew from the gym. He broke in, she shot him in the left shoulder. He was spared prison, she spared him his life. Lisa divorced him again. He fought for the last time in 2003, finishing with 31 wins, two defeats, no world title and no money. In 2004, he was arrested in a car. He had no licence, he was speeding, and he had heroin. He spent ten years in prison. He was released in 2014 and was trying to get his life together, working as a trainer at the family gym in San Antonio. It was in that gym that he went off on his own, to end his life. He had first started to train there when he was five; he died there when he was 52.*

19

STEVE ROBINSON
— v —
NASEEM HAMED

WBO FEATHERWEIGHT TITLE: CARDIFF, 1995

Hamed was British boxing, flaws and all, for a long time.

The fight was not the fight that Steve Robinson wanted but it was the fight that he had to have.

Naseem Hamed was unbeaten in 19 fights, he had a new Mercedes, he had a Rolex, and he was hated by Robinson. Actually, a lot of people hated Hamed. The WBO's long-time boss, Paco Valcarcel, arrived in Cardiff for Robinson's seventh defence and told the Welsh boxer that he had 60 days to agree terms. It was a brutal ultimatum.

Robinson agreed, married his girlfriend, Angela, went on his honeymoon and came back four weeks before the planned showdown. Robinson was dismissed. The BSkyB publicity followed a simple narrative: 'See The Prince Crowned King.'

'How do I get respect?' Robinson asked us. 'What do I have to do?' None of us could look him in the eye – we never had the answer, but we had not tried too hard to find it. That is the British boxing writer's shame from that time. That sounds harsh, but it is true.

Hamed had rolled into Wales with his entourage. I was staying in Newport with him at a nice hotel in the hills. There was a carnival atmosphere there: ten or 12 crammed into the sauna, late-night runs to McDonalds. It was the Naz way.

Robinson was looking old that week. His face was puffy, there were dark marks deep under the skin from 31 fights. He was a warrior and his wins over world champions Colin McMillan, Paul Hodkinson and Duke McKenzie in defences were impressive.

'McMillan was meant to be the Golden Boy, what a joke,' Ronnie Rush, the devoted trainer of Robinson, reminded everybody in the week of the Hamed fight. 'Hodkinson was going to knock Steve out. Remember that? The experts got that wrong.'

Rush had a point, a good one. Robinson beat McMillan about nine to three in rounds and was nine rounds up when he knocked out Hodkinson in the 12th and last round. Hamed had dazzled, was unbeaten in 19 with 17 ending early. Robinson was his hardest fight to date.

'The Naz fella will not have it easy; Steve has proved himself on so many occasions,' said Brendan Ingle, the man who found Hamed when the boy was a kid of six or seven. Brendan had to keep Hamed focused and that is why so many of his friends, boxers at Ingle's Wincobank gym in Sheffield, were in Newport at the hotel. They were Hamed's calming distractions. The room-service ruse had finished, but they were all packed in.

Two nights before the fight, Hamed decided that he would drive to Robinson's Ely home and stand outside his house at midnight and scream abuse at him. Muhammad Ali had done the same in Denver on Sonny Liston's doorstep.

Hamed drove, John Ingle was in the front, and I was squeezed into the third and invisible backseat. We never got very far on the A48 before the police pulled us over. They recognised Naz, they talked, we left and returned to the hotel. No charges for the speeding. The night, however, was not over. An underwater swimming competition was organised and the pool was opened. It was gone 2 a.m. when it was over. I think Ryan Rhodes won.

It was a wet and miserable September night outdoors at Cardiff Rugby Club and 16,000 had braved the conditions. They had also ignored what they felt in their hearts. Everybody knew it was going to be a tough night for Steve Robinson.

Hamed was hit and cut by a £1 coin as he made his way through the hate-filled mob. Robinson was welcomed like a hero. At ringside, with plastic bags on his boxing boots, Barry Jones huddled against the cold and watched. He was the swing bout – he was ready for five hours to fight, but never did. He got paid. 'Hamed was so nasty that night – there was nothing that Robinson could have done; there is nothing that anybody could have done that night,' he told me. At the time, we were having a steak in Phoenix after watching Sunny Edwards lose his world title. It was December 2023 and Jones had total recall.

It finished in round eight. Hamed never lost a round, he was brilliant and Robinson's role in this fight is always overlooked. He took seven full rounds of Hamed's best and that is monumental. Robinson took it and never stopped trying. It was hard to watch at times.

In late 2023, I was with Hamed at a fancy boxing gym in Belgravia. He is a different man now to the boy in 1995 and that is to be expected. 'You know who never gets the respect? Steve Robinson. He was brave, man.' He most certainly was.

Naseem Hamed: *The Cardiff night was just the start of five incredible years. Hamed was British boxing, flaws and all, for a long time. He was avoided by the very best fighters in the world until he started to lose his way – they queued up then to fight him.*

20

GEORGE KIMBALL:
A TOP MAN

AUTHOR OF *FOUR KINGS*: LAS VEGAS, 2011

'Not a single American had to watch this fight – why should *I*?'

There was every chance that George Kimball would leave a foul-mouthed message at 3 a.m. He kept a permanent check on any stupidity in the writing side of the boxing game. And we are all capable of being stupid.

He wrote *Four Kings*, a book of love and devotion, fights and brilliance. He lived every second of the fights between Marvin Hagler, Tommy Hearns, Sugar Ray Robinson and Roberto Duran. He wrote for the *Boston Herald* for 25 years and had columns all over the world; one of his poems about the decline of Muhammad Ali still makes me choke. I like Kimball because he was there and that is crucial for me. He travelled, dined, wept and drank with the men from the game. They were his friends; he was their friend.

He slaughtered me in 2009 for claiming that Tyson Fury would rule the heavyweights one day and went for me in 2004 when I wrote something kind about Maurice Termite Watkins. Sweet George spoke his mind and he was an old-school, hard hack. And he could write. He was also a funny man.

He was not funny when he wrote about his great friend, Pat Putnam, after it was revealed that Putnam had never been in the Marines, had never been in the Korean War, was not a hero and was not imprisoned, after being captured, for 17 months. It was a helluva story and Putnam told it in boxing's last-chance saloons. The Flame, the legendary Las Vegas lounge, held some of those tales until dawn. Putnam wrote for *Sports Illustrated* and might just have been the best boxing writer of his whole generation of great boxing writers. I interviewed him once for a BBC show and I knew all about his war exploits. Kimball was on the floor after the news but crafted a heartfelt defence.

There are some real fantasists and outright liars in the boxing media in Britain – men that just lie about fights they claim to have been at and fighters they claim to have known. We have a few, real chancers.

'I know he never fabricated a single word in any of his stories. He didn't have to. He could write circles around the rest of us anyway,' Kimball said. Others were less convinced, and the debate raged.

In 2005, when Don King arrived in Baghdad with plans to deliver world title fights, Kimball was in great form. At the time, Saddam Hussein was in custody. King waved his flags and made his mad promises. In 2022, King would make the same crazy promises to me in Miami about taking world title fights to Ukraine to help deliver peace and punches. King waved Russia and Ukraine flags that afternoon.

Back in 2005, King had promoted the heavyweight title fight and bore-fest between Nikolai Valuev and John Ruiz. It was a bad fight. Kimball imagined Saddam's response to King's invasion and, in a typically brilliant column, he had the despot say: 'Not a single American had to watch this fight – why should *I*?'

George spent hours with me in Las Vegas coffee shops. Idle hours of wonder. Big George could spin a story.

George Kimball: *King never delivered world title fights to Iraq or Ukraine. And George was wrong about Fury.*

21

MIKE TYSON

— v —

DANNY WILLIAMS

RETURN FOR REVENGE: LOUISVILLE, USA, 2004

'He's a bully and I will stop him by about round four or five.'

There was the end of a love story in the fabled Freedom Hall in Louisville in the hours after Danny Williams finished Mike Tyson.

There were tears, some were mine.

In the ring, Tyson had slipped down, bloody and broken in the fifth round. It was the end. He had taken 16 big shots to the head as he started to slide down. The iconic picture of him sitting comfortably in the corner, on the wet canvas with blood trickling down his right cheek, is significant because it is obvious that he knows exactly what has happened. That is the look of defeat and utter despair.

Williams had been lifted off his feet, but he was not knocked over in a brutal first round. It was sickening and I still have no idea how he survived. He did, he had a plan and on the Tuesday of the fight week, he had told me what would happen.

'He fades away after a couple of rounds and I will go back at him,' Williams told me. 'Tyson don't like having it, Steve. He's a bully and I will stop him by about round four or five.' I listened, I wanted, I hoped, I prayed, but I never believed. Sorry, Danny.

A deal with Bob Arum was ripped up before Tyson left the hospital, after an MRI on his damaged left knee and stitches in his right eyelid, and took a private jet out of Louisville. The celebrity ringside included Mr T and Rahman Ali, the brother of Muhammad, but nobody could get to the broken man.

There was real drama in the hours before the first bell. I was rushing from ringside to the hallways near the dressing rooms. The fight was off with 45 minutes to go – Danny was not told, he was warming up, but the promoter, a former stripper called Chris Webb, had repeatedly failed to hand over a 50 grand advance. Finally, at 10.40 p.m., just 33 minutes before the first bell, a bag of cash was given to one of Williams' team – the man missed the fight because he was in a locked room counting the cash.

When the fight was over and before Danny's face started to swell from the first-round beating, there was a moment of unforgettable tenderness. It is hard even now to type this without getting emotional. First, at the end of the fight, Williams was jumping about wildly with his trainer, Jim McDonnell, then he stopped. He had caught sight of his family for the first time. He had no idea they were there, no idea. Zoe, his partner, and his two children had arrived the night before and had been hidden from him. Danny went over and through tears – I was close enough to see – he proposed and through tears she accepted. Three hours later in Freedom Hall's South Wing, Williams had his six-week-old baby, Melia, on his lap and his five-year-old Nubiah was resting her tiny hand on his giant thigh. I wrote this piece for the *Sunday Herald*. What a story.

'I will fight him again, no sweat, to prove it was not a fluke,' said Williams. It never happened.

In the dark, Freddie Roach, Tyson's latest trainer, walked away from the Freedom Hall. 'Mike got hit too often tonight and I think he has to make some hard decisions,' said Roach. I wrote that

Roach was 'plagued by his honesty in a business that has always treated the truth like some type of disease.'

A year later, Big Kevin McBride stopped Tyson and that was it for him.

Danny Williams: *There is no happy ending, sorry. Danny fought for far too long and was still fighting in 2023. 'I have school fees to pay,' he told me in 2019. A lot of his fights are hard to trace; some bad people keep offering him work in obscure locations. His last 14 traceable fights have been in nine different countries. He is, remember, the man who knocked out Mike Tyson. It is possible that he has fought over 60 times since beating Tyson. In one fight in 2020 in Russia, a man having his first fight hurts and wobbles Williams, and then tells the referee to stop it. It is pathetic and so wrong.*

22

JAKE LAMOTTA:
RAGING BULL

NEW YORK CITY, 2001

'Woody Allen? Good friend of mine . . . I'll introduce you.'

La Maganette on New York's Third Avenue once had a party trick that was the envy of the city.

On the same night and for over 20 years, Jake LaMotta arrived with his latest wife or squeeze and sat at the same small table in the Italian restaurant. One night in September 2001, just two weeks after the attack on the Twin Towers, I was with Jake and the woman who would become wife number seven. Her name was Denise, and she was not impressed with me.

The table was in the centre of the restaurant, and there was VIP red rope forming a ring on all four sides. The maitre d' lavishly opened the corner and we three slipped in. There was not an empty seat in the place. The Raging Bull himself was 79 that night, a human machine of war and love and outrage and comedy. He had lived a wild, wild life: 106 fights, some the most savage in the sport's history, he had served time on a chain gang when he was nicked for being a pimp and then the movie saved his soul. *Raging Bull*, it's one of our holy items in the boxing business. Its dialogue is our psalms.

'You know, I made a good fighter out of (Robert) De Niro, he could have been a pro,' he told me. 'They made a good movie out

of me.' They did. I listened as Jake told the wife jokes, told me about
Sugar Ray Robinson and told me about his truthful little talk with
De Niro. The one where he gets De Niro in private and puts it on
him: 'Did you have sex with Vikki?' De Niro says no, but LaMotta
is not sure. Vikki, who was wife number two, was a beauty. Is there
a finer night out in New York? C'mon, you know it's legend when
LaMotta is telling me what he said to Robinson at the end of the
St Valentine's Day Massacre. And asking Bobby if he banged Vikki.
The piano player dedicated another song, there was applause
and Jake raised a hand. A bottle of red arrived from a man called
Tony. 'Ciao,' Jake offered across the heads of 30 diners. And then
it happened.

He tapped his fork gently against a wine glass. There was
instant silence. Jake wiped the corner of his mouth and stood up.
My God, it was true – I had thought it was a myth.

Jake LaMotta delivered every word. It was Jake playing De Niro
in *Raging Bull* playing Jake playing Terry Malloy in Bud Schulberg's
On The Waterfront. In the film it happens in a dressing room before
his stand-up in Miami in the early Seventies. De Niro is the fat
LaMotta in the scene. It is beautiful stuff – here it is in full, with
the movie notes:

INT. TAXICAB. EVENING. (NEW YORK BACKGROUND)

TERRY: It wasn't him. (Years of abuse crying out in him.) It was
you, Charley. You and Johnny. Like the night the two of youse
come in the dressing room and says, 'Kid, this ain't your night
– we're going for the price on Wilson.' It ain't my night. I'd have
taken Wilson apart that night. I was ready – remember the early
rounds throwing them combinations. So what happens – this
bum Wilson, he gets the title shot – outdoors in the ball park
– and what do I get – a couple of bucks and a one-way ticket
to Palookaville. It was you. Charley. You was my brother. You
should have looked out for me. Instead of making me take them

dives for the short-end money. I could've been a contender.
I could've had class and been somebody. Real class. Instead of
a bum, let's face it, which is what I am. It was you, Charley.

That is what Bud wrote, that is what Marlon Brando said and it
is what De Niro and LaMotta used. There is some history in those
words.

Silence and then a standing ovation. I heard somebody crying.
Jake moved close to my ear as he sat back down. 'Every word was
perfect, I can guarantee you that,' he whispered. I'm not sure De
Niro – he was just Bobby that night at the table – uses Palookaville
in the film.

That is Jake LaMotta's long-running party tricky at La Maganette. The meal cost me nearly $400. For that, I got the greatest seat
in the city.

It was after midnight when we left. The night was not over. I
had told LaMotta that I was a fan of *Broadway Danny Rose*. 'Woody
Allen? Good friend of mine,' LaMotta replied. 'C'mon, let's got to
Elaine's; I'll introduce you to him.' I will leave it there, otherwise it
sounds like I'm ripping the arse out of it.

The Raging Bull: *LaMotta was 95 when he died in 2017. I have
no idea when the La Maganette gig finished. Three days after the
meal, I had breakfast with Budd Schulberg – yes, I know. Budd got
an Oscar for his screenplay of* On The Waterfront. *Yep, he wrote the
Contender speech. He was no fan of Jake the man. 'He always made
a play for the wife, he was a bully. But he could really fight.'*

23

NIGEL BENN

— v —

MAURO GALVANO

WBC SUPER-MIDDLEWEIGHT TITLE: MARINO, NEAR ROME, 1992

The boys snarled, threw a few punches, slapped a couple and got through the tunnel of hate.

Three rounds of bloody boxing and then ten minutes of bloody confusion. It was a fight in Italy and that is never easy or simple.

Nigel Benn was the away fighter, the man with the heavy entourage, on a mission to win a world title behind enemy lines. The champion was Mauro Galvano; the enemy lines included his personal ultras.

It was a beautiful location, the venue just minutes from where the Pope spends his long and hot summers. There was a lake, a mountain, the autumn was warm and there was a lot of al fresco going down. The travelling press pack – in suits and ties for the airport – had come out in numbers; I reckon about a dozen seasoned British newspaper men made the journey. We had arrived in Rome together after a very boozy plane journey.

Later that night, Benn came to the hotel, and we sat around him on chairs as he told us about his hopes for the Galvano fight and a rematch for revenge against Chris Eubank. 'I hate that man,' he told us. That was fine, just about everybody in the press pack above the age of 40 hated Eubank: Only Steve Lillis and I were under the age bar and we both loved Eubank.

It had been a long road to Galvano's door after the loss in 1990 to Eubank. Those of us in the Benn-watching business knew just how deep the wound was. And those of us still breathing and working were witness to the proposal for a generational opening of hostilities in 2022: the fight between the sons, Chris Jr and Conor, over 30 years later, was made and collapsed with about 24 hours to go before the first bell. The animosity was still deep. Back in 1992, Benn had fought six times since the Eubank loss.

It was probably Wednesday when we sat with Benn. Jimmy Tibbs, his trainer, was there and a few of Benn's closest friends. Tony Tucker and Patrick Tate were there, and they were big lads. In the Seventies, Alan Minter had travelled with some lively friends to fights overseas – Tate and Tucker were the extreme end of 'lively friends', that is for sure.

In the fight, Galvano was cut above the left eye and there was a lot of blood. Benn was coming on top, as we say. He was snarling and, in the corner, Jimmy was happy. And then at the bell to sound round four, Galvano stayed on his stool in the corner. The fight was over; well maybe.

There was a problem and a bad one. The Italian's corner was screaming that the cut was caused by Benn's head, and they wanted the fight to be called off and a technical draw declared or a No Contest. Anything but a loss. It was an expected stroke. Benn was, incidentally, in front after three completed rounds on all the scorecards.

'It was a perfect right cross over the top of Galvano's jab and that did the damage,' growled Tibbs. And if Jimmy growled, you tended to listen.

In the ring the wait continued, Barry Hearn joined the ring-side debate and he was very strong in his argument. I could hear him from the opposite side of the ring. 'It was a legitimate punch,' Hearn repeatedly said and demonstrated.

'How can they do this?' Benn mouthed to friends at ringside.

In the ring, both boxers were on the shoulders of their people; Galvano was a lot happier than Benn. His title, it seemed, was staying in Rome and Benn was coming home empty handed. And then it changed – Barry Hearn had justice.

'He tried some dirty tricks, but I'm way too cool for that type of stuff,' said Benn.

The decision was changed, and Benn was the winner, the new champion. That made him smile. He went to the ropes and leaned through to speak with ringside guest, Eubank. It was five feet from me.

'Now, we can do business,' said Benn.

'That's OK, now I accept,' Eubank replied. Their rematch was one year later.

In the arena it was getting ugly. The armed carabinieri arrived and they were *abbondanza agitato*.

'Justice is served, the kid deserved it,' said Joe Cortez, the referee. Galvano would later admit that it had been a punch and not Benn's head. Five months later in Glasgow, Benn retained the title on points when he gave Galvano a rematch.

Outside the ring, the new decision was announced, and it did not go down too well. The missiles started to fill the air. Benn had left the ring and was making his perilous way through the gauntlet of predictable hate. The guns came off the shoulders of the carabinieri – it was a genuine standoff. He was shielded on either side by Tate and Tucker, Tibbs was also in the thick of it. The boys snarled, threw a few punches, slapped a couple and got through the tunnel of hate. They had done their job – they had protected their friend. It was messy and the British press were held behind at the end. It was still hostile when we went out in search of taxis a little later.

There was a party somewhere that night, I was just relieved to get out in full health.

Nigel Benn's friends: *Tony Tucker, 38, and Patrick Tate, 37, were shot dead in a Range Rover on a farm road near a place called Rettendon in December 1995. It became known as the Essex Boys' murders. In Rome they were heroes, that is all I know.*

24

RAHMAN ALI:
A GENTLEMAN

LOUISVILLE, 2004

'I can't believe I just had Muhammad Ali's brother in my taxi.'

In the early Sixties, Muhammad Ali called his devoted brother 'little Rudy'. They were inseparable.

In the days leading up to the Danny Williams and Mike Tyson fight, a fixer called Gene Kilroy arranged for 'little Rudy' to be our guide to Louisville. Rahman Ali, as he had been known for nearly 50 years, was a gentleman.

I went with Rahman to the house where he and his brother grew up. The part of Grand where the house is has seen better times. It was a bit neater when Cassius Marcellus and Rudolf Valentino lived there from babies and boys to men. It was a smart little home.

I had seen the pictures of the two dreamers on the steps outside the house, read the stories about playing marbles there and of the young Muhammad talking endlessly about being the world champion. Our taxi, driven by a man called Steve, pulled up outside the house. The house needed some love, that is for sure. Rahman went quiet – he had not seen it for a long time. He seemed a bit shocked.

There was an ugly sheet of blue tarpaulin over the front door – the porch had come off in a storm. The house badly needed some work. We walked to the door. The place was sad, it looked like it belonged in a shanty town.

A young woman answered the door; she had three kids, one in her arms, and I couldn't help but notice, only three toes on her otherwise perfectly formed right foot. She was polite but had no idea about the house. Rahman went in to have a look; it felt like an intrusion and I gave that a swerve.

'My brother would sit on that step when he was just 11 and 12 and tell me that he would be the world heavyweight champion. I believed every word.' Rahman was also a pro, having 18 fights between 1964 and 1972 – has any boxer ever fought under such a heavy shadow?

We sat on the step. Rahman, me and Mick Costello, the BBC's voice of boxing back then. We listened; it was the ride we expected.

'I remember when we first went to a Sonny Liston fight in Las Vegas,' Rahman told us. 'At the time Muhammad was the leading contender and we were shocked to find out that we could stay in the best hotel and order room service.' The Steaks in Las Vegas story is one of the classic Ali tales – being told it by his brother, on the steps of the Ali family home, was mad. Louisville had been a magical city in my mind for decades.

'I think we ordered six steaks in total because we had never been able to do anything like that before,' Rahman added. The boys were not free to eat at the best restaurants in Louisville when they were young and even when Ali had his gold medal from the Rome Olympics in 1960.

The house should have been a shrine at that time, but it was not. The woman there had no idea about the brothers. Not a clue. 'I'm gonna speak to my brother and tell him to buy the house, fix it up and turn it into a shrine.' I have no idea if that happened, but

Costello told me that at Ali's funeral in 2016, the house was a shrine to the mourners. The blue tarpaulin was gone.

Rahman got tired and we drove in Steve's taxi to drop him off at his apartment opposite the Greyhound station on Muhammad Ali Boulevard. Rahman and Mr T sat together for the Williams and Tyson fight.

It was a staggering week in Louisville for the monumental fight, the day with Rahman, the bird shit on Tyson's bed from the pigeons he was living with in his suite and, last but by no means least, a story for the ages from Steve, the taxi driver.

After we dropped Rahman off, Steve was still shaking his head in wonder. 'I can't believe I just had Muhammad Ali's brother in my taxi,' he said. He then told a few tales of his own. Steve was 51 at the time and can remember drinking from the wrong fountain, he could also remember getting a kicking from one of Ali's 'kinfolks' one day, but he saved the best for the stop outside a fish restaurant called Moby Dick. The building was shaped like a whale. It was to fish, what the Colonel is to chicken.

'Yeah, that's the place,' said Steve and he told me his story. 'It's a normal black-man tale, trust me, brother,' he assured me.

One day he had picked up a passenger outside Moby Dick. The guy seemed normal, he gave Steve the address and off they went. Steve had never seen the man before in his life. Suddenly, the police had Steve's taxi trapped. There were guns everywhere. It turns out that the passenger had just held up Moby Dick with a busted and rusty .45 and fled the scene with a pathetic $50. He had also ordered two fish wraps and fries and he had not paid for them. It seems Steve was guilty because the man had ordered two Moby Dick famous fish wraps and not just one. Steve was the cod accomplice.

It's not funny, really. The *Louisville Courier* dubbed them the Fish Wrap Bandits and Steve was sentenced to five years for his role in the robbery. 'No damn robbery, I was given five years for being black.'

Rahman Ali: *In late 2023, Kilroy was still looking out for Rahman. Steve the taxi driver, Rahman and Gene belong to a different time.*

25

JOHNNY TOCCO'S GYM

LAS VEGAS, 1994

Tocco's was in the middle of nothing. But it was something.

Imagine walking back in history and being in a room surrounded by memories from a quarter of a century earlier. It can happen, and it did happen to me one afternoon at Johnny Tocco's gym in Las Vegas. The other Las Vegas, by the way.

Tocco was a good friend of Sonny Liston. He trained him and remained until the very end a defender of the fighter, a devoted advocate.

Tocco ran a gym in Las Vegas for 41 years. The one I was in was on the corner of Charleston and Main and it had once been called the Zebra Lounge. Too often people get a bit nostalgic for all things 'off-the-strip' in Las Vegas; they talk like there is a glorious other side to the place. A place packed with hopeless romantics, Elvis backing singers, Liberace's dressmaker, a lost poker-playing millionaire. Hey, once upon a Vegas time there might have been.

Even I knew the infamous Flame, the sacred drinking hole of the world's greatest boxing scribes. But, in 1994 there was no real chance. There was nothing much to see, trust me. How many Eighties burnout crack fiends, pushing a trolley packed with what is left of their life, do you want to see? There were car repair garages, very bad bars and the occasional chapel for doomed marriages. There was no romance in those streets. Downtown is different now and there are pioneer bars, alternative places to eat. Back then Tocco's was in the middle of nothing. But it was something.

Tocco's credentials are ancient: he worked with Liston, Larry Holmes and the doomed Michael Dokes. The gym was real, and it attracted real fighters. Lennox Lewis liked it. Mike Tyson loved it and boxing men like Teddy Atlas always used it.

Tocco on Tyson: 'They ruined a wonderful fighter. He would sit with me and ask questions; he spent hours here.'

Tocco on Atlas and his heavyweight, Michael Moorer: 'Teddy can really work a fighter, and he's a good guy.' Tocco was pointing his wet and dead cigar at Moorer for the last compliment. Moorer shocked Evander Holyfield outdoors at Caesars at the end of that week. Tocco was 83 at the time and you better believe that his opinion was still respected.

Moorer, Atlas and Tocco finished the session in a whispering huddle. I watched it. I had been in the gym a few hours before Tocco gave me an invite to travel back in time.

I entered Tocco's office and saw history in a half-dozen Polaroid pictures. The office was like both a sanctuary and a museum to Tocco's life. There were notes on the walls with the names of the greatest people in our fighting game and their numbers. There were more of Tocco's cigars on a desk cluttered with snippets.

There was a signed and dedicated photograph of Jack Dempsey and Sugar Ray Leonard. But it was the Polaroids, those glorious and candid snaps of a smiling Charles Sonny Liston, that were unbelievable. Liston had been dead since New Year 1970, but the snaps looked like they had been taken the previous Sunday at a family barbecue.

'He loved kids,' said Johnny when he saw me looking.

Liston with children, not his own. Liston with a beer in the sun in a garden somewhere. Liston with an apron cooking some meat on a barbeque. Liston was smiling, relaxed, happy.

Liston was 38 when he was found by his wife, Geraldine. It was thought he had died of an overdose, a heroin overdose. Tocco was not impressed, he handled his boxing affairs, and he was looking to make another fight at the time.

'Sonny hated needles, but the coroner says he found needle marks in his arm. I think he had some type of convulsion, like a stroke,' said Tocco. He told me that a long, long time ago. It felt like a giant exclusive, especially being in that tiny office surrounded by all the intimacy of the Polaroids.

'We were due to go out for New Year's evening. I tried to ring,' Tocco told me in that office. Liston died at some point near New Year's Eve. He was alone and there is a debate about his death: accident, suicide, murder. It rages on.

I left there that day with Dokes. He believed that he would get the call from Don King for the first fight with Mike Tyson when he was released. He was training hard but using even harder. Still, he blagged 50 bucks from me in the taxi back to the MGM. I think I even paid for a buffet. No sweat, Dokes had been a very good fighter at one time. He fell harder than most.

A day later, I made my first trip to Paradise Garden Cemetery, out under the flight path at the airport. It was easy to find Liston's stone. 'Look for all the toys,' Tocco had told me. I found teddy bears, tiny cars, Barbies and then I found Liston. The most feared heavyweight in history was buried next to the children, a minder for the end of life. The oddest guardian of their safety, but I had seen the pictures and heard the testimony. Liston was in the right place. His stone on the lawn was simple:

Charles 'Sonny' Liston. 1932–1970 – A Man.

That will do, thanks.

Johnny Tocco: *He kept secrets and loved the man he helped to make. Tocco died in 1997 when he was 87. I have no idea whatever happened to the Polaroids. They would be priceless today and I'm* *privileged to have been shown them by Tocco. And Dokes never got the call from King. He had won the WBA heavyweight title in 1982, and he was sentenced to ten years for attempted murder in 2000. He died a free man in 2012 at just 54. No sign of my nifty.*

26

JOE BUGNER
— v —
FRANK BRUNO

WORLD HEAVYWEIGHT FIGHT. WHITE HART LANE, LONDON, 1987

'Where's 'Arry?'

A man called Kenny Peanuts made me a press pass. It was hard cardboard, it said 'Press Pass' and there was a picture of me. It was inside a plastic sleeve and about the size of a cigarette box. I used it without rejection for about five years until my NUJ card came through; the press card was more impressive.

Kenny worked in the 'print', as it was known, and he also sold peanuts at Highbury. He would leap from row to row, selling his packs of peanuts at home games. I saw him, it was true. He also was a so-called keep-fitter at the Fitzroy Lodge: a regular face, one of the chaps. That is how I knew him.

Anyway, in 1987 I used Kenny's Press Pass to get into the Frank Bruno and Joe Bugner fight. I was writing for the *South London Press*, the *Boxing News*, the *Daily Telegraph* and the *Sunday Express*. However, all legitimate roads to the ringside were blocked. Kenny's pass opened the doors, and I went in on that wet October night.

It was a shambles at White Hart Lane. One of the promoters, Barry Hearn, used the pages of the *Boxing News* to apologise to the paying public. It was shown on ITV, but 37,000 were there on the night. There was a problem with the seating, the stewarding, there were skirmishes and there was a general atmosphere of intimidation. It was not a nice experience. The fight was fun.

'I did it for the money and no other reason,' Bugner told me several years later.

In 1996, he was back in London from Australia, and he had been denied a British licence; he would have to fight British heavyweight champion Scott Welch in Germany. Bugner was 46 when they met and an icon. Two decades later in 2008, I got him and Henry Cooper together at a fancy Mayfair hotel for a BBC show. I sat them down for an hour and Cooper was still bitter about the result in their fight in 1971. Bugner finished Cooper's career with a tight decision over 15 rounds. I walked Cooper to his car and when I came back there were real tears in big Joe's eyes. 'He still hates me,' he said. And he did. In all fairness, Bugner did say to me in 1996: 'In my opinion Cooper couldn't walk in my shadow as a fighter. I am a legend.'

At White Hart Lane in 1987, Bugner was stopped at the very end of round eight when the towel and the referee came in at the same time. The post-fight interview with Bruno and ITV's Jim Rosenthal was funny. 'Where's 'Arry?' Bruno asked Rosey. It was not funny the tenth time. Bruno and the BBC's Harry Carpenter had become a fixture when he fought, a comedy double act.

'He will beat (Mike) Tyson,' said Bugner when it was finished, and Bruno had cleared the way to a world title fight. Bugner knew how to sell a fight.

Joe Bugner: *At the end of 2023, Bugner was in a care home in Brisbane. He has dementia, and apparently he has no memories of any of his fights. And he is right, he is a legend. Kenny Peanuts still works with boxers in the East End of London. The peanut game is over.*

27

AZUMAH NELSON: AN AFRICAN HERO

ACCRA, GHANA, 1995

'I'm a man of action – I need to fight.'

The passport went missing somewhere between the car park and the check-in desk. Our fixer asked for the passports, we handed them over, we walked 50 feet to the check-in desk. I was last in our line of four and when I got there the woman told me there was no passport. It had been five minutes and a 50-foot walk!

The handler said he gave them to an airline official; the woman said she never received them, but she had the other three. It was late afternoon in Accra and the flight was only about an hour away. I was taken to a room and two security guards explained how serious the situation was. They never took their boots off the desk as they warned me about prison and the chance of being refused entry to the UK. Guess what, there was a solution. It would cost $1,000 and I could travel with ease. It had to be cash and it had to be then.

John McDonald, the ring MC, had an alternative plan. He used the phone in the security guard's den to make a call. The boys seemed happy, assuming their bag was on its way. How wrong they were.

McDonald, using his trademark blend of Ghanaian English, was speaking to the one man in Accra that could solve my problem. After the call, we sat in silence, John nodding over at me.

After about 20 minutes I could hear a commotion outside and the door flew open – that is the only way to describe the entrance. And there stood Azumah Nelson, Africa's greatest boxer and Ghana's greatest hero. He was all of five-foot four in his leather sandals, but he was a beast. The guards jumped up and Zoom Zoom slapped the pair of them, backhanded. *Bang Bang*. He then gave them the facts of life and out we walked, straight onto the plane and into the cockpit to say hello to the captain. Nelson left, I sat down in first class; seven hours later, the customs officer in London shrugged and waved me through. That's how you exit Africa, baby.

Three days earlier, I had gone to Nelson's bungalow in the Achimota district of the city. His iron gates were between the Blood of Jesus church and Tina's Chops Shops – and that is the correct spelling of Tina's place. There were street traders at the gate selling pictures of Nelson and pieces of fruit. There were other traders and each day they set up a full market. It was known as Champ's Market. It sold everything from chickens to three-foot tall wooden statues of their champ.

'A champ must be simple like his people,' he told me. He would buy his produce from the stalls. He refused a painting because, he told the woman, it made him look ugly. The gathering in the market laughed and cheered. She offered him an alternative, one of Nelson Mandela and one of the country's leader, Flt Lt Jerry Rawlings. He smiled and declined; they were both friends of the champ. Nelson never had to boast, he was regal.

Nelson had huskie dogs and a swimming pool shaped like a boxing glove. But we went inside and sat in darkness, the curtains pulled tight, and we watched his fights. Hours and hours of his exceptional fights. He had won and lost world titles at that point in his career. He could have retired then, and he would still be Africa's greatest. He refused.

'I want money because glory is no good to an old man like me,' he told me. He was 36 at the time and not finished with the glory or the money.

'At night I go outside, and I stand by the pool, and I have visions of fights,' he continued. 'I'm restless, I'm a man of action – I need to fight.' It was a wonderful remark, a beautiful vision of the African fighting god in the moonlight with his huskies at this side.

Less than six months later, he ended his 18-month exile when he shocked Gabe Ruelas to win the WBC super-featherweight title. He was 37 then, his status secured for eternity; over 60,000 met him at the airport and the four-mile drive to his home took six hours. I know it takes about ten minutes and so do the two security guards.

'This is a great fight, one of my best, but I lost,' he said in the darkness. It was a bad recording of the night at Madison Square Garden in 1982 when he lost to the Mexican king, Salvador Sanchez. It finished in the 15th and final round, Nelson was up on one card. What drama. It remains one of boxing's true gems. The fights rolled on; he had fought in 21 world title fights when I sat down for the first of two days of endless fights on tape. The sun shone very bright through a few cracks in the curtains. We never sat by the pool, not even for a break. The huskies were obedient. Nelson made cold baked bean salad both days. I filled my pad; I listened as he talked me through the Jeff Fenech fights. He knocked out the Australian idol in front of 50,000 in Melbourne; it was a rematch after the draw in their first fight.

In the shadows in that room, Nelson moved and threw the shots. He was reliving the fight in his darkened room, and he could remember, like so many boxers, the exact punches. What a time it was.

One of the punches he threw was similar to the first he landed on the chops of security guard number one; the man was lucky it was a backhand and not a fist.

Azumah Nelson: *He is still a boxing god in any country. He fought on after my visit and even had a mad exhibition/fight with Fenech in 2008; the less said about that, the better. My passport never surfaced.*

28

LENNOX LEWIS
— v —
OLIVER McCALL

WBC HEAVYWEIGHT CHAMPIONSHIP: HILTON, LAS VEGAS, 1997

'I was waiting for God to let me know when to knock Lewis out.'

Lennox Lewis was up at six, fell into the referee at eight and was stopped on his feet. It was a nightmare that he had lived with for three years before his rematch with Oliver McCall.

'The ref was right,' said McCall. 'It was 31 seconds – there was no way he survived the round.' Lennox had to live with McCall beating him and it was not easy.

It was a very different Lewis in Las Vegas for the second fight. He prepared at Johnny Tocco's gym under the watchful eye of Manny Steward – in the first fight, Steward had trained McCall. In boxing, we have an alternative word for loyalty: we like to use 'business'.

'If Lennox loses, he will be just another bum,' said a brutal Steward to a few of us during the week of the fight. 'In America he's seen as an inconsistent fighter, and he needs to win, and he needs to win by knockout.' When Manny Steward was in full, fighting flow, he could be harsh with the truth. He was the same in the corner.

'Lennox is stronger now than ever,' Kellie Maloney insisted.

McCall was not stronger – he was bad, very bad. There was a story that McCall had only left rehab seven weeks before the first bell; he had gone berserk and thrown a Christmas tree from a balcony at a hotel. He had been arrested and rehab followed. It was true. He had with him his personal drug counsellor, Ruth Ferguson. He was erratic at public appearances that week. He looked off his nut, to tell the truth. And he was, it turns out.

Only 3,800 people paid to watch the fight, and nobody will ever forget what happened. I will never forget that tiny attendance.

McCall arrived in the ring with his face twisted and tears falling from his eyes. He was disconnected from his cornermen, George Benton and Greg Page. The referee, Mills Lane, looked concerned before the bell; Lewis never noticed.

In the first couple of rounds, not a lot happened and then at the end of the third, McCall refused to go to his corner. He was still crying and talking to himself. Benton and Page were patient, they knew what they were witnesses to. In the fourth and fifth rounds, McCall kept turning away and refusing to fight; Lennox held off, confused. At the end of the fourth, Don King, the promoter, went to McCall's corner: 'Get out there and fight, Oliver,' he demanded.

In the fifth, Lane told McCall to defend himself and he never listened. At 0:55 of round five, it was stopped. McCall ducked straight through the ropes and ran to the dressing room. There were boos, but they could not hide the giant sobs from McCall as he ran for his life from the ring.

The fight was on a Friday and late that night, I spoke to Benton. 'I seen it before, men crying and stuttering, and it is a terrible thing, withdrawal. I know what I'm talking about.' Benton's own career was finished when he was shot, left for dead and finished up in intensive care.

Steward was brutal as ever when asked what he thought had happened. 'He was very much intimidated and afraid of being hurt.'

I had written a dramatic preview and it still fell short: 'Lewis is fighting for his future, but McCall is fighting for his life: a boxing combination that seldom fails to deliver.' We knew, but we never expected such a shocking and sickening public breakdown.

Late that night the calls came through and messages were left on hotel phones. Next morning at the Hilton, McCall would tell his side of the story.

We gathered and in came the main players: King and McCall. There was a psychiatrist now to replace the drug counsellor. 'I was never hurt; I was waiting for God to let me know when to knock Lewis out. My tactic was to confuse him.' Wow, that was his defence. Dr Leonora Petty, his overnight shrink, just nodded her head. Yep, all makes perfect sense now! 'His mental state is just fine,' she told us.

McCall continued talking and his wife, standing behind us, kept on crying. It was gentle, a pain she was trying to hide. On the top table, Jose Sulaiman, the boss of the WBC, reached a hand over and comforted Oliver with a pat. A stroke as gentle as a master pickpocket at work.

Benton was not there for the big reveal; perhaps he just cared too much to listen. 'The drugs messed him up and ruined his career,' he said. And McCall echoed Benton's words that Saturday morning at the lunatic conference. 'I will always have a problem,' McCall said and then he told a truly harrowing story about his still-born daughter. 'I was high, so high and I asked the Lord not to let a child come into this world bearing my name.' The sobs continued.

It was a heavy morning. Lewis was the new WBC heavyweight champion of the world, but the message got lost somewhere when the ridiculous life and times of Oliver McCall took over.

And the final word must go to King when he was asked about the Nevada Commission holding back McCall's $3 million purse.

'It's not the money, it is Oliver's health that matters.' Get in! King never lets you down when you need a mental quote.

Oliver McCall: *It was McCall's 35th fight and he would retire in 2019 after 75 fights. It would be petty to list all of McCall's crimes and misdemeanours. I remember something that Greg Page said in the minutes after the fight ended and during a scramble at ringside. 'Pray, that it never happens to you or to somebody you love.' He is right. And finally, McCall got paid in full.*

29

NICKY BOOTH: EXTREME

THE STRELLEY ESTATE, NOTTINGHAM, 2004

'People tried to help me, but the addict always knows best.'

It was liver failure in the end, and he was just 40.

Nicky Booth had one of the briefest and craziest reigns as British champion. He was a genuine home-town idol in Nottingham. He was from the Strelley Estate, and he fought eight of his last ten fights at the Harvey Hadden Sports Centre. He had nine title fights in four years; he was loved. He defended his British title four times at the Hadden.

He was just 24 and the reigning British bantamweight champion when he smashed his way into a local crack house and stole the supply. It was not the work of a vigilante; it was the work of an addict. A bad addict.

He was caught, he lost his British title outside of the ropes, and he was sentenced to two years for 'burglary and theft' in June 2004. I went to the Strelley to see him in December when he was released. He still had his dreams, and he knew the truth. 'Nicky Booth has never tried to deny the months on the pipe that led to prison.' He was clean that day – I went back the following year, when he still wanted to make a comeback, and he was not clean.

His addiction cost him his title and access to his daughter. He knew that there were no excuses in his life. 'People tried to help me, but the addict always knows best.'

When I went to see him, he was getting help from a former pro called Matt Scriven; they had a plan to get his British Boxing Board of Control licence back. It never happened. Scriven is now a war-zone junkie; in a crazy turn of boxing events, he was my personal security when I went to Saudi Arabia for the Tyson Fury and Francis Ngannou fight. That was easy work. Matt has been behind enemy lines in a dozen forsaken places; his skirmish with Booth's enemies on the Strelley was good preparation.

Booth once told me that he wanted to swim the English Channel. 'When?' I asked. 'What about today?' he replied. He was deadly serious. He was extreme.

It is amazing that a boy like Booth was not protected. I know the arguments about how junkies can't be helped, trust me. I know that story. But they can be helped to become addicted. Booth and his brother, Jason, topped the bill at the Harvey Hadden, even walking from their homes to their fights and often leaving the packed arena with part of their money in a bag. The lights in the distance, seen from the entrance at the Harvey Hadden, were burning bright – some of those intoxicating lights were in crack dens. It was a crazy situation: fight in front of 1,000 adoring fans, defend your British title, get a few grand in cash and walk towards the lights. Hard to believe.

When I went back to Nottingham in 2005, Booth had a new girlfriend and was trying to get his life back. We arranged to take him to a show in London to watch a fight for his old title. He was excited, he was also using heavily once again. When we went to get him, his girlfriend was in tears. She showed us the new suit that she had spread out on the bed for him. It looked like the suit for a dead man. It was pitiful and damning: a reminder of a life lost. So neat and hopeful. She had such pride in it.

Nicky Booth never knew or cared, and he had vanished; we went to the show without him. I wanted to scream. And I never spoke to him again. He died in 2021 surrounded by the people that never stopped loving him, holding his hands and sobbing as he left. Go on, Nicky. Go well, my son.

Nicky Booth: *One of the saddest tales in modern boxing. British champion, swimming dreamer and addict.*

30

SUGAR RAY LEONARD
— v —
TERRY NORRIS

WBC LIGHT-MIDDLEWEIGHT FIGHT: MADISON SQUARE GARDEN, NEW YORK, 1991

'I had heard thuds and bangs and heavy wallops, but never the crisp crack of every blow that cut down Sugar Ray that night . . .'

Mean Streets was on at 2 a.m., a perfect way to finish a night at the Garden after a visit to Fanelli's cafe. Now that is a New York boxing tale.

Sugar Ray Leonard lost against Terry Norris and only 7,495 paid to watch his debut under the roof and exit from boxing's elite level. It was a disturbing pleasure to witness this piece of sad history.

Three days earlier, I had pushed my way up some stairs above a filthy McDonalds next to the Port Authority to watch Sugar train in a gym. It was a squalid and dangerous part of New York in 1991. It's no resort now, to be honest. I had about three feet of fax paper confirming my credentials, and I waved it like a magic wand to get up those stairs. I still have it in a folder, but now it has faded to nothing, with just my scribbled notes in the margins as a ghostly reminder that it was once a critical sheet.

Sugar was 34 at the time, his gold medal had been in 1976, his greatest fights a decade earlier, his cocaine addiction had raged through the last few years and yet, as I stood there six-layers deep against the cold, I watched a true genius at work. He was brilliant. Sure, there might have been a bit of Grecian on his hair, his face and eyes scarred for life, but he still moved like a boxing god. In that shithole, I watched one of the true greats.

I got a few minutes with my whirring Dictaphone. He talked of turning back the glory clock – it never happens – and of some unfinished business – always the same. He smiled and he moved on. We now know that the addictions were following him in New York that winter; the addictions were Sugar's safe place. That is the truth. I filed a few quotes to a few British papers, using the free-phone numbers. I nicked back a few quid, not much. I was staying on a friend's couch.

Leonard had lost just once, had not fought for 14 months and was, oddly, the betting favourite. I'm still shocked at the small attendance; it was freezing, but still, it was Sugar's Garden debut. And mine, obviously.

I was in the Garden early, eating as much free popcorn as possible. A trio of British boxing writers met me at one point. 'Well, who you doing it for?' Colin Hart of the *Sun* asked. He was flanked by Ian Gibb of the *Daily Mirror* and Ken Gorman of the *Daily Star*. 'Anybody who will take it,' I replied. I think I was filing for the *Daily Telegraph*, *Today*, and the old faithful, the *Sunday Express*. I bet I never made 300 quid on the trip. I did, however, watch Willem Dafoe remove a woman's bra in a SoHo bar on my way to Fanelli's that night. They both seemed happy. He loved his boxing, Willem. And obviously, a good set of tits.

Terry Norris was a special fighter. He was far too much on the night for Leonard. It was a lost memory fight for the ghost of Sugar that night; he was fighting on basic instinct, not memory. He was exposed by age and abuse. Norris won clearly, dropping Leonard twice. I remember one thing about Norris, and it was the sound, the crack, that his tiny gloves made each time he caught Leonard; it was a sound I had never heard. I had heard thuds and bangs and heavy wallops, but never the crisp crack of every blow that cut down Sugar Ray that night in the old temple. That is a living memory.

At ringside, there was a sideshow attraction. John Gotti, the Teflon Don, was there in a fur coat, his pinkie ring dazzling from the opposite side of ringside. He took applause and mini bows on a regular basis. Two seats from him and topless in the frozen night, was Mitch 'Blood' Green, a one-time street-gang leader and at that time a retired heavyweight. Blood was the man involved in the 3 a.m. scuffle in Harlem, outside Dapper Dan's suit emporium, with Mike Tyson in 1988. They clashed, Tyson broke a hand, Green's eye was closed and he needed stitches. They had met at the Garden over ten rounds in 1986; Green had kept singing after losing on points. The big house, as the Garden is known, was rocking.

Leonard was tiny and beaten when I saw him at the very end of that night.

I left the Garden late; I was in no hurry to end the night. In my lift was Norris and his manager, a real cowboy, Joe Sayatovich, and a few of their team. Joe wore Wrangler jeans and could catch a cow with a lasso. They ignored me and talked of fights against big names. It was another world for me – I had been, one week earlier, at the schoolboy championships at a school in Wembley. That night had probably ended at the Golden Kebab in Stratford.

After the end of Sugar Ray Leonard's last great stand, I walked about 50 blocks to Fanelli's cafe and then went back to my digs and watched *Mean Streets* from the start. That is what is so wonderful about my job.

Sugar Ray Leonard: *In 1997, Leonard had his last fight. He lost again. Leonard is still on the circuit, still adored. Norris won and lost world titles for the next seven years. He is not in great condition now. Fanelli's is still there, a haven.*

31

FOUR NATIONS TOURNAMENT

ST PETERSBURG, RUSSIA, 2004

I had been to a killer's lair the night before and paid homage to the blood spilled.

The assigned guide was called Fedor, and he was desperate to tell us all about Afghanistan. He knew nothing about television or the BBC, but he knew a thing or two about covert wars.

It was 2004, the Olympics in Athens were just seven weeks away and I travelled to a nearly mythical tournament to see the very best from Russia, Ukraine, Uzbekistan and Kazakhstan fight each other. I was on BBC duty, part of the *Path to Athens* series, an Olympic preview show. I went on after Russia and did a water-polo film from Budapest the following week. Four winners from St Petersburg would win gold medals in Athens. And the Hungarians won the gold in the pool.

It was the summer and that meant the white nights were in full force. We filmed the first day until about 3 a.m. and then went to eat. Fedor knew a place – obviously he did. He also loved his Russian literature and at about 4 a.m., just as it was about to get dark for three minutes, he took me and the producer, Stephen Lyle, to some flats. We left the meal and followed him.

'You know Raskolnikov?' he asked. I did, it turns out. He was delighted. Lyley wondered if he was the new Russian defender at Stoke.

We entered a building, not flats and not a house. I guess it was about six floors tall. There were hundreds lining the stairs and landings. Fedor, who was armed, led us up, straight to the door. I knew where we were. There were candles everywhere and graffiti on the walls. It was a shrine.

'This is where Raskolnikov killed the old woman,' Fedor announced. Lyley couldn't work out how Stoke City's number four had managed to get a visa. Ten minutes later we were back in the restaurant, and it was light again. That was enough for me.

The boxing was magnificent, but we were excluded at first. There was a demand for payment, and it was all a bit ugly, a bit Russian and then the man with the most winkle picker of winkle picker boots in history arrived. The man from Green Hill: Khan and his trademark pointed boots. I had admired those rascal babies in Budapest, Houston and Belfast at the amateur world championships. His company had an exclusive deal to supply the gloves for major amateur tournaments. Hey, I have no idea if that was an ethical deal, but what did I know? I had been to a killer's lair the night before and paid homage to the blood spilled.

Khan laughed when I said there was a problem; five minutes later he solved it, and we were in and filming. There had been a mistake in communication, Fedor told us.

The Russian coach was Aleksandr Lebziak, one of the most fearsome amateurs in history. He had crazy power. He won Olympic gold in Sydney, and he also won the Worlds and the Europeans. He also smoked like a trooper. He knew Alexander Povetkin would win gold in Athens, and he did. Lebziak looked like the Soviet fighters from the Seventies, tall, cold and vicious. He was a cultured man, a delight to talk with, but he also looked like he could order your execution with about the same amount of stress as buying a new pair of socks.

It was in St Petersburg that I was given an education on Russian boxing politics and what it was really like under the Soviet banner. Back in the Seventies heyday, the Kazaks and Uzbeks struggled against the blue-eyed boys from Moscow and Kiev. At the national championships in Belarus each year, the judges always favoured the Russian and Ukraine boxers. The men from the republics of Uzbekistan and Kazakhstan were the poor relations in the boxing business; if they somehow got selected for the Olympics and won gold, they were brilliant. I took testimony and Fedor was not too happy.

So, the takeaways from St Petersburg: it is a stunning city, white nights are a wonder, Raskolnikov is worshipped, Khan could fix anything, the Russian bride thing is real and Chicken Kiev at 4 a.m. is essential.

Four Nations: *The tournament has gone forever and that is a pity. Lebziak remains a boxing idol. And, by the way, Fedor was not his real name.*

32

JOE JOYCE
— v —
DANIEL DUBOIS

BRITISH HEAVYWEIGHT TITLE: CHURCH HOUSE, WESTMINSTER, 2020

As Daniel went down in calculated surrender, I could hear a shriek of despair from his sister, Caroline.

In the very thick of the Covid restrictions a great heavyweight title fight was made.

Joe Joyce was unbeaten in 11, with ten ending quick; Daniel Dubois was unbeaten in 15, with 14 ending quick. Dubois was the British heavyweight champion and Joyce had won a silver medal at the Olympics in Rio.

Inside the glorious hall, about 50 people had managed to secure a ticket; it was officially behind closed doors. All of us working on the fight for BT had taken Covid tests. It still felt like a big fight.

Joyce was magnificent and calm. Dubois only seemed to realise he was in trouble when it was too late. And then he was in trouble; his left eye was slowly closing and his cheek swelling. He was damaged and for two or three rounds he could not see a thing out of the eye. That degree of damage meant that he could not anticipate Joyce's thunderous right hand.

In the tenth, Dubois was hit with a jab, he backed off and went down on one knee. There was a collective intake of breath. He had quit in one of sport's most naked arenas, a sacred square where bravery was demanded, and every dubious action is analysed. He had damaged his orbital bone and that can be repaired; he had also damaged his reputation and that is harder to mend.

It was a truly shocking end. The barren hall was shaken and as Daniel went down in calculated surrender, I could hear a shriek of despair from his sister, Caroline. He was blind in one eye and his punches had not hurt Joyce. I had no problem with Dubois taking the knee. It is an act that always divides people in the business, but let's be honest, only boxers have a say. It annoys me when journalists, broadcasters, managers and promoters declare a fighter a coward.

Dubois and Joyce have been on a mixed path since that odd night.

Daniel Dubois: *In Saudi Arabia in late December 2023, Dubois got his redemption. He stopped the American, Jarrell Miller, with just eight seconds left of the tenth and last round; Dubois had been in trouble in about the fifth or the sixth. It was a hard fight. The truth is, he looked close to quitting. His father had been moved to ringside and it worked. Dubois dug very deep and broke Miller. In 2023, Joyce lost back-to-back fights to Zhilei Zhang. He was meant to win and get a summer world title fight with Oleksandr Usyk; Joyce lost, and it was Dubois who got Usyk in Poland.*

33

GIL CLANCY:
TRAINER OF CHAMPIONS

THE POCONOS, 1989

'Balance, it is all about the balance, it's the most important thing.'

Gentleman Gerry Cooney needed more than Gil Clancy on the night he met George Foreman in Atlantic City. Clancy knew it would be hard, he was not a fool. He got Big Gerry too late.

On a bitter cold November day, I joined Clancy and a dozen or so other boxing people for the short journey from outside Madison Square Garden to Caesar's resort in the Poconos. It's the place, I found out, with a Perspex six-foot tall champagne glass jacuzzi in the suites. No expense spared in pursuit of class.

Clancy had worked with a broken Foreman after the unbeatable man of the heavyweight division was beaten by Muhammad Ali in the Rumble in the Jungle. Clancy knew Foreman, knew him well. 'If you stand with George, you are in trouble,' he said that day.

On the bus, the first thing I heard Clancy say was: 'He'd knock out a horse if he hit it clean.'

Clancy belonged to that lost breed of trainer, confidant and fight guru. A man impeccably turned out, his second's jacket starched, the tools of his corner trade stashed in a tiny bag. I guess he was in his mid-sixties that day on the beano to the Poconos and Cooney's training camp retreat, and he looked distinguished.

George Francis, the north London boxing genius, had the same classy look. They were the 'been there, done it' men.

We had barely left Manhattan before Clancy started to talk about his greatest fighter and one of the sport's finest, Emile Griffith. There was silence on that wayward boxing bus.

Clancy had worked with Griffith from the very first moment he walked into the gym: he had taught him balance, footwork, tucking in your elbows, simple stuff. 'Balance, it is all about the balance, it's the most important thing,' he said. Their relationship remains one of the greatest bonds in boxing. Griffith won and lost world titles and Gil was there each time.

On that bus, he talked about the death of Benny 'Kid' Paret. It had been only 27 years before that journey, and it was fresh in Clancy's head. It is the most famous death fight in the sport's tricky history. The ending was truly sickening and there are iconic pictures of Paret helpless and dying, trapped in the ropes in a corner. He's not on the ropes, he is *in* the ropes, tangled up. Griffith had been merciless, determined to make Paret suffer for a sexual slur. Clancy had to try and help Griffith deal with the guilt in the fight's high-profile aftermath.

'It was not easy,' Clancy said. 'Emile was not a killer, that was not what he was. He had to deal with a lot.' Clancy was like a father to the boxer he made.

'We watched that in slow motion,' said Clancy. 'Emile landed 17 punches in five seconds; don't blame the referee, I'm the one who told him to keep punching if he had Benny hurt.'

It felt like Gil Clancy told that story again and again, a form of penance. That makes sense.

In the gym with Cooney, there were tiny things that he kept telling Gerry. I was too far away to hear, but that is the way the craftsmen in our game work. No stupid, showy thrills. It's no good bellowing, 'that's right, champ!' from 30 feet away. A true coach talks and talks. Clancy taught the art of boxing, and for a few hours I was one of his students.

Gil Clancy: *In January of the following year, Foreman walked through Cooney in two rounds. Gerry stood still. Foreman was on his way to the world title; Cooney was on his way to a lethal freefall. 'That fight pushed me over the edge,' Cooney told me in 2022. Clancy left the Boardwalk that night and no doubt his second's jacket was folded neatly away.*

34

MIKE TYSON
— v —
JULIUS FRANCIS

HEAVYWEIGHT CONTEST: MANCHESTER, 2000

'A plan? It's impossible to have a plan, because I will find out what I'm going to do when he hits me.'

Nobody knows where the boots are.

Julius Francis was paid £35,000 (it could be more; it was probably less) by the *Daily Mirror* to have their logo on the soles of his boots. The thinking was a bit cruel, but it worked: if Mike Tyson could drop Francis, the logo would be visible. In the end, Francis was over five times in four minutes and three seconds. Francis was paid £308,000 for the fight; Tyson received £5 million.

'Those boots will be worth a fortune,' Francis told me in 2023. 'I gave them to (Kellie) Maloney and I think he [she] gave them to a charity.' Maloney, now Kellie and living in Portugal, had no idea what happened to the boots.

It was a perfect end to the fight in many ways. Frank Warren, the promoter, kept calling it an event and not a fight. He was right.

There had been moves to ban Tyson from entering and fighting in Britain. The boxer had been convicted and sentenced to six years in prison for the rape in 1991 of Desiree Washington. The broadcaster, Trevor Phillips, was dismayed at Tyson's imminent arrival 'It will stick in my craw,' he said. 'He molested women.'

Members of his family knew Washington. Tyson would later be banned from entering Britain.

It was a genuine wild ride once Tyson touched down in London in early January. A cameraman called Dave Varley was imbedded with Tyson and the boxer's initial entourage of 17 from the first day. Crocodile, aka Steve Fitch, was the main cheerleader. That was his job: shouting, wearing combat fatigues and being the centre of attention. 'Loved by few, hated by many, but respected by all,' he would bellow. He wore the same clobber, but kept his mouth closed when we walked down Oxford Street looking for a money sending bureau. He was just a wayward dad, with an odd job. He had to send a few dollars home that day.

The entourage grew to 36 by the time the boxer moved to Manchester for the fight. With Varley, I went with Tyson to Brixton and that was crazy; we ended up taking shelter in the police station with thousands and thousands outside on the street. Tyson waved at them from a window, Varley filmed it all, including Tyson's escape in a secretary's little car. He was on the floor in the back. A mile or so down the road, in Kennington, he got out and got in with his security detail. Varley filmed it all. The extraordinary documentary went out on BBC Two, just 48 hours after the fight. *Mike Tyson in the UK* was a pure gem, never seen since and Varley has no idea where any of the unused film is. There was one exchange that obviously never got used where Tyson and Frank Warren are talking about their experiences with Don King. It was x-rated, not one for the kids.

'I have no fear of him, Steve,' Francis told me the week before the fight when I visited him at the army's Hammersley Barracks in Aldershot 'A plan? It's impossible to have a plan because I will find out what I'm going to do when he hits me.'

Mark Roe trained Francis and he seemed captivated by Tyson at the press conference in Manchester. I had seen that before, seen people fall under Tyson's spell. 'He had a dignified manner,' Roe said. 'You're looking at someone of magnificence.'

The venue was sold out in 48 hours – every single one of the 21,000 seats. It was mayhem on the night. I somehow got my wife a ticket, which was a rare event. It would backfire, trust me.

Francis was 35, the reigning British heavyweight champion, a former felon and the first, so he claimed, black Millwall hooligan. 'They thought I was an undercover copper at first,' he told me. He remains to this day a good friend and funny man. He tried; he took it to Tyson on the night and went down swinging.

Tyson told me, in the last day or two in Manchester, something that has haunted me. 'Man, I'm young, but I seem so old.' Tyson had seemed so old for many years; the kid from the Eighties had gone forever. There was still an endless fascination with Tyson, the boxer, and what he had left. There were still flashes of the heavy-weight champion in the gym, and that is why it was sold out.

Mike Tyson in the UK: *At about two in the morning, I traipsed back with my wife to the hotel. It was the Midland, the hotel where Tyson was staying. The lobby was busy, too crazy to be honest. We went up to the room, which was at the end of the landing. Outside the rooms next to ours, five or six of the ring card girls were sitting, obviously locked out of their rooms. In nearly 40 years at ringside, I don't think I have ever spoken to a ring card girl. As we approached, a few of them jumped up, beaming and said: 'Hi, Steve, can we use your toilet? Thanks.' What could I say?*

35

AMIR KHAN:
THE TEENAGE SENSATION

BOXING DEBUT. BOLTON, 2005

'I'm made for the pros – British boxing is ready for me.'

It was one of the most chaotic nights to ever take place in a British ring – the day started with a vanishing and ended with a bomb scare. In the middle, Amir Khan, still only 18, arrived on the pro scene.

Khan had reached the Olympic final the year before in Athens and had been chased by every decent promoter in the world – and a few indecent ones. Turning pro was not as easy a decision for a wide-eyed teenage boy to make as people think. He was still a kid, the lights were very bright, and the bold claims were crazy.

'If it was the money, I would have turned pro after the Olympics and not waited nearly a year,' Khan told me on the Thursday before the debut in his home town. 'I sat with my dad and the rest of the people, and we considered every option.' In the end, Frank Warren won.

'Amir is a role model for young British kids of all colours and races,' gushed Warren.

The journey to Bolton on that hot summer night had been something to behold; in Athens, at 17, he defied the odds again and again and again. I was ready to fly home when he met the European champion in the second round. No British boxer had won a European amateur title since 1961. Khan had failed in Pula earlier in the year. He had no chance, and he was, remember, the only British boxer at the Olympics. Khan boxed the ears off Dimitar Stilianov and then he stopped the Asian Games champion in the first round in the quarters. It was a fairy tale. There was one more win and then he met the great Cuban master, Mario Kindelan, in the final. Kindelan was the defending Olympic champion. Kindelan was also Fidel Castro's favourite boxer.

Khan lost on points, but he was fearless and pushed Kindelan all over the Greek ring.

The debut was set; the main event on the night was Matt Skelton defending his British heavyweight title against Brixton's Danny Williams. It was a fight with a bit of anger and needle. Williams had been giving Skelton stick for months. It was all set and then at midnight before the fight, Williams vanished, went back to London with the 'flu'. A man called Dean Powell, a matchmaker, contacted Mark Krence, a butcher from Chesterfield at 8 a.m. 'Do you want the fight?' Powell asked. Krence had a mouthful of corn flakes, but he accepted. He retired after seven rounds of Skelton taking out his anger on him.

Powell had found David Bailey for Khan's debut. It was a good choice. Bailey was from London, was getting five grand and was tough. He had lost four times in seven fights; he had never been stopped and two of his defeats were by a single point. My personal stat of the fight, and I used it in the *Independent*, was an old-fashioned piece of boxing journalism: Bailey was a southpaw like seven of Khan's last 11 opponents. There was only one place you would read that, son.

Khan was a very excitable boy that week and that night. Just under 6,000 people had packed the arena. It was a Khan party. I guess nobody really imagined that the teenager was going to stay calm and box sensibly. No chance. 'I'm made for the pros – British boxing is ready for me,' Khan said.

So, there is an unbelievable atmosphere and noise. Bailey looks fired up; Khan is flying. Ding-ding and then it was a dong. Bailey rushed at Khan, charged in like a banger. Khan found a punch or six and Bailey was over. 'Khan was merciless,' I wrote in the *Observer*. Bailey took a nine count on his knees after the second knockdown. There was total bedlam in the place, mayhem. It was wonderful. 'Fuck's sake, ref, stop it,' hollered Eugene Maloney in Bailey's corner. The ref let it go a bit longer and finally after 69 seconds the debut was over. Khan was on his way.

Ten minutes later there was a bomb scare and the entire building had to be evacuated. Tony Doherty and Ernie Smith were in round two of their six rounder, and they had to flee with their gloves on.

It was the start for Khan and the end was a long and crazy distance away. Khan told me that week, when we were in a takeaway shop in Bolton that had named every dish after him, that he wanted to simply win world titles at two weights, make £50 million and get out in five years. One out of three is not bad.

Amir Khan: *He became the star of British boxing. A real celebrity, but I still see that little boy from Athens each time I'm with him – even after his many scrapes. Bailey never fought again. Skelton eventually won and lost in fights with Williams; his last fight was a defeat to Anthony Joshua. Big Matt never liked me, and I have no idea why. Nobody was ever prosecuted for the bomb scare.*

36

CUBAN BOXERS:
THE ULTIMATE DEFECTORS

VICTOR'S RESTAURANT, NEW YORK, 1998

A lot of Cuban boxers struggle to deal with the excesses of life in the West.

There was a time when the most expensive cargo in the world was a Cuban boxer. They managed to escape Fidel Castro's gaze by boat, jet ski, dressed as women, in helicopters and on local buses. Their journeys were funded by secret accounts. The defection of Cuban boxers was an ugly business. And a lucrative one.

In the summer of 1998, during the Goodwill Games, I stumbled on a proper scene at Victor's restaurant on 52nd Street. Two years earlier, at the Atlanta Olympics, a consortium of professional boxing people had unveiled Joel Casamayor, a defector, and a gun had fallen from a Cuban official's tracksuit. It was wild stuff, a conference with a bit of real edge.

The Russian and Cuban boxing delegations travelled all over the world to events with a dozen men posing as 'trainers' or 'officials'; only they weren't, they were part of the secret state police. The job of the travelling and armed police was to prevent any of the talent defecting.

In Victor's, Ramon Garbey, who had gone over the wall one night at a pre-Olympic training camp in Mexico, was in charge. Garbey was the world amateur champion. Five days after Garbey vanished, Casamayor claims he simply walked out of some Mexican training camp, got on a bus to Tijuana, met up with Garbey and walked across the border. He was the reigning Olympic champion, the first Cuban gold medalist to jump over the wall. The bit missing is the bit where Garbey makes contact with his American handlers, and they smooth the border crossing. They were elite cargo.

Garbey was running a dining club with a difference behind a curtain at the back of the swanky restaurant. He had some familiar faces back there. Casamayor loved the pulled pork, one of Victor's signature dishes.

I did ask a couple of questions, but I was not very popular. Anyway, the food is excellent. Garbey had become a fixture in Miami's Little Havana; the big lad was revered for sending money back to his grandmother in Havana. Casamayor won major world titles as a pro; his defection changed it all for the Cubans.

Ramon Garbey: *It never worked out for the Big Lad. I heard that he was working on the door at Victor's in Miami. I looked for him in 2022 when Daniel Dubois boxed there. A lot of Cuban boxers struggle to deal with the excesses of life in the West. Money, food and women, baby.*

37

ANTHONY JOSHUA
— v —
ANDY RUIZ

WBA, WBO AND IBF HEAVYWEIGHT TITLES:
MADISON SQUARE GARDEN, NEW YORK, 2019

He was fast for a fat little man.

It went spectacularly wrong for Anthony Joshua at the Garden in New York in the early summer of 2019.

We missed every single sign until we were cast out of the Garden in the small hours and convened over eggs and beer at the Tick Tock diner. Even then, we were still missing the clues.

Joshua was meant to be fighting a big, slow, foul-mouthed and dangerous lump called Jarrell 'Big Baby' Miller. The fight collapsed in late April when it was revealed that Miller, who was getting $5 million for the fight, had failed a drug test. He failed in spectacular fashion, old-school East German style. No juiced-up recovery drink for Big Baby. He was caught with so many ancient illegal drugs in his system – he looked doomed forever. No chance. He was out, banned, disgraced and in came Andy Ruiz at short notice.

Ruiz was a very small six-foot two, but he was a big boy, and he could fight. His only loss was on points in a WBO title fight to Joseph Parker.

Ruiz arrived in new jeans, with a new diamond necklace and a smile. We all noticed his belly. Joshua arrived from Florida, and it all seemed fine. We missed how agitated he was. We missed how many demands there were for his time. We missed the stye on his eye. We missed the cough. We ignored the stories about being chinned in the gym. We also missed that look in Ruiz's eye. He was AJ, unbeaten in 22, with 21 knockouts and perfect at 29. Forget Ruiz's confidence. What could go wrong?

There would be a good house inside the Garden on the Saturday night, but what we really wanted that week was the mayhem that Miller would have delivered. Still, we went through the week and watched the open workouts.

We watched out of the corner of our eyes as Katie Taylor and Callum Smith, both on the bill, went through the motions in a ring pitched in a fancy shopping area. Then Ruiz stepped in the ring and my old partner in the BBC podding caper, Mick Costello, went silent. And me. We watched and were stunned by the speed and the movement. And we decided to ignore it. Sure, it got about three seconds on the preview show from New York. In private we talked about it and then dismissed it again. The dumb detectives, hands up.

'This is a tougher fight,' said Eddie Hearn on Friday at the weigh-in. Joshua told us again that he wanted Tyson Fury. It was all normal, but the crazy stuff was getting closer. Could Ruiz really get inside and let his hands go? He was fast for a fat little man. Sounds harsh? Forget it, those are his words. We ignored all the warning signs.

People in the AJ business were still calm; well, not all of them. Some hinted that there had been problems, not massive, but still problems. AJ, you see, never liked problems.

And then, as the clock ticked towards 3 a.m. in the Tick Tock, all the warnings came together. It was a Colombo moment. It had been there all the time: all the signs and we had ignored all of them.

Ruiz was the first man since Dillian Whyte, in my opinion, to get in the ring with AJ and to genuinely believe he would win. Yep, we also ignored that.

So, Agatha Costello and I sat down at ringside and then the fun started. What a fight, what a night at the Garden.

Joshua did look a bit apprehensive when he got in the ring, not nervous, just a bit cooler than normal. Ruiz was laughing. The first two rounds were close, I gave them to Joshua.

In the third, Joshua sent Ruiz down heavily, but I saw his eyes clear as he started to stand. I had seen that before with Joe Calzaghe. It is weird. Ruiz was completely recovered when the ref said, 'Box on'. I think Joshua missed that. There was 2:06 left. Thirty seconds later, Joshua was on the floor, and he was hurt. He got up, there was pandemonium at ringside and in the Garden. He was down again, got up again and then the bell came to his rescue. It was a third round to sit anywhere in any list of great rounds.

Joshua survived and started to get his boxing back together in rounds four and five. They both seemed tired in the sixth. In round seven, Joshua was face down with 2:17 left. He was over again, up on a knee and then standing in a corner. He was not moving or responding, he had no idea he was in the boxing ring in New York. The ref had to stop it and he did.

An hour later, I spoke to AJ in one of the big service lifts. I had staked out the lift – Costello was at the other exit. I had just followed AJ, his team and his boys into that lift when they came out of the dressing room by a back door. It was packed with about 30 people. AJ was six inches away from me, he was as stripped back and raw as any boxer I had ever seen. He was standing and facing the mess: 'I got involved. What a fucking fight.' He was still gone.

'It's about the rebuild now,' Hearn confirmed at midnight. 'He didn't know where he was – he will be back in November or December.' That was it, the final cue for us to go over to Tick Tock. The fighting was over.

Anthony Joshua: *Outdoors in Diriyah, on the outskirts of Riyadh, Joshua won every round to get his titles back and get revenge over Ruiz. It was December and Ruiz had lost his battle with the fridge since the win. He was 15 lbs heavier, had not prepared a bit. He was still smiling, even when he lost. Miller came back, eventually, and fought on the Days of Reckoning bill in Saudia Arabia in late 2023. He got in AJ's face at every opportunity. Three weeks later he was in trouble for allegedly trying to steal a truck from a dealership in Florida. I believe it was a misunderstanding, just like the drugs.*

38

STEVE ROBINSON: CINDERELLA MAN

WBO FEATHERWEIGHT CHAMPION. CARDIFF, 1993

'I know how this business works and I had to take this opportunity.'

Steve Robinson was fighting for respect a long time before he was dismissed for not being a proper world champion. It was hard and he was dismissed for a long, long time.

This is a tale seldom told and that is because, even in the boxing business, there is just too much romance. It's a fairy tale, a real one.

In April of 1993, Robinson and his girlfriend, Angela, were watching television when they saw that Ruben Palacio had failed a routine HIV test. Palacio was the WBO featherweight champion of the world, and he was fighting John Davison in Sunderland on that Saturday. It was Wednesday night in Cardiff. There is one version where it is Thursday morning. Whatever, you get the idea.

As they watched the news, the phone in his Ely home started to ring. It was, first, his manager, Dai Gardiner, and then his trainer, Ronnie Rush. They told him that his name was on the list to replace Palacio. It was the type of break all fighters from the wrong side of the tracks dream of. At that time, Robinson had lost nine of his 23 fights, he was not ranked by the WBO, but he was a full-time boxer. Robinson had given up his job in the Debenhams warehouse to train just three weeks earlier. He had walked out on a guarantee of £52 each week. He was already starting to worry about making ends meet, and then the calls came. This is like a story from 1949 and not 1993.

With about 48 hours to go before the first bell, a contract was signed. Robinson and Davison would meet for Palacio's vacant title. Meanwhile, in London, Colin McMillan, who lost the WBO title to Palacio, was taking and passing his own HIV test.

Robinson and his team travelled to Sunderland by train. He was on weight, always ready. Davison was on the floor at the news of the change and the ups and downs. I have seen many fighters broken by late replacements and cancellations; Davison looked like a ghost at the weigh-in. Robinson was twenty grand richer and he had nothing to lose or fear. He had been in with good men; he had taken jobs at short notice. It was not new to him.

'I know how this business works and I had to take this opportunity – I don't want to miss out,' Robinson said at the weigh-in.

Robinson had lost on the road in Paris seven weeks earlier and before that had won three on the spin when he was meant to lose all three: he was a live underdog in all three fights. He could fight, make no mistake. And all four fights had taken place in the last six months. He was fight-fit, raring to go.

'I'm not here to make up the numbers, I'm serious about this business now,' he said. And then he told us about quitting the job in the warehouse and waiting each day in the gym for a fight to come in. There was something in the air long before the fight.

Over 3,000 local fans watched their man lose to Robinson on a split. Robinson won it on two cards by just one point. It was slender, but it was enough. Robinson then went on a great home town run with defence after defence in Cardiff's dilapidated Ice Rink. It's gone now and there should be a plaque, a reminder of so many great nights inside the building.

A British boxer with a record like Steve Robinson's is unlikely to win a world title again. That is sad – we love fairy tales.

Well, there is one more thing to add. Palacio returned to Colombia, believing he had failed a medical because of a blood disorder. When he landed, he found out it was HIV. He was determined to fight again. He never did.

In May, three weeks after his cancelled fight, he became a father for the fourth time. He named his son John Davison Palacio. It was a permanent reminder to him of his ongoing fight, so he said. I like that.

Steve Robinson: *Naseem Hamed would stop Robinson in round eight in 1995 to eventually take the title. Robinson made seven successful defences – every defence was in Cardiff. He was meant to lose three of them, that is the truth and that is how often he was dismissed. Davison had one more fight. Palacio was arrested in Miami for cocaine trafficking a year after the Davison fight collapsed; he went to prison, serving four years. He died of AIDS in Colombia in 2003. Not such a happy ending.*

39

TERMITE WATKINS: THE RATCATCHER OF IRAQ

FITZROY LODGE, LONDON, 2004

'I never travel with the team because that would increase the chances of them getting killed . . .'

When Termite Watkins tried to get his boxing team out of Iraq, he lost five of his seven boxers.

'They said they fit the profile of various wanted men,' Watkins told me. It was April and we were in the Fitzroy Lodge gym in Lambeth, not far from the War Museum. The incident at the border with Kuwait had been two weeks earlier.

Watkins was actually travelling ten miles behind the boxers, in an unmarked car, but he was a marked man in the region. He was listed as a rat catcher in Baghdad, a pest controller working on an American government contract in the most dangerous city in the world. It was the family business.

'I never travel with the team because that would increase the chances of them getting killed and they are already at risk because of me,' Watkins told me that night in the old railway arch gym. I had first walked through the doors there as a skinny boy of ten. I knew the place and the people running it, and that is why I was tipped off that the 'Iraqi boxers with some noisy septic' were there. I went to see them. Termite being a typical noisy Septic Tank, that's yank.

A man called Ubdelzahia Juraid was also there. He had lost his gym in Hillah when it was destroyed by bombs. He had lost fighters, but not his belief in an Iraqi team and an Iraqi boxer at the Olympics. Six months before the night in the Lodge, Watkins had started working with the boxers. A British colonel, Steve Bruce, had helped fund the first gathering of the scattered team; 24 of the surviving boxers from Iraq's boxing programme showed up that day. Uday Hussein, one of Saddam's sons, had kept the boxers as his pet project. The team was short on a few names and for obvious reasons. The men and boys were also scared; they could be viewed as collaborators.

'Everybody has deaths. Everybody. Under Saddam or during the last year, death is death,' Juraid told me. 'The boxing had to stop, we had to just try and survive.'

Termite was far more than just a noisy American. In 1980, in Las Vegas, he challenged Saoul Mamby for the WBA light-welterweight title. He lost on points over 15 rounds. He was the chief support to Muhammad Ali against Larry Holmes. Those are credentials, the slippery old rat catcher. And there I was, thinking he was just a straight CIA conman.

At that point, the Iraqi boxers had failed to qualify for the Athens Olympics. They were all going to Pakistan the next week to try and qualify at the last event. It was a dream, that was for sure. Nearly 20 British boxers tried to get to Athens and only Amir Khan succeeded.

'The boxing had to stop, I understand, but now it is back,' said Najah Salah, the light-flyweight. 'I waited for the end of the fighting. I had to believe.'

'He can fight a bit, the little fella,' Mick Carney told me, pointing at Salah. Mick had been in the gym nearly half a century at that point. He knew a bit.

Najah did get to the Olympics, and he won a fight, beating the North Korean. He was known in Athens as Najah Ali; he entered the ring with 'Iraq is Back' written on his back. The American coach, Basheer Abdullah, helped Termite in the corner. That is a victory under any circumstances, and against a backdrop of war it is a miracle. George Kimball, the great scribe, saw it as a political message and was scornful. Sure, Ali was given a wild-card entry, but then he returned to Britain, turned professional, won five of his ten fights, was known as Little Ali and last fought in 2013. In the last decade, he has drifted away from the sport. He has driven a cab, served kebabs and lived in the Welsh valleys. It is hard to invent this stuff.

Maurice Termite Watkins: *Termite is still killing rats in Texas – it is the family business. He has had many offers to make a movie about his life. In 2020, Sly Stallone's company, Balboa Productions, were in talks with Termite. However, even I draw the line at suggestions that Brad Pitt wanted to play the ratcatcher.*

40

RICKY HATTON
— v —
FLOYD MAYWEATHER

WBC WELTERWEIGHT CHAMPIONSHIP: MGM, LAS VEGAS, 2007

'I got it all wrong last night.'

It was that simple: if Ricky Hatton beat Floyd Mayweather, then he would win the BBC's 2007 Sports Personality of the Year. And obviously it would be one of the greatest wins in a ring by a British boxer.

I had the trophy in my room at the MGM Grand in Las Vegas. And I also had the small runner-up version.

Joe Calzaghe was in town, and he had beaten Mikkel Kessler in a unification masterclass in front of 50,150 at the Millennium Stadium earlier in the year; if Hatton lost, Calzaghe would win SPOTY. It was close – a lot closer than the Mayweather fight.

Hatton and Mayweather had a combined record of 81–0. The venue, the Garden inside the MGM, sold out in seconds and tickets were being sold by agents for as much as $8,000. Hatton was only allocated 3,900 tickets and over 33,000 of his fans applied. The capacity was either 15,150 or 16,000 – the capacity at a venue is liquid, trust me. I invented the capacity at the MEN in Hatton's home town, I really did. The tickets were officially priced from $150 to $1,000. There was an invasion, and it was Hatton's third fight in Las Vegas that year.

There were also 20,000 seats in closed-circuit venues in Las Vegas. The fans were there, they took over the MGM. They took over the city. They also backed their idol with $20.1 million being placed on the underdog. There was a lot of hope in Las Vegas. Hatton was the most backed British boxer in history – he still might be.

On the morning of the fight, I came down for a coffee and a 5 Live hit from the media centre, and I saw a queue in the hotel's lobby. It was three or four wide and it stretched away, deep into the casino and kept going. I walked the length of it. It was a Hatton-fan, winding snake of thousands of men and woman all queuing and singing and drinking on their way to the SportsBook, the official betting office. They were backing their boy with dollars – often just ten. Hey, a bet is a bet. The Hatton faithful kept that fat line growing and paying for hours.

I spoke to Budd Schulberg a day or so before the fight. He was not happy with Mayweather referring to himself in the third person. 'Even Charlie Chaplin, the genius, never did that.' Budd had high standards and a contact book full of the world's greatest names. At the end of World War II, Budd had helped convict Nazi criminals; in the Fifties he won an Oscar; in the Sixties he covered Muhammad Ali. He could use Charlie Chaplin for anything – when you have done what Budd has, you are not a name-dropper.

Mayweather was brilliant on the night and Ricky was chasing shadows. Ricky had done a very un-Ricky thing at the weigh-in when he ran his finger across his throat – the crowd of 6,000 loved it; I hated it. He had never got that involved and getting involved emotionally with Mayweather was a mistake. Floyd Mayweather, you see, is heartless and cold in the boxing business. It finished in the tenth. It was ugly to watch.

After the fight, the fans were still singing at midnight and at 3 a.m. and at 6 a.m. when I was making my way to record some radio or to grab a coffee. You could hear the singing before the lift doors opened. The Betty Boop bar was dry long before dawn. The place had an apocalyptic feel. Nobody will ever forget that night and that week. The collective energy, the unbridled love for Ricky Hatton will never be repeated in my business. Not a chance. There really is only one Ricky Hatton. Gawd bless him.

Ricky Hatton: *The following day, after getting Hatton to his seat next to the empty ring at the MGM, it was Calzaghe who got the BBC trophy and was crowned Sports Personality of the Year. Ricky was a runner-up. It was a blur that crazy day. The trophy stayed with me in Las Vegas and went on a tour: swimming pool, bars, roller-coaster and poker table. The main memory from that Sunday was Ricky's arrival at 11 a.m.; he had shrunk during the night, he was cut and bruised and cried. 'I got it all wrong last night,' he said. Jennifer, his girlfriend, had her arm on his shoulder and for the entire two-hour broadcast, she never once took that arm off her man. Not for a second.*

41

PEOPLE'S CHOICE TOURNAMENT

CASINO MAGIC, MISSISSIPPI, 1993

There was a meeting of fighters and trainers and conmen and fixers and wayward drunks.

This was the craziest day of boxing that I have ever attended. There is not even a close rival.

There was mutiny in the air in south Mississippi during the week and just utter bedlam once the tournament started inside Casino Magic, a vast building built on a swamp. Ten minutes before the first bell a whole crate of beer was placed under my table.

This is how it ended. This is taken from my ringside story. At 11.20 p.m., Tony Tubbs, the former world heavyweight champion, left the ring after beating Olympic gold medal winner, Tyrell Biggs. It was his third win of the day, and the final was just minutes away.

At 11.25 p.m., in a tent in the car park, Tubbs was flat on a massage bed and his people were desperately trying to help him by rubbing ice all over his body. He was close to naked and close to collapse. It was a race to get the big lad dressed, on his feet and back in the ring. His hands were swollen, ruined from the punishing day.

'I can feel my aching bones,' Tubbs told me as he left the tent for the walk to the ring. All fights were over three three-minute rounds.

The bell for the first round of the final and his fourth fight of the day tolled at about 11.40 p.m. Tubbs was facing a Romanian called Daniel 'Bazooka' Dancuta, who had started the day as a 500-1 outsider. Dancuta had a bye in the semi-final when Australia's Craig Peterson was withdrawn with concussion and dehydration. Peterson had been in a war with former world champion, James 'Bonecrusher' Smith, in a truly brutal quarter-final. Smith and Tubbs had once been in major world title fights, men of glory and also part of the Lost Generation. The Casino Magic gathering was unique.

The plan was simple, I guess: offer a lot of prize money with a few extras and invite the fighters to Casino Magic. The problem was the money – the million-dollar winning purse on offer was, by the Wednesday of fight week, reduced to $150,000. The $15,000 bonus for a first-round knockout was dropped. All fighters had been guaranteed $20,000 for entering. That fee dropped to $6,000. On that Wednesday night, in the Waveland Tavern next to the casino, there was a meeting of fighters and trainers and conmen and fixers and wayward drunks. Men had guns, but they were just the regular customers and not part of the wild bunch. It was outrageous. The organisers, two Canadians, Don Arnott and Trevor Wallden, tried to reassure everybody that they would all get paid. The full quote was: 'most of their money.'

At the meeting, tempers were running high. A mysterious backer had withdrawn and that was the problem. It was claimed that he was injecting £1.2 million; it was then revealed that Wallden had never met him, and the negotiations were being conducted by a former glamour model. It was said she knew both. Casino Magic stumped up £1 million, Wallden and Arnott had invested £600,000. The figures never stacked up. They tried and failed to come up with the money that was promised.

Henry Tillman, an Olympic gold medalist, withdrew. It was too big a risk. Tillman beat Mike Tyson in the 1984 USA Olympic trials. Norway's Magne Havnaa, a world champion, also withdrew that night. Tillman was ready to fight anybody and for free and with his fists that night. It was ugly. A lot of the others were stranded – they needed some cash to get home. Some never had the dollars to pay for the cab to the airport and then pay the small fee to change their flight. They had no option; they had to stay and fight.

The organisers had asked a boxing writer called Bert Randolph Sugar to liaise with the press. Sugar was a cigar-smoking fun guy. He had run various boxing magazines and owed me a considerable amount of money for articles. I thought it was a good time to ask about my money. He ordered a drink, took a sip and vanished. That was $7 I would never get back.

One guy, fresh from a four-year prison term, was making his debut. In prison he had lost seven fights and been stopped in all of them. He was beaten in the afternoon. Biggs had stopped a lumberjack called Shane Sutcliffe in his quarter-final – Biggs was an Olympic gold medal winner and Sutcliffe was seven inches shorter, a veteran of a dozen Hard Man fights – street fights with kicking where they all seem to wear a lot of denim and drink beers. Peckham's Derek Williams lost in the first series to Jose Ribalta on a dodgy split decision. He had knocked out Ribalta in the first, but the aging Cuban was given time to recover; there was no danger of that knockout bonus ever getting paid.

'I want to go home,' Williams told me on the Thursday, the day before the event. A day earlier, at the meeting, Williams had declared that he had 'signed for the million and that is what I plan on making.' He ended up having to split $6,000 with his team.

Casino Magic was a beauty: 'Having been designed to withstand hurricanes it has been painted lime green and peach to dumbfound visitors. The interior is an attempt at high-rolling style and glitz which even makes Las Vegas seem tasteful.' It was a lively preview in the *Daily Telegraph*. I can't ever remember having the same feelings of dread, genuine fear and glee as I walked to a boxing show.

The men had fought in Olympic finals, the MGM in Las Vegas, Sing Sing prison, York Hall, San Quentin prison and Wembley

Arena. There were some great fights – they fought like their life depended on winning.

Tubbs had risen from that table, stood in the water and ice in his tent and tried to roar as he walked to his final fight of the day. I went back to ringside; the beers were untouched. It was unforgettable.

Tony Tubbs: *In the final, which was slow, Tubbs knew enough to win. There was a suggestion that Dancuta and Tubbs had agreed to split the fee for victory, although they both fought hard through their exhaustion. Obviously, nobody knew for certain what the fee would be. The fighters were told that no money was available until the pay-per-view revenue came in. Tubbs was not finished with the game. 'He deserves his blood money.' That is how I finished the report. Sugar died still owing me a lot of money.*

42

LENNOX LEWIS
— v —
FRANK BRUNO

WBC HEAVYWEIGHT TITLE: CARDIFF, 1993

'I proved I'm a better boxer than people thought.'

Frank Bruno had no idea how to lose and Lennox Lewis knew exactly how to win.

On a wet night in Cardiff, outside at the national stadium, the two British boxers met in a perfect storm just after 1 a.m. I was under a plastic poncho, perched on the ring apron and silent witness to the flaws, the heroics, the suffering, the pain and the drama.

During the weeks before the first bell there had been some ugly exchanges. Bruno had been called names, unpleasant names. Bruno had been dismissed. The thinking was that Bruno would lose badly and never fight again. The bookies supported the sound and sensible thinking of the insiders, outsiders, press and other hangers-on: Bruno had no chance. There was even some envy because he would get paid £1 million. Hate and jealousy run deep in the boxing game. Lewis was guaranteed £3 million.

It was the first time that two British-born boxers had fought for the heavyweight world title. It was, at that time, the richest fight in British boxing history. It was also a battle between bitter rivals on the so-called safe side of the ropes. Lewis had Kellie Maloney and

Panos Eliades, a liquidator by trade, and the promoter on his side; Mickey Duff, the ancient voice and face of British boxing, delivered Bruno. It was never pleasant.

I was banned by Duff at this time, and he had me thrown out of a press conference for Bruno in Brentwood, Essex. No sweat, I sat in the lobby. Years later, Duff admitted to me that having me banned never worked. He is right – being banned allowed me to write the truth about a lot of Duff's fighters. In the end, Duff won his case against me and accepted a settlement figure. It was not a Mickey Mouse ban; it was a Mickey Duff ban and he meant it.

Duff believed the fight should have been in London, at Wembley. Eliades went with Cardiff and needed 15,000 to break even; he got somewhere between 20,000 and 25,000 on the night.

Duff had a private five-grand bet with Maloney at 5–1; it made it seem like he was backing his man, but Duff was a good gambler and a big gambler; he would have had 50 grand had he truly believed.

Bruno was getting abused all week. It seemed like it was open season on Big Frank. Sure, it was his third attempt at the world heavyweight title, and he had been stopped in the previous two, but the anti-Bruno stuff was hurtful and personal. I never thought he could win, but I drew the line at accusing him of never having won a single hard fight. He was basically called a fraud and that is wrong: he always went down trying to throw punches. He might have frozen when clipped, been trapped, hurt, dazed, but he never quit. Never. The previews in the papers were like unkind obituaries. At the time, I might have been a tiny part of the problem; as I said, when you are banned, you have a new freedom to write.

Obviously, the crowd still loved him and was massively pro-Bruno. The show, however, was all about Lennox, the champion and the man who would be king. The Americans were in town – they had big plans for Lennox. They had no plans for Frank.

If Lewis won, he was going to fight the WBO heavyweight

champion, Tommy Morrison, at the new MGM Grand Hotel in Las Vegas on 5 March 1994. Morrison was not there because he was preparing for an easy defence later that month, but his trainer, Tommy Virgets, was in Cardiff. The fight was a done deal, and it was worth a lot of money. Morrison was going to come over to Britain to prepare in December as part of the publicity for the massive fight. There was also talk of a Riddick Bowe fight and a Mike Tyson fight. Bruno did not feature in any plans.

Maloney made a promise to walk naked to John O'Groats if Lewis lost. He did that type of thing several times. I think he still owes Don King a nude walk around Piccadilly Circus.

On fight night, as midnight approached, the rain eased. Mickey Vann, the referee, inspected the ring to check for sodden spots. There was a real sense of excitement finally at ringside. Under my poncho, a phone had been installed for me to file a 'runner': at the end of each completed round I would dictate copy to a woman in a room somewhere in Yorkshire. It sounds like something from the Fifties, and it was, it had not changed.

Bruno appeared first, wrapped in blankets and with his boots taped inside a couple of plastic shopping bags. He looked calm, George Francis at his side looked sharp. Lewis was next, his music ringing out but not drowning out the boos. Anthony Gee, a promoter from Brixton, was carrying the WBC belt. 'It was nasty,' Gee told me. Incidentally, Gee also made my wedding rings. To my left was Bruno's corner and I could see his wife, Laura, hovering. She had been in a couple of run-ins that week with members of the press. She backed her man. It must be no fun reading that your husband is going to get knocked out and that he is better suited for pantomime. One senior writer had even suggested that he might have to end up as the arse of a pantomime horse. Another had questioned if Bruno was smart enough to ever play anything but the arse of a horse. It was brutal.

The first bell was at 1.05 a.m. The fight was on.

Bruno was older and a bit heavier. He started well and hurt Lewis in the third round. Lewis and his team would later explain that the fight had been brought forward 20 minutes and that Lewis had been sleeping. They had to wake him and do a quick warm-up. There was also mention of the cold; they were not excuses, just facts. Pepe Correa, Lewis' trainer, was very defensive of any criticism. He was quite aggressive when the fight was over: 'Only people who know nothing about boxing would say that Lewis fought without a plan.' Lewis knew he would win, and he knew he would find a way.

By round six, Bruno had slowed, and his left eye was closed. It finished in the seventh and it was unpleasant viewing. Bruno was once again too brave. Vann finally jumped between them after 72 seconds. Bruno was standing but gone, which is not a medical term, but it perfectly captures that moment when the fighter has nothing left to give. George Francis was in the ring quick, and Bruno's battered and swollen face seemed to melt onto his shoulder. Bruno's left eye was closed and as he left the ring, he raised one fist to cheers. Right then he did look like a man we would never see again.

In the ring melee, Maloney tried to be positive and said to Laura Bruno: 'That's boxing.' She spat in Maloney's face, but she was comforted by Lewis' mother, Violet. The peace never lasted long and at the press conference in the middle of the night, she said: 'At least Frank is British.' That had been the unofficial sales pitch for the fight.

Late into the night, there was a long inquest into why it had been so difficult for Lewis. Nobody at the time was giving Bruno too much praise for making it difficult. When the fight finished, one judge had Bruno in front and the other two scores were even. Virgets, on duty as the eyes and ears of Morrison, was not convinced. 'Lennox is not ready for Tommy,' he said.

'I would tell him to retire if I handled Bruno,' said Maloney.

'Frank should retire now, the British public don't want to see him hurt,' said Lewis.

The finest from Fleet Street went to work. It was not for the squeamish and Lewis never escaped their harshest evaluations. But the full storm was for Frank Bruno. His so-called last attempt at glory held no romance for the men I worked with.

One headline was a mix of glee and savagery: 'Time to end the brain drain'. There were too many references to Bruno's intelligence, a result, it seems, of his beatings in the ring. This stuff was damning.

'I proved I'm a better boxer than people thought,' said Bruno at about 3 a.m. 'I'm a proud, proud hombre.' There was still a noticeable shortage of respect and certainly no mutual affection between the boxers or their teams. The hate was deep with resentment and some jealousy. 'I'm a proud man, I never liked what he said,' Bruno reminded me.

It was nearly 5 a.m. when I got to my room. I was still soaking wet. My pal, Ron Shillingford, who wrote for *The Voice*, was kipping on my floor. I'm not sure we slept before it was light. There were a lot of nights like that. I had other writers on my floor at fights in Las Vegas, New York, Dortmund and most cities in Britain. I had the sofa a few times myself at fights in America.

Frank Bruno: *Well, here we go. Tommy Morrison was knocked out in just 93 seconds by Michael Bentt and lost his WBO title later that month. Lewis missed that giant payday and in September of 1994, he was knocked out in two rounds by Oliver McCall. And then, well, you probably know the rest: our Frank won the WBC heavyweight title when he outpointed McCall outdoors at Wembley – it was less than two years after all of his ring obituaries. Lewis went on and became a legend in the game. Bruno remains a troubled but adored man – he won the world heavyweight title at his fourth attempt. That is also legend.*

43

HEPATITIS NIGHT

MADISON SQUARE GARDEN, NEW YORK, 1998

The show collapsed in a perfect storm of medical dramas.

I wrote that the 'fight that nobody wanted was cancelled last night.'

It was New York and a very hot summer. The fight was a world heavyweight title defence by Evander Holyfield against Henry Akinwande, who had been born near Peckham, south London. Holyfield's WBA and IBF belts were meant to be the prize at the Garden. It was cancelled with just about 24 hours to go before the first bell; it was that late I had filed my copy, my preview.

Akinwande failed a pre-fight medical when he was diagnosed with hepatitis B. That ruined the top of the bill. Ray Mercer, a former world champion, also failed a blood test for hepatitis B and that stopped his fight. There is more: Marcia Nieves-Garcia, a 21-year-old mum of one, discovered that she was five months pregnant and her fight with Christy Martin was scrapped. Nieves-Garcia said she had been sparring up until the week before – that is week 20 in pregnancy terms. The show collapsed in a perfect storm of medical dramas.

Martin, incidentally, turned down a 9–0 replacement; Nieves-Garcia was 2–1 and had not fought in 15 months. Nieves-Garcia demanded three tests to prove she was pregnant. She had originally insisted that it was impossible.

There were some frank exchanges at the hastily called conference to announce the cancellation. It was a Don King show, but

King had not been there all week. And that is odd. It was revealed – no shock – that only 4,000 of the 18,000 seats had sold. It was officially announced that 6,500 tickets had been 'distributed'. There were quite a few conspiracy theories.

The world title fight between Roberto Duran, having his 116th fight, and champion William Joppy on the undercard was just collateral damage. Duran at the Garden would have been fun. There was also an injunction by a Florida judge to stop the promoter paying Duran his $250,000 because the boxer owed $41,000 in unpaid child support. The unpaid money could be taken from the promised purse. It was a crazy week.

The show, which was dubbed 'D-Day', was scrapped. Joppy stopped Duran a few months later.

King had been absent because he was attending a trial for an alleged false insurance claim following a postponed fight, over which he was cleared. Another claim would be coming in for Hepatitis Night. It was a lovely empty weekend in New York.

Henry Akinwande: *After a break of nine months, Akinwande was back. He never got another world title fight but fought for another decade, having 20 fights, before finishing his career in obscurity on small shows in Turkey, Russia and Germany.*

44

SHEA NEARY
— v —
ANDY HOLLIGAN

WBU LIGHT-WELTERWEIGHT TITLE: TENT, STANLEY PARK, LIVERPOOL, 1998

A policeman on a white horse was gently pushed in through the revolving doors.

'The fight belongs to Liverpool and that is why it is being held here,' said John Hyland in January.

Hyland had found a tent, a fancy marquee that could hold 5,500 spectators, he found a park and he had his two Scouse fighters. Less than six weeks after it was announced, it all came together. The fight was live on Granada television.

Neary had been filling the Everton Park Sports Centre on nights that were a lot of fun. He was a throwback fighter: brave, dangerous, prone to cuts and with the ability to win a lost cause with just one punch. Holligan had been British champion and had once lost a world title fight to Julio Cesar Chavez at a bullring in Mexico.

On the night, beers were being sold by the dozen from lorries, the tent was heaving. It was Hyland's greatest night as a promoter. As a fighter, he boxed at the 1984 Olympics, and as a promoter he delivered a lot of good nights.

In the end, 5,800 witnessed one of the fights of the year and that was expected. There was far too much Scouse pride on the line. They stood toe-to-toe, bloody, their eyes bruised, and they fought for any, tiny advantage. Neary had once been a sparring partner for Holligan and that added to the merciless action inside the ring; they refused to take backwards steps. All the belts, all the promises were lost somewhere, and it was just two men with something personal to prove.

The action slowed in the fifth and Holligan's faithful thought their man had come through and would go on and win. He had the experience, but it was false hope. In the sixth, a right dislodged Holligan's shield and then he was dropped; he regained his feet at eight, but it was stopped 20 seconds later. Holligan's right eye was closed, the left eye was fluttering, and he had nothing left. Neary had his own scars, his left eye was damaged.

In the mobile hut, which was the dressing room, Neary was still bouncing when I got back to talk to him. He was flying, smeared with a bit of blood, and fuelled by pure adrenaline. He still had his gloves on, and he was prowling. It was a pleasure covering his fights. Later that night, at the Moat House, the fight hotel, the crowds outside were massive. It was the place to be. I was on a table with John Hyland, near the bar, when a policeman on a white horse was gently pushed in through the revolving doors. That is how you finish a night of fights in Liverpool.

Neary was there for the arrival of the horse, his hands sore, his face bruised and a giant smile on his face.

Shea Neary: *In 2000, Neary was stopped by Micky Ward. It was from a body shot. 'Never known anything like it, Ste,' he said.*

45

ERROL CHRISTIE:
THE END

FREE TRADE HALL, MANCHESTER, 1993

'It's been my life, but it's over now.'

Less than 200 witnessed the boxing wake of Errol Christie on a Friday night at the Free Trade Hall in Manchester. The end, in all fairness, was a few years earlier; this was just the final physical end. The last beating, if you like. The last sacrifice.

Christie was the boy who had it all – well, that was the plan, that was the thinking. When he turned professional, he was just 19; he had won ten national titles and a European under-19 championship. His achievements were in the *Guinness Book of Records*. He was expected to join the global greats at the time, men like Roberto Duran, Marvin Hagler, Sugar Ray Leonard and Tommy Hearns.

'I was the first real star of the Eighties, before Watson, Benn and Eubank came and took all the limelight. I was there, now I'm here, and it's over.' It was a sad confession to hear, and I wrote, 'his words as soft as his punch resistance'. Errol had been a hero of mine, an amateur god in the Seventies.

Before he turned pro, there were rumours about his stiff legs, his lack of movement. Just rumours, it seemed, and he went 13–0 without a problem. He had knocked out 12 and been in Las Vegas training and fighting. He was living the high, high life as one of boxing's young superstars. He was destined for greatness and riches and then a giant Belgian with a hefty mullet ruined him one night in London. It was 1984 and those that knew held their tongues.

It never went right again. His last fight was nine years and 26 fights later; he lost another six times, five by knockout, before climbing through the ropes to meet Trevor Ambrose, a kick boxer from Leicester. Ambrose was on a losing streak of five; he was a safe bet for Errol.

Christie was dropped three times in the second and that is when the fight and his boxing life finished. He had no idea where he was after the final knockdown.

'It's over,' he admitted. In the ring at the end, Billy Graham and Phil Martin of Champs Camp went and helped him up from the last knockdown. I wrote: 'They went to their man, their fighter, their brother.'

Later, in the dressing room, he was talking to me and Steve Lillis of the *Daily Sport*. It was such a sad scene. The boxers from Martin's Champs Camp gym liked him, he was part of a team. It was hard not to openly weep.

'What round was it?' he asked.

'The second,' said Frank Grant.

'I'm finished. I have been boxing so long, but my punch resistance is gone. It's been my life, but it's over now.'

Nobody from the gym disagreed; one of Errol's brothers kept telling him that it was not over.

'He needs to shut up,' Martin said, pointing at the brother. 'That's it for Errol Christie – I wish he was with me from the start because he would have been a world champion.'

Christie's fall from his hopes of glory, to defeat on that Friday night, is a warning to all boxing dreamers. He had dazzled in the Kronk under the watchful eye of Manny Steward – Christie's horizons were not invented, trust me.

'He could box, but he couldn't fight. He was left to his own natural ability. It is sad,' added Martin. The boxers, Eric Noi, Grant and Maurice Core stood over the dejected Christie.

The hall had been so empty that when Graham, who would go on to take Ricky Hatton to the world title, was cleaning Errol's face in the ring at the end, I could hear the boxer saying: 'I'm alright, I'm alright.'

Errol Christie: *I'm afraid there is no fun ending here. He had a market stall in Catford, he tried comedy as a stand-up and he worked on doors. That is the mixed life of a fallen star. Two days before he died, I went to see Errol at his hospice near Penge in south London. He had been diagnosed with lung cancer two years earlier. He had been diagnosed because he had been jumped by a special police unit; they suspected he was a terrorist. The mistake was quickly realised, they all laughed. That was typical Errol, but he had hurt a rib, and they took him for an x-ray – it was not his rib, it was lung cancer that they found. He was a friend.*

46

MICHAEL WATSON
— v —
CHRIS EUBANK

VACANT WBO SUPER-MIDDLEWEIGHT TITLE. WHITE HART LANE, LONDON, 1991

'Five minutes after that fight was stopped, I started to die in the ring.'

In late 1981, Michael Watson walked across the canvas and shook my hand. He had just lost the NABC semi-final to Roy Connor at the Stantonbury Leisure Centre in Milton Keynes.

I was handing up to Mick Carney on the day – it meant I washed the boxer's gumshield, put the stool in the ring and held up a filthy spit bucket. I thought nothing of that fight for years, it was just another championship, but in the late Eighties I reminded Watson about the loss. 'He was slick,' he said.

I did think of that fight at some point on a diabolical Saturday night and Sunday morning in September 1991.

On 21 September 1991, Watson's life stopped. He believes he died at some point after midnight.

At 10.54 p.m. on 21 September, Watson was stopped on his feet after 29 seconds of the 12th and last round of a world title fight. 'That's it, son,' said Roy Francis, the great referee. And it was. Seconds later, Watson fell forward into the arms of his trainer, Jimmy Tibbs. In just a few moments, he was on the sodden canvas in his own corner. A doctor was in with him, Watson's head was placed on a briefcase. On the opposite side of the ring, Chris Eubank could hardly speak as he was being interviewed by ITV's Gary Newbon. The interview should never have happened. A simple glance at Watson's corner should have been enough to shut the men up in the television production truck and the man in the ring with the microphone. It was a terrible call, and they were desperate to hear from the winner in the few minutes they had on air before they cut to Cilla on *Blind Date* or something else.

'Five minutes after that fight was stopped, I started to die in the ring. It's that simple,' Watson told me during one of our sessions when I sat with him to help him put together his story for his book. I have no idea if it was used in the book; it seemed to me that most of the truly evocative stuff was taken out by the editor. She dropped me out, that is for sure.

Watson also told me that he sat up in one of the ambulances – he went in two ambulances on the night of the fight – and spoke to the medics. 'I knew I was dead,' he said. Obviously, he never moved in any of the ambulances, he was incapable of movement. He was sedated and on the edge of death. It is a memory stuck somewhere in his head. I'm sure it never made the book.

In his witness statement for court, Watson wrote: 'I am not sure what my last memory was on 21 September 1991 or when my next memory occurred. It was some years later.' I was a witness in court in his case against the British Boxing Board of Control. He won a settlement figure and Frank Warren, who never promoted Watson and therefore never made a penny out of him, was the independent broker on the deal. 'Right,' Warren said when he entered the closed room and sat down with representation from both the Board and Watson. 'Let's get this fucking thing sorted.' It was sorted, Frank made sure of that.

On that September night, Watson finally went for surgery after 1 a.m. He had left North Middlesex hospital at 11.55 p.m. The drive to St Barts was simple, the neurosurgeon, Mr Peter Hamlyn, was coming in from home. The night was long and full of prayer, led by Pastor Joe White and Watson's mother, Joan, and her sisters from their church, the Evering Pentecostal Church in Tottenham. Michael's brother, Jeff, was also there. Jimmy Tibbs and his son, Mark, joined in, dropping to their knees to pray. Watson's agent at the time, Jon Robinson, who weighed over 30 stone, bent his head in respect – he could do no more. The glare of the neon light in that waiting room exposed my presence and I too went down on my knees. The miracle we were praying for seemed unlikely. Watson had collapsed over two hours before he was anywhere near surgery. The golden-hour rule was gone.

There are always numbers when a boxer ends up in intensive care. At 4.20 a.m., Joan was taken to see her boy. At 5.10 a.m., Jimmy was taken to see his boxer. At 6.05 a.m., Hamlyn appeared. 'He's in a critical state.' Watson had a bad Sunday afternoon. He was close to death several times. He kept battling, fighting. I was at a gala dinner at the Grosvenor House hotel in Park Lane. Henry Cooper was there, but Muhammad Ali failed to show. I went from there, with Big Jon, to the hospital.

He still looked great; his body was in fantastic shape. The first time I saw him on the Sunday night he was still and calm in the intensive care unit. There was a scrawled message on his bandaged head. It said: 'No bone flap.'

There was also a bloody fingerprint next to the words.

He left the ICU and was placed in a recovery ward. He had a window in the ward, and it was overlooking Smithfield meat market. Less than eight weeks earlier, Watson had been at that market holding up a giant beef carcass 'to illustrate what he intended to do to his opponent in the return'. In June, Eubank had won a narrow and controversial decision in their first world title fight. Their rematch at White Hart Lane was by public demand.

It was in that recovery ward, on the 38th day after his loss, that Watson tapped the pictures of boxers he knew in a magazine I was holding up. 'Where's Duke, Mike?' I asked. He slowly, slowly tapped a picture of Duke McKenzie. I wrote about that in the paper and was then invited to a meeting and offered, by a national paper, ten grand to take a picture of Watson in hospital. I think I got 150 quid for the article. I could have got 15 grand had I told them about the yellow roses that Elton John kept sending and snatched a picture. The dirty bastards. I also had a chief sports-writer from one of the Sunday papers kicked out of the waiting room. He was in there reading a paper. Dirty bastard.

It was also on that ward that Michael watched the fight for the first time. He had to turn the sound down, it was too much to listen to. He couldn't speak because of the tracheotomy tube in his throat. He watched in silence.

On the tenth anniversary, I went to see Watson at his home in Chingford. The walls had boxing pictures and religious relics. His life in those frames. 'What was the fight really like?' he asked. I realised that we had never spoken about the fight. He then added: 'When I watch it back, I feel like I'm not there.' It is hard to tell him how dramatic it was, hard to explain the 11th round when Eubank finally crumbled and he went down, tangled, hurt, exhausted and close to defeat. The fight was won and then, with a few seconds left and just one punch, the fight was lost. Eubank regained his feet, set them and connected with a right uppercut. Watson is down, the bell sounds. Watson is groggy. I told him how amazing that was. He never said a word. Watson tells Jimmy Tibbs in the corner: 'I'm fine.' He is not. The bell rings, Watson struggles to walk forward. They fight on, Watson is trapped, and Eubank lets both fists go and then it is stopped at 29 seconds of the 12th.

'That was some fight,' Michael Watson tells me. It was, I told him. I leave an hour later. 'I pray for you, Steve,' he tells me. Heart-break. Ten years later, another anniversary, I repeat the story.

It has been a battle since then. Watson remains a miracle man.

Michael Watson: *The head of sport at ITV, Brian Barwick, put an embargo on the fight. I have only ever watched it once, and that was when I helped Michael with his book. I never want to watch it again. I saw it in all its brutal glory and tragedy the first time.*

47

BERNARD HOPKINS:
A GOOD MAN

PHILADELPHIA, 2008

'Oh beautiful, for heroes proved in liberating strife.'

Stabbed and left for dead. Prison as a boy. The champion of the world. A good man. Bernard Hopkins is a Philadelphia fighter with a proper story.

In 2008, a few months before Hopkins met Joe Calzaghe in Las Vegas, I went to Philadelphia to find the man behind so many myths.

We went through his city, the meanest of streets and the changed neighbourhoods he was involved with. We went to the school where he had spent thousands to install computers, we walked on some corners only after he had taken his watch off and left it in the car with his minder. We dashed all over the city and ate fresh bison meat in his apartment.

He told me about his criminal history. The stabbing that left him with a collapsed lung and needing six months of hospital care. He was sentenced as a minor to five years for aggravated assault. Think Omar from *The Wire*. He was sent to an adult maximum-security prison. He told me that for the first six months at Graterford he acted crazy. 'I knew the men there would not rape a crazy man.' He was 19, some of the men had been incarcerated for longer than he had been alive.

'The business of boxing couldn't break my spirit. The ghetto life couldn't break my spirit. The penitentiary couldn't break my spirit. That's what makes you a man. I'm a man first. I'm prouder to be a man than a fighter.'

I went to Graterford Penitentiary with Hopkins. He served 56 months there. He was saved there and won four penitentiary boxing titles. In the gym, there is a giant mural of Hopkins. It is a mark of utter respect. It is his place and when I went, there were still men there he had lived and trained with.

When, at 22, he was released, he was given nine years of parole. 'That was hard, that was the challenge. They expected me back,' Hopkins told me. He washed dishes, he trained, he fought. He was still on parole when he became the world middleweight champion. He beat it, but there was other damage.

In Philadelphia, he showed me the dirty piece of land between buildings where his brother was shot and killed. We had coffee opposite his apartment and two police in a car spotted him and crossed their arms and smiled. Hopkins was known as the Executioner and would enter the ring with his arms crossed. In his apartment, he opened a window and asked me to be quiet. I could hear kids playing. He took me to the window and down below, about 12 floors lower, was a playground. 'That's not a school, Steve,' he said. 'That's the juvenile detention centre. I was held in that place dozens of times. That is why I live here; it is a permanent reminder to me.'

Bernard Hopkins: *Each fight Hopkins walked into had Ray Charles singing 'America the Beautiful.' The opening lyrics could and possibly should be dedicated for life to Hopkins. 'Oh beautiful, for heroes proved in liberating strife.' I believe that is Bernard Hopkins, the King of Philly.*

48

FRANK BRUNO
— v —
OLIVER McCALL

WBC HEAVYWEIGHT CHAMPIONSHIP. WEMBLEY STADIUM, LONDON, 1995

**'He turned southpaw, danced and bemused McCall with
a flurry of jabs.'**

It was the very last chance for our Frank. It was his fourth world
heavyweight title fight and the previous three had ended in heart-
break.

He was fighting the American, Oliver McCall, a man with a
documented drug burden, but with the ability to end a fight with
just one punch. A year earlier, McCall had won the title when he
knocked out Lennox Lewis.

McCall often said the wrong thing, but when he landed in
London, he said a few vile things. Seven months earlier, Nigel Benn
and Gerald McClellan had been in one of the great fights; it ended
with McClellan requiring surgery to remove a blood clot from the
surface of his brain. He had survived but would need 24-hour care
for life. McCall said: 'I will take him out and try to do to him what
he (Benn) did to my friend Gerald. This is not sport – it's about
vengeance and revenge.' He also said that McClellan was 'blind
and a vegetable.' We ran with it in the papers – it was a savage time.
'He's jet-lagged, but that is still no excuse,' said Frank Warren, the
promoter.

The ringside pit was packed, the tables heaving with installed landline phones. There was real excitement and the noise of men shouting as they desperately tried to file copy, the drama from the commentators on television and radio and the screams of the faithful and concerned turned the place wild. There is no place like it on earth for a big, big fight – my seat, about five feet from the canvas, was a privilege.

Bruno had been cool and calm all week; he entered the ring skipping and happy. At his side, George Francis and 'Bloomers', Johnny Bloomfield. McCall came out with most of his entourage of 27 at his side. He was swaddled in blankets and crying and wiping away snot and tears with his gloves. He liked to get emotional; it helped him, he said, get his head ready.

Our dread was simple: Bruno would run out of energy and take another bad beating. McCall had that style, that great American heavyweight style that suited a patient man. He could wait, our Frank would gas and then McCall would break all our hearts. Don King was there, and he knew – two of his men had done it to Bruno before. But we hoped and we prayed, and the first bell sounded. Bruno still looked relaxed; McCall looked demented.

After six, Bruno still looked relaxed. In a remarkable eighth round, he turned southpaw, danced and bemused McCall with a flurry of jabs. Francis in the corner stayed cool, but it was hard in the last two rounds. King got up and went to McCall's corner at the end of the 11th and Benn and Naseem Hamed had been on their feet living every punch from about round ten. It was feverish and then the bell to start the 12th tolled and 30,000 people stood, jumped up and down and willed Frank Bruno on. It was agonising – I was half up and half down throughout the last 180 seconds, the phone trapped between my ear and shoulder as I hollered my copy down the line. I also ducked, just like Bruno, every single one of McCall's wild swings.

Bruno just got to the bell. He had done enough; he was the

world champion. 'Land of Hope and Glory' was played. Bruno's face was swollen from the fight.

The next day, at a motel near his Essex home, Bruno met with us to talk over options. There was a photo opportunity on a fallen tree – Bruno was so stiff and exhausted that Lawrence Lustig, the photographer, had to lift the heavyweight champion's legs up. That is sacrifice.

After Bruno was helped down from the tree, champagne was served. In a field next to the motel, King and Warren had wandered off to make a deal. Bruno would get Mike Tyson and that would be it for Frank.

Frank Bruno: *Not many people know this, but without me there might have been a problem. I had to give £100 to a man called 'Big' Dave Carrol, who was in charge of paying the doctors for the pre-fight medical; Dave found himself a bit light, he asked me, and I stepped up. My pocket saved the day. Bruno remains a national treasure. A damaged and fragile one. I'm still a ton short. And, amazingly, McCall was not fined for his outburst. At a hearing, held by the British Boxing Board of Control two weeks later, no action was taken.*

49

ANGELO DUNDEE: MASTER STORYTELLER

FRANK WARREN'S OFFICE: BLOOMSBURY, LONDON, 1992

'Muhammad, you gotta suck it up.'

It was the first time I had met Angelo Dundee.

I had read his book, seen a zillion pictures with him and Muhammad Ali and knew all about him, but in April 1992 I was lounging with him in Frank Warren's boxing office. And it was clear that all the stories were true.

Dundee had flown in for a fight at the Royal Albert Hall. He had been training Peckham's Derek 'Sweet D' Williams in Miami and Williams was fighting Lennox Lewis for the British, European and Commonwealth titles in the old building.

'Frank, I'm telling you, Del's the greatest I've seen in the gym,' said Dundee. 'He's the best, untouchable in the gym. We can beat this guy.'

'Fights are won in the ring, not the gym,' Warren reminded his old friend.

That afternoon he talked about all of his 'guys' and their best fights, his greatest nights. He talked with love about Sugar Ramos and Jose Napoles. He remembered fondly his lazy, hot days in Mexico City. A year later, I would get to spend a few lazy, hot days with Dundee in Mexico City.

He talked about walking to the train station in Miami to meet

Muhammad Ali, known then as Cassius Clay, in 1960. 'He was a nice kid.'

He talked about the Thrilla in Manila. 'I looked at my guy at the end of the 11th round. He was exhausted. I hadda grab him and I told him: "Muhammad, you gotta suck it up." He did.'

He talked about 'kidology', which was his way to convince a fighter to do something without actually telling the fighter to do it. 'That way, they think it is their idea.' Dundee was a marvel that afternoon.

A few years later, I spoke to Sweet D about his time with Dundee and he just laughed. 'They were great days,' he recalled and then he told a lovely little tale. 'He would say to me: "I like the way you hook off the jab, that's fantastic." It made me feel great, but then I realised that I had not thrown a hook off the jab! The next day in the gym I would throw hundreds of hooks off the jab. He was a great man and he made everything positive.'

Angelo Dundee: *At the Royal Albert Hall on the night, where Dundee was treated like a visiting dignitary, Williams never hooked off the jab. Lewis stopped him in round three. In the loser's dressing room after the fight, Dundee was praising Sweet D in defeat. He was loyal to his guys, that is for sure.*

50

FRANKIE LUCAS
— v —
TONY SIBSON

VACANT BRITISH MIDDLEWEIGHT TITLE: ROYAL ALBERT HALL, 1979

**He [Frankie] . . . looked about as cool and mean as
you could get.**

The Frankie Lucas story is one of injustice and deep, deep sorrow.

Lucas could have been and should have been a great fighter, a champion. Instead, he fought dreadful battles on both sides of the ropes and finished with nothing.

He was my first real hero, a boxer that I had seen fight in the flesh as an amateur and as a pro. He had signed my green autograph book one night outside Manor Place in Walworth. It was probably 1973 or 1974; Lucas was still an amateur at the time.

When he turned professional, he did fight for the vacant British title one night at a packed and fevered Royal Albert Hall. I was there, just sweet 16 and in the cheap standing area at the top of the ancient venue. It was a very lively night: Sibson had arrived with his Leicester boys and Frankie had his troops from south London. The fight was brutal – Sibson won in the fifth.

The story starts on the streets of Croydon in south London. It is the early Sixties – can you imagine how grey and bleak Croydon was then – and Lucas had left St Vincent and been reunited with his mother. He is nine. He finds the Sir Philip Game boxing club.

He needs something, he is troubled. I don't care if that sounds like a weary cliche, it is true.

Injustice number one: he beats Alan Minter on his way to becoming the ABA champion in 1972. However, Minter gets sent to the Olympics in Munich, wins a medal, makes a fortune and is a national treasure. Lucas cries his eyes out when Minter wins.

Injustice number two: Lucas wins the ABA title again in 1973 and beats Carl Speare on his way to the title. A few months later, Speare is selected to represent England at the Commonwealth Games in New Zealand.

This was an outrage in south London at the time; inside my boxing bubble, it was all we cared about. Lucas was one of our own, he won the South-East London Divisional Championships and us juniors looked up to him. He had an afro, large collars, a smart jacket and he looked about as cool and mean as you could get. In the language of the time, he'd fuck Shaft up, no sweat. Deep inside, we all knew why Frankie had missed out on selection for the Olympics and the Commonwealth games: he was just too bad, Frankie Too Bad. The truth.

And then there was a bit of magic, and I'm not kidding.

A policeman called Ken Rimington, a committee member at Sir Philip Game, created a boxing federation for St Vincent and the Grenadines. The Commonwealth Games accepted the new federation; money was raised, the Scottish team helped, and somehow Frankie Lucas, the boxing reject, was on his way to Christchurch. He carried the flag at the opening ceremony – he was the only member of the St Vincent team.

Lucas won twice and, in the semi-final, he met England's Speare. It was meant to be, that is the way the boxing gods work. Lucas won, but in the final, he was up against the Cuban-trained Zambian, Julius Luipa. It was a lost cause; Luipa had knocked out cold two of his three victims. He had been prepared in Fidel

Castro's boxing gyms in Havana. Lucas was wearing second-hand kit – Luipa was like an adidas model!

Des Lynam, the smooth BBC voice, was on boxing duty in Christchurch. Lynam loved the semi-final win and the sense of justice. I have listened to the final many, many times. But nothing compares to watching it live.

Lucas is cut badly in the first round; both were hurt. It was wonderful. Nobody was sitting in my parents' living room. 'C'mon, Frankie, c'mon on my son,' We loved an underdog on the estate. And then, *bang*, Luipa was down and hurt. Lynam was losing his mind.

Lucas just looked at Luipa. It was a look of raw defiance, hate, emotion and ten years of rejection – had Luipa got up, there was no telling what Lucas would have been capable of. The Cuban coaches were pounding the canvas, but their man was done. There is an iconic picture of Lucas, hovering in that ring, his halo lit by the glare of the ring lights. He went for gold, that is what he told everybody.

Lucas did turn professional with George Francis, but it was hard. He was ill with demons in his head. The stories started when he stopped boxing: Frankie topless in the freezing cold and shadow boxing, Frankie with his mutilated hands, Frankie on a final run over Parliament Hill fields with his afro now grey. Some true, some invented. I was repeatedly told he was dead. I found him in the late Nineties, but I left him alone in care. That was the request from his nurse. Sure, at every Commonwealth Games since, I have retold the story and that has upset some people. I was accused of 'cashing in on Frankie's suffering'. If £125 for a *Boxing News* column is cashing in, then I'm guilty. But it turns out, I might be responsible for a great ending.

Out of the blue in early 2023, I got a call from Michael Bovell. He was Frankie's son. Frankie was still alive. There was a play coming out. One of my articles had inspired the play. The playwright, Lisa Lintott, had served Frankie in a shop when he was boxing and she was a child. It was 1974 and the man with the afro had left an impression. She read the column and that was it, she had the words, and she was on a mission. 'You gotta be there, man,' Bovell told me. And then, in the days before the play opened, Frankie Lucas died. The play, *Going For Gold*, was exceptional. On the opening night in London, Ken Rimington was in the audience, the old guard of the Sir Philip Game faithful. There should be a film.

Frankie Lucas: *His funeral was on a sunny day in south London. A week or so later, the play opened. Lucas fought 17 times as a professional, losing seven and I'm not sure he was meant to ever win a single fight.*

51

MIKE TYSON:
LICENCE TO FIGHT

THE HEARING: THE HUGHES COMPLEX, TRENTON, NEW JERSEY, 1998

**'I'm a husband, I have a wife and I'm a fighter, and those
are the priorities in my life.'**

Here is the simple story and it is simple. Mike Tyson lost his licence
to fight because he bit off a chunk of Evander Holyfield's ear. He
was fined $3 million by the authorities in Las Vegas.

Fast forward a year, and Tyson wants his life back and his right
to fight. He had decided to apply for a licence in New Jersey. I
made the journey by train from New York. It was worth it.

Tyson was raw, open and then angry. 'I am here today just as
a man. I am not a good guy or bad guy. I'm a husband, I have a
wife and I'm a fighter, and those are the priorities in my life.' He
had to answer 34 questions and listen to an endless list of people
praising him.

Finally, before question 35 from the Commission, Tyson
delivered the deathless line: 'Why do I have to relive my fucking
life?' His attorney, Anthony J Fusco, was quick to calm him. Tyson
dropped his head in his hands and Fusco powered on. My old
friend, Tim Smith, of the *New York Times*, uttered 'he went from
tears to swearing.'

Fusco tried his best. 'It's time for the crucifixion to come to an
end and for Mike Tyson to fight again.'

The hearing did have its truly mad moments. Chuck Wepner, the original Rocky, was there to provide testimony. He insisted that Tyson was a good guy and he just 'goes in there and knocks your head off'. But it was good pro, Bobby Czyz, who dropped a beauty. 'When you are in the zone, nothing else matters and there is a total performance blackout. If an opponent's eye fell out, Tyson would eat it before the guy could pick it up.' Cheers, Bob.

In the melee at the end, Tyson told Larry Holmes: 'I messed up, I messed up.'

Tyson's outburst had changed the temperature in the room; what had looked like a walkover, was now a debate. Before the hearing I had assumed it was a simple job and put this in the paper: 'Las Vegas will grow dimmer as Atlantic City, the cesspit by the sand, prospers from his return.'

We knew Donald Trump was involved – his casino and hotels were in Atlantic City on the New Jersey shore. Tyson and Holyfield had bumped into each other outside Trump's office. Holyfield v Tyson III was big, but Trump wanted a freak show for the ages: Tyson v George Foreman. That was a big possibility and Trump had connections, obviously.

It was a pure circus. I had been in Las Vegas for the first hearing the previous July and that had been dry, sharp and lacking in emotion or comedy. It was serious. A few months later, Don King and Tyson had a fight outside a hotel in Los Angeles. Tyson was suing his paymaster for $100 million. It seemed, on that July day in Trenton, that New Jersey, was his only lifeline. What did I know?

Mike Tyson: *A week or so after the hearing, and the day before the New Jersey Boxing Commission was due to deliver their decision, Tyson told Fusco to withdraw his application. Then, he announced that he would go back with King to Nevada and apply again. Out-of-control chaos does not come close to capturing this craziness. Trump was not happy.*

52

QUEENS OF THE RING: SAVANNAH MARSHALL, CLARESSA SHIELDS AND QUEEN ELIZABETH

O2, LONDON, 2022

It was the best fight to be made in women's boxing.

It had been a great week, the O2 would be sold out for an all-female bill – and then came the bad news from the Palace. The Queen was dead, the show was off.

It was pushed back from 10 September to 15 October and that was fine. The American fighters had enough time to go home. On the night, it was very special with ten fights. It was a first.

The main event was a rematch that took a decade to make; Savannah Marshall had beaten Claressa Shields at the World Championship in 2012, the only loss amateur or professional that Shields had suffered. It was all she talked about; Sav was not a great talker, she just got on with her business. She had called Shields a 'daft cow' and that made me chuckle. Shields had gone full gangster and that is what she got back – that happens when you mess with a Hartlepool lass. They met for all four middleweight belts at the O2, which was packed. It was the best fight to be made in women's boxing.

Both were unbeaten in 12 fights and had not lost a round: Marshall had stopped ten of her 12 opponents, Shields had only stopped two. It was a good stat and a rare one in the women's game: prime v prime, unbeaten v unbeaten.

'Shields has the speed, Sav has the power,' said Peter Fury, who trained Marshall at a secret gym inside a compound on the outskirts of Macclesfield. 'It's a 50-50 fight and that is how it should be.'

On the way to the O2, the underground trains were packed with mums and girls. I had seen that before when a boyband was playing. This was different, this was a night of fights. I have heard a lot of people in the business dismiss that night, insist it was not sold out, claim it was fake. It was a great night for women's boxing, make no mistake. It is also true that all the women on that bill would have claimed Katie Taylor as their inspiration – in ten years, who knows, new champions will tell you they were at the O2 on that night.

Let me tell you a quick story about what influence an unforgettable fight and night and boxer can have on a girl. One day in the summer of 2012, I was making my way to the ExCel to cover the Olympic boxing tournament. I was on the DLR with Darren Fletcher, the commentator, when I had an 'Oi, mister' moment. A girl of about 12 asked me if I was going to the boxing. She was going to watch Katie Taylor. I spoke to her mum, got their contact details to get the girl on my old BBC London show. We stayed in contact, her young career continued, she boxed for England, she turned professional and in 2023, she won the Commonwealth title. Her name is Emma Dolan, and we still speak; the day at the Olympic boxing watching Katie Tayor changed her life forever.

I saw that same look in the eyes of the young girls waiting to get in to watch Marshall and Shields. I like that look, some might stick with their Barbie and Action Man toys and dolls, others we might get. Why was there never an Action Man Rocky? It is a mystery.

Shields won the fight. It was a terrible drain on both; fights like that take a toll and leave a hidden message. In 2023, they managed just one fight each and in 2024 they were both looking to fight in the MMA octagon. It is obvious that a bit more happened in the ring on that October night – they both had to go to some dark places to get through the rounds. The intensity up close was impressive. 'Did you see Shields digging in her feet?' Natasha Jonas asked me. I did, she was burying her toes to get every ounce of power in her shots. The fight was personal and from the ringside pit it was loud.

The following day, I went to an Islington Boxing Club show at the Boston Dome in north London and met a dad with his boxing daughter, Hayleigh Cosgrave. She was just ten and had been at the boxing the night before. 'She was standing on the chair the whole time,' her dad told me. It was her first bout that day, three one-minute rounds, a skills contest. She lost that Sunday afternoon. I have no idea if she is still in the gym.

Emma Dolan: *In February 2024, Dolan withdrew from a fight for the vacant British super-flyweight title. It was a late, late injury. But in June 2024, Dolan won the British title. The journey continues. Never underestimate the influence of childhood heroes in the boxing game.*

53

MARTIN BOWERS:
A TRUE BOXING MAN

PEACOCK GYM, LONDON, 2020

'You need to save them from themselves.'

The Peacock gym in Canning Town has been at the centre of British boxing for over three decades.

Just about every quality fighter passing through London has trained there. It has opened its rings to Lennox Lewis and Floyd Mayweather and a thousand cranks, unidentified men, quality dreamers and champions. At the very heart of the gym is Martin Bowers.

There was once an illegal wooden bunk house on the roof; the bunks were three high, and at one point boxers from 11 countries lived there. It was mayhem.

In 2022, the Peacock gym relocated to a remote farm and field in Essex, but the old gym, the place of smells and history remained in place. There is every chance that one day, a billion pounds' worth of flats will be built above it, but it will live forever. There was a statue outside the gym of Bradley Stone: he fought out of the gym, lost a British title fight just a couple of miles away at York Hall and then died from his injuries. The statue is lovely.

'We see it every day, we remember him every day,' said Bowers.

One night in late November 2020, deep behind all the Covid restrictions and in front of an invite-only crowd of about 60,

Bowers had a tough night in the corner. The lack of crowd meant that every word he uttered in the corner could be heard; the Covid fights were raw because of the voices heard in the silence. And the pain being inflicted and the noise that made – if a boxer was hurt to the body, you felt it and heard it.

Bowers had his heavyweight, Daniel Dubois, in a real test against Joe Joyce at a venue in Westminster called Church House. Dubois was just 23, unbeaten in 15 with 14 ending early. Joyce was 35, a veteran in years, but he had only fought 11 times. Something had to give, and it was Dubois.

There was damage to Dubois' left eye from the fourth, it was closing by the sixth. At the end of the sixth, Bowers sat Dubois down, took a breath and fixed him with a look. 'This is the fight game, and you're in it. You have to get through this. It's what we do.' It got harder for Dubois and the eye shut. Bowers kept Dubois in the fight in rounds seven, eight and nine. He worked him in the corner. It was belief, hard work. A trainer can save a lost cause and Dubois could finish a fight with just one punch. And, possibly with just one good eye. It was drama.

In the tenth, Dubois went down on his knee. It was over. 'I was going to pull him out at the end of the tenth,' said Bowers. 'You have to give that kid a chance. It's a long road back.' It was a long road back. Bowers and Dubois split after that fight.

'You need to save them from themselves,' he said late that night.

Martin Bowers: *Dubois got his career back on track in late 2023 with a win over the American Jarrell Miller. He had another big win back in Riyadh, in May 2024. Bowers still has an interest in the kid. 'I told you it would be a long road, Steve.' The road back was getting shorter.*

54

JAKE PAUL

— v —

TOMMY FURY

RIYADH, SAUDI ARABIA, 2023

This fight was not a pantomime and they each reached the walls of their limitations.

On Friday evening, at a sports centre on the dusty outskirts of Riyadh, a Saudi princess lost in the Central Region Amateur Boxing Championships. A real princess, not an invented one.

Two nights later, outdoors, Jake Paul dropped Tommy Fury, but still lost a tight decision at the historic Diriyah site, in the same city. Same sport, two very different events.

In early 2024, Turki Alalshikh announced that there would be no more 'YouTuber boxing; I just want real fighters'. The man behind the Saudi boxing revolution had not yet taken control of the sport when Fury and Paul had their fight. It was a real fight, but they each had a toe in the celebrity world.

Fury against Paul was a lot of fun. They became the two highest-paid novices in history, and they fought like their life depended on victory. It would be nice if other six- and seven-fight novices, especially ones who have been heavily protected, had to scrap as hard. It was not a classic, but it was full of commitment, intensity and errors. That is a perfect mix for a good fight. They were each short of defensive skills, but brave. Fury was dropped in the eighth and last round but got the decision. He did his post-fight interview in tears: 'I have been under so much pressure,' he said. And he is right: his father, Gypsy John, and his brother, Tyson, had promised to disown him if he lost. They might not have been joking.

This fight was not a pantomime and they each reached the walls of their limitations. They fought each other to a standstill, swinging at each other in hope and desperation. So much money, so much pressure and so few fights: it was Fury's ninth and Paul's seventh.

A topless Gypsy John, who seems to lose his shirt every time he is at a fight or press conference, was also emotional at the end. 'He's from my loins, I'm proud of him,' he said. Whenever Big John is around, there is a lot of loin chat.

Fury made a fortune eight months later when he outpointed the darling of the YouTube boxing business, KSI, in Manchester. It was six rounds of mauling and reluctance; the three judges all returned a slender one-point win for Fury. It was a poor, poor fight, but a great event; just under 20,000 filled every seat at the MEN and stayed in place from before the first bell until the very last punch. 'Did you see that crowd?' asked Eddie Hearn, a ringside guest. The fight will not show up on Fury's legitimate boxing record.

So, away from the carnival back in Riyadh in February, I got wind of the defeated princess and made a few calls. A man called Kevin Smith, from the Rotunda boxing club in Liverpool, had become the Saudi national amateur boxing coach. I tracked him down; he invited me over and I went to the sports centre on the Saturday before the Sunday Fury fight. I was stepping into a world I had not seen in three visits to Saudi. It was a world that people told me did not exist. Men and women together in shorts and vests. I saw it, I'm not inventing this.

I stepped back in time when I walked in. I had covered the Schoolboy Championships in dirty halls like that 25 years earlier. I was only there ten minutes when a female trainer was evicted from the corner for excessive shouting and abuse. My Arabic is shaky, but she was not joking. She was letting the judges have it in no uncertain terms. Two of the judges were also women. They were giving it back.

Smith just shrugged: 'It's like a normal amateur show,' he said, and he was right. Smith had been involved with Rotunda for 20 years. In the ring, one boxer asked the ref for a break so that he could ask his coach a question; a losing woman hurled her gloves at the officials in anger (she does it every time she loses). It was great.

Smith got me a big chair, a pot of tea and a plate of biscuits. I had visitors all day, it's the Saudi way. First, Naseibah Al-Jeffery came over. She is a referee from Jeddah, and she once worked on the breakfast show on BBC Stoke. She had fallen in love with boxing when she attended the Anthony Joshua and Andy Ruiz fight in Diriyah in late 2019. Smith had sent her out to the Asian Under-22 championships in Bangkok to get some experience. That is a one-off podcast right there.

The princess that lost was meant to be travelling with Smith to Europe for training and fighting experience. It is hard, apparently, to arrange for Saudi royals to travel. It involves the secret service, a zillion phone calls and other silent men with guns. 'Next time,' Smith told me.

'See the big lad, he can fight a bit,' said Smith and he could. He was Ahmad Alzahran, and he had won a bronze at the Asian Under-18 Championships in Cairo. It looked like Smith was running an alternative, but legitimate, boxing movement – nobody back at the plush hotels and in the land of Fury and Paul had a clue about this – I was five miles and a galaxy away. It was amateur boxing, the real thing. The fancy PR company, hired by the Saudis to help promote the fight, looked at me like I was lying when I tried to tell them about the event. Well, actually, they looked at me like I was mad when I told them a princess had lost a fight and that the referee was a woman.

I was back in Riyadh twice in 2023 and still nobody involved with all the cash and mayhem of the professional fights had any idea about Smith and his low-key revolution. Smith has a couple of secret female fighters, and they really can fight. He is looking at the Paris Olympics and not banking on a handout of a wild card. One had dyed red hair; the other won the equivalent of £220,000 when she won the Saudi Games. The woman she beat in the final made her professional debut the following night on Fury's undercard. I'm not kidding, this was a strange new world.

Kevin Smith: *The irony is that on the day I went to the Regionals, there was a fancy press junket to a gym to see a Saudi woman train. That was a trip with perks, as they say. Instead, I saw a dozen women box, I saw female referees, judges and officials. I never got any expensive gifts on my trip, but I did get tea and biscuits. I paid for my own cab, by the way. Entrance to the boxing was free. I must add an alarming footnote: in October of the same year, back in Saudi for the Tyson Fury and Francis Ngannou fight, an American woman, stylishly draped in full Saudi clothing, came over and introduced herself. She was, she told me, setting up boxing clubs all over the country. She had Saudi funding, she told me. 'Great, Kevin Smith must be delighted,' I said to her. Bemused, she looked at me and said. 'Sorry, Kevin who?' Not a clue. Ouch.*

55

WOMEN'S US AMATEUR CHAMPIONSHIPS

MIDLAND, TEXAS, 2000

The circus of slappers, nudes and foul-mouthed sluggers had no future.

Cindy Zamudio torched the toilets at her school and was ordered to fight in a boxing ring or go to prison. She picked the boxing.

In Midland, Texas, an old town famous for oil, Zamudio, who was aged 18 and weighed 19 stone, became the super-heavyweight amateur champion of the United States. That is better than being known as an arsonist from Los Angeles.

Big Cindy beat Debbie Grim in the semi-final. Grim tipped the scales at 20 stone and was on a mission of discovery. Back in New York, she was a singer, and she was often arrested for fighting men in bars. They were in one of the must-see fights in a long week in the Texas town. I made a documentary about the championships. It was called *Ladies Who Punch* and it was brilliant. A film about women's boxing, shown on BBC television in 2000: it was way ahead of the curve.

Zamudio won in just 83 seconds. Grim was stuck, frozen in fear. 'I shit in all their faces,' Zamudio said. 'They said I was fat, they said I was too slow and that's all I needed.' Three days later, she won the final. Grim went back to New York and two weeks later, in the ancient and sacred ring at Madison Square Garden, she won the Golden Gloves. I'm telling you that Grim, forget her size, could really shape up.

Grim and Zamudio were just two of the stories and by no means the best of the tales. It was a mix of comedy and chilling emotional stuff; women and girls on journeys, desperately looking for something in that illuminated ring. At that time, the professional women were often the daughters of famous men, glamour models or raw, raw sluggers. The business was bad, and it never had a future; the stuff I was watching in Midland was the start of where we are now. The amateur game was the only future for the professional game. The circus of slappers, nudes and foul-mouthed sluggers had no future. Slappers is a bad boxing style, not a lifestyle choice.

In Midland, we filmed the start of the revolution. In late 2019, I tried to get the band together – Jim Bentley, the producer, and the cameraman, Dave Varley, to go back and find our women. And then Covid came and then the 20th anniversary was gone. It's still a plan. The documentary from then can still hold its own.

Zamudio travelled with her mother. Others had different people with them, friends, lovers, grandparents, kids, husbands even. An undercover vice cop from New York had her new wife with her – boxing is very open and all we require is that you can fight, and that you want to fight. We are not bothered by who you kip down with.

Amber Gideon, who would go on and fight in the World Amateurs in Turkey two years later, had both her kids in one car. It looked like they had left Chicago for good. She had to drive the 1,300 miles with Dante and Devon because there was nobody available to look after the boys. She arrived with the kids, but no coach; a week later and after four wins, she left as the new lightweight champion of America. I was walking in fairy tales in Texas, trust me. On finals night and the next day when they all started to leave, I was sobbing like a child. I had a reunion with Gideon in Antalya at the Worlds.

Julia Day, from Lexington, Kentucky, had run away with her boyfriend, Gerald Reed, who was also her coach. 'The problem with women,' Reed explained, 'is nobody takes them seriously.' Reed had made Day balance on paint cans, the type of ancient trick that Mickey used in *Rocky*. Her parents were not happy with Reed and that is why they had run off together to Texas. Day was just 20 in Texas, Reed, a professional fighter with about 50 bouts at that time, was nearly 20 years older.

Julia Day: *'What are those motherfuckers gonna say now?' screamed Reed when Day won the bantamweight title. In the dressing room, her hands still in bandages, she tried to smother the tears as they fell. 'I told you; I told you,' Reed continued. 'I told you that sometimes you gotta do things that your parents don't understand.' Varley was in close, getting the intake of breath and every single tear. Ten minutes later, I let Julia take my mobile, go into a corner and call her parents. There was not a dry eye in the place. It would still be a great film now.*

56

NASEEM HAMED
— v —
KEVIN KELLEY

WBO FEATHERWEIGHT TITLE: MADISON SQUARE GARDEN, NEW YORK, 1997

'This young punk arrives on the scene, and everybody is down on their knees licking his boots.'

It was the Monday before the fight and Hamed was behind closed doors at a fancy boxing gym called Blue Velvet in New York. The place was years in front of any curves.

Hamed and all his people were there, but nobody else. I was tucked in under a speedball, watching. There was a bang at the door, somebody opened it and Michael Jackson came in. Hamed had been at his Neverland ranch in October. Jacko had on full Jacko kit: gloves, hat, shiny shoes. The works.

I wrote: 'In the ring, Hamed performed some of Jackson's dance routines and at the ring's edge, the singer squealed with delight. It was weird cabaret.' That is the breaking story you need in your paper over your eggs in the morning.

Hamed stayed in the ring, moving, shadow boxing, smiling and shouting out at his friend. Then the pair were doing a synchronised moonwalk – one in the ring and one outside. The most important fight of Hamed's career was about 100 hours away.

Jacko removed his smog mask when he was ringside, left his shades on and took his gloves off to shake hands with the Hamed team. 'He never does that,' his security guy told me. And, yes, Jackson was a strange-looking dude.

At the Blue Velvet, there was a veteran trainer called Victor Machado and he had a wonderful line. He told me: 'This kid, the Prince, he can do the double-fake quicker than a snake, man. He is an old fighter.' Who finds these men from central casting and their quotes? Get in, love it.

Hamed's boxing life in New York was more settled than normal. Hamed was not sharing a room, just a suite with Thomas Bradley and Johnny Nelson. The rest, including Anas Oweida, Kevin Adamson and Clifton Mitchell, were in rooms down the hall. There had still been long, long nights. They were all fighters; they had all known Naz when he had nothing. In New York there was endless talk of his new super deal, worth $40 million. It was a deal with Frank Warren, and it specifically excluded Don King's involvement.

The training team of Brendan Ingle and his son, John, were a couple of floors below. There was a rift growing, make no mistake. In New York it was strictly business.

Welcome to Naz's world.

On the Wednesday of fight week, Brendan Ingle was in great form. Inside boxing's most revered venue, he conjured up the sport's greatest men when he talked about the boy he had found. Brendan Ingle in the Garden. I wonder now if that was his first time, the first time for the kid from Dublin, a struggling and jobbing pro boxer in the Sixties and Seventies. Ingle had fought hard men in hard venues, once mixed it with an Olympic gold medal winner and walked away from boxing in 1973 with 19 wins and 14 defeats. He never had a single easy fight. He knew fighters, that was his trick.

'All the Naz fella does is what the great fighters in history have done. He has taken a bit of Willie Pep, a bit of Kid Gavilan and a bit of Sugar Ray Robinson and turned them upside down, inside out to get his style.' Ingle, the great whispering guru, played his part. A few people knew that the relationship was falling apart; the week in New York was odd in so many ways.

And there was more testimony. Hamed and Ingle, in an attempt to break clear of the New York fight rumour mill, had gone over to Jersey City to train at the Rocky Marciano gym. They had met Rocky's brother, Lou, and he had watched a session. 'The kid can fight,' he declared.

Kelley had also done his best to raise the fight's profile. He had lost just twice in 50 fights, held a version of the world title and was not happy with being a supporting actor in his beloved city. He had said some mildly offensive things. It all helped shift some tickets; it never helped his chances. The expected box office was about 7,000 tickets and that would have been a success.

'This young punk arrives on the scene, and everybody is down on their knees licking his boots,' Kelley said when we gathered round him. 'If Hamed ever finds himself lost on a New York street and he tries any of his acts, guys that couldn't kill him with their bare hands will shoot him.' Late on the Monday night, at a gym out on Long Island, Kelley and his trainer, Phil Borgia, were going over the final details. It was all about pressure, and it was dependent on Hamed not being ready. Hamed was ready: he was on weight at that time, strong and ready. Kelley had fallen for the stories about Hamed not preparing seriously. It had been a Brendan Ingle con.

'He has put himself in a bad place and there is no way back. Listen to his voice,' Hamed said.

It also needs to be said that Kelley was getting $600,000 for fighting the 'punk'. It was by far the highest purse of Kelley's career.

Hamed was only 23 when he left his dressing room on that Friday night at the Garden. He was unbeaten in 28, with 26 knockouts.

It was a crazy fight. It finished in the fourth with Kelley counted out. Hamed had been officially dropped three times and Kelley three or four times. Naz touched down a couple of other times. Hamed was dropped near the end of the first and was clearly still hurt during the break. Ingle worked furiously. At the start of the second, Hamed touched down, got up and was then dropped. It looked like it was all over – the money, the fame, the career. The Garden had taken another boxer; in 2019, it would take Anthony Joshua. Kelley had two minutes and ten seconds left to change history. One minute later, Kelley was flat on his back and Hamed was standing over him and smiling. I'm not inventing this stuff – inside five minutes of boxing, Hamed had been over three times and Kelley was looking up at the lights.

They both survived to the fourth. In the fourth, Kelley was over again, this time heavily, and then he caught Hamed, and Hamed went down. Then Hamed dropped Kelley for the last time. The native New Yorker beat the count but stared at oblivion and the count reached ten. It was over. There had been real fear in the Hamed camp.

'We all saw what went wrong; I just hope people recognise what went right,' said Warren at ringside. 'An unknown from Sheffield went to New York, set a record for featherweights at the box office, attracted 12,000, climbed up from three knockdowns to take out the local hero in the fourth. That's what happened and that's a bloody good British success story.' Hard to disagree with that.

Naseem Hamed: *The papers in New York were harsh. 'He came in like Kid Confetti and fought like Kid Counterfeit' was one headline. Warren is right, it was a success. Hamed sold nearly 5,000 more tickets than Sugar Ray Leonard had done, 2,000 more than Roy Jones and he did it in the middle of a bleak winter and just six days before Christmas. There was a fallout, there always is. 'Do you think I will ever be that bad again?' Hamed asked me on the Saturday after we had watched the fight in his suite. I hoped not.*

57

KELLIE MALONEY: STORM AT RINGSIDE

PECKHAM, SOUTH LONDON, 2014

I saw Maloney take control at ringside, letting everyone know that she was not there to be jobbed.

When Kellie was just Frank, she dined with the most powerful people in the business she had chosen. She was the manager of Lennox Lewis, one of the greatest heavyweights in history and people wanted her to be their friend.

When Kellie, then as Frank, got married in Lake Tahoe, I was one of three men tasked with passing her the ring. We were dressed in summery shirts and yellow shorts. We should have guessed that she was struggling with her sexuality from the way she dressed the three of us in a sea of pastel. And strappy sandals. We were dressed like Liberace's backing singers.

Also, a couple of nights before the wedding, Steve Lillis and I had left the bachelor party at a suite in a hotel on the lake when three Jack the Rippers arrived. No thanks, guvnor. Lillis and I slipped out and, as the lift arrived about 30 doors down, Kellie charged out of the room in her underpants and carrying her clothes. 'Wait, hold on, son. I'm coming with you.' I guess that was another sign. Anyway, it makes no difference, because until about midnight on a Saturday in August 2014, I had no idea she had been battling her body. I knew Kellie and I had no idea.

I sent her a text and told her that she was brave. 'Either brave or stupid,' she replied. Maybe a bit of both, who knows or cares. Maloney finally has a private life now after a few years of scrutiny. Thankfully, the pictures of her frolicking in the ocean have dried up. At the end of 2023, she was living in Portugal with her own little menagerie. Happy, so she said.

During her reign as the manager of Lewis she battled Don King and won, she refused Donald Trump's offers, she had a long struggle with her addicted fighter, Scott Harrison, and she discovered her unbeaten Irish boxer, Darren Sutherland, hanged in his bedsit. Darren had dined with Kellie, her wife and their children the night before. She also had a heart attack after the first Tyson Fury and John McDermott fight in 2009. Fury dodged a bullet that night and, according to doctors, so did Maloney. It was not a shock when it emerged that she had undergone full gender reassignment treatment.

When I was 17, I boxed on one of Maloney's shows at the Trinity Club in Albany Road in Southwark, south London. Maloney ran the Trinity ABC (amateur boxing club). She gave Mick Carney, who was the legendary trainer at the Fitzroy Lodge some expenses. The Lodge is about two miles away. I got a tenner – that was a fortune. A few fights after me that night, Frank Bruno boxed. He beat Hughroy Currie from Catford. He never got a tenner.

Maloney never lost touch with her roots at the lower end of the boxing business. She knew about stuff that most successful promoters and managers never knew. The hardships of young boxers struggling, the bad days, the letdowns. She started with nothing before landing Lewis. To be honest, that was a fluke. Still, she did a great job with the Big Lad.

When she was still Frank, we went on a trip to Paris with Crawford Ashley in 1997. We were with Bob Paget, Ashley's trainer. Ashley was up against it in a European title fight in a town called Alfortville on the outskirts of Paris. Pascal Warusfel was his opponent, and his uncle was meant to be the mayor. I saw Maloney take control at ringside, letting everyone know that she was not there to be jobbed. Ashley got a majority decision; one judge returned a draw. I believe Maloney won Ashley that title fight before the first bell.

Long after midnight, we traipsed the streets of the dark and silent town trying to buy a bottle of champagne. No luck. The next day, we did our best to drink dry the lounge on the train. She was a proper boxing person. I have heard liars claim that when she was overseas on fights, she indulged her secrets and dressed as a woman. Well, she did all that without a frock or lippy on our Paris trip. She stormed that ringside, all five-foot four of her, and gave them all the facts of life.

Kellie Maloney: *We have mutual friends, and some have still not spoken to her since the revelation came out in the paper. Brave, stupid, it makes no difference. Kellie is happy now with her old donkeys in the sun.*

58

MIKE TYSON

— v —

LENNOX LEWIS

WBC HEAVYWEIGHT TITLE: MEMPHIS, 2002

**'If I would have had my proper crew with me that day,
Lewis would be dead.'**

'Elvis Presley and Dr Martin Luther King Jr did actually die in
Memphis, but Mike Tyson only went through the motions and it
was not a pretty sight.' That was an early line in my fight report.

This was how the Lennox Lewis and Mike Tyson heavyweight
fight at the Pyramid in Memphis finished; it started ten years earlier and that week in Memphis was unforgettable. The fight was a
one-sided massacre. Tyson came to take a beating; it looked to me
that it was his mad attempt at being forgiven for all his sins on both
sides of the ropes. He never flinched.

I arrived in Memphis on the Sunday. My cabbie told me that
he had watched Ricky Hatton fight the night before in a war with
Eamonn Magee. I had been at that fight in Manchester. It was the
start of the Memphis blur.

On Monday, we waited for an audience with Tyson. It never
happened. Steve 'Crocodile' Fitch, the king cheerleader, was back
in Tyson's gang. He had been away winning custody of his little
boy. I liked Croc, others believed he was a nuisance. But this was a
troubled city. There was a story on the news about a man who was

left for dead; he had been beaten, wrapped in barbed wire and a bomb was attached to his chest. The newsreader never batted an eyelid when she warned Memphis that the culprit is 'more dangerous than most'.

On Tuesday, three busloads of press went on a 60-minute journey to Fitzgerald's casino in Tunica. Tyson kept about 200 members of the media waiting another 90 minutes. Tyson never spoke. His trainer, Stacey McKinley, never stopped: 'Lewis is a coward.' There was a lot of bad history.

In New York, four months earlier, at a press conference to announce the fight, Tyson and Lewis had got in a scuffle and Tyson bit Lewis on the thigh. He drew blood, Lewis had to go for a tetanus shot. 'Lewis had his chance, and he will regret not killing me when his punks had me down in New York,' said Tyson. 'If I would have had my proper crew with me that day, Lewis would be dead.' In Memphis, separate locations were needed – there was a real fear that something truly bad could happen. It was expected.

On the Wednesday, we were back in Tunica, and at the Lewis camp in Sam's Town. It was fine, typical Lewis. The story of the day was the touts complaining that $1,000 tickets were selling for $500. The local paper had hundreds of cheap ticket ads. It was bad for the British travelling fans because they had paid top, top dollar. It still felt odd, the fight was spread over too many locations.

They weighed at different times on the Thursday. Lewis would have a 15-lbs advantage, six inches in height and 13 inches in reach. The mayor of Memphis, Willie Herenton, put on a barbecue, pork and beans, but food would not lift the dark cloud of violence hanging over the fight. Over 4,000 tickets were returned. The streets were suddenly noisy and full. There were still people out at 6 a.m. on the Friday; the fight was taking on a life of its own.

On that Friday, Ricky Hatton arrived to go in the corner with an old friend, Jason Barker, but a variety of crazy reasons meant Barker never fought. Ricky was out until 6 a.m., no worries. Memphis was a dangerous place, the sirens never stopped. An Irish pub called Dan McGuinness had become the hub for all touts. There were bargains and there was the constant threat of something in the night air. On the night, 15,300 paid and about 4,000 seats were empty. An empty seat on that night remains one of boxing's mysteries: the fight would sell 100,000 at Wembley Stadium in about three minutes in the modern business. Still, they each cleared $25 million after the pay-per-view generated $103 million.

On the fight day, Saturday, the car park opposite the Pyramid was a no-go area. It was crazy. I saw my old pal Crocodile walking out, shuffling with the look of a man in a hurry trying not to look like a man in a hurry. They were selling everything in there – drugs, flesh and tickets. He never made it clear to me what he had been shopping for. It was a scary atmosphere.

Lewis won in the eighth round. The first round was worth the ten-year wait, it was a glimpse of what we all missed out on. From the second round, Tyson was finished, Lewis was clinical.

I walked back on my own at 4 a.m. and the night was crackling with raw excitement. The car parks were buzzing, and the city seemed lawless. The next day, the local paper reported that one fan was shot and killed, and another was shot in the face. At my cheap hotel, I placed a damp towel along the bottom of the door to avoid a contact high and then I listened to the sirens until I faded at about seven in the morning.

In the tunnels backstage when it was over, Violet Lewis, the champion's influential mother, spoke to a few of us. She also, I think, spoke for a lot of us: 'I didn't want Lennox to hurt him. I want Mike to go back to being a nice man.' Make no mistake, Lennox did not want to spare him. Lennox made it last – it was vicious.

Shortly after Violet's words, Tyson emerged, he was cradling his young son, Miguel, and finally and thankfully his gang of cheerleaders had fallen silent and dropped back. Mike Tyson was all alone, just him and a child, as he left the Pyramid that night. It was a procession, the endgame in Memphis.

It was an oddly dignified finish to a week and a fight that had raised real fears. The sport was under the spotlight; Tyson had talked of death in the ring and Lewis had found his voice. 'Tyson has been a millionaire for 15 years and I'm sick of hearing about his hard life,' said Lewis. By 2002, Tyson's persecution complex was established.

In the ring at the very end after Tyson had got up from the chilling knockout, he embraced Lewis. We asked Lewis what had been said when Tyson pulled him in close. Both were smeared with blood – Tyson bled from cuts above both eyes, his nose and dark, dark blood from his mouth. Lewis also had some damage. 'He said to me: "I'm sorry."' Lennox left it there to let it sink in.

Lennox Lewis: *A rematch with Tyson the following April was just one of the plans. It never happened. Lewis had one more fight, a bloodbath with Vitali Klitschko, and then walked away. 'I had nothing left to prove,' he told me in Toronto in 2024. Tyson is still deep in the boxing game and considering all offers for freak fights.*

59

BRENDAN INGLE:
MAKING FIGHTERS, SAVING FIGHTERS

SHEFFIELD, 2018

He worked some miracles in that Wincobank gym.

Brendan Ingle was the whispering guru of the ring, a man so deep inside the boxing business that just being in the same room as him increased your knowledge.

He made fighters, he saved fighters, and he loved every part of the dear, old, dirty game. He was not, it has to be said, universally loved in return.

We sat in steam rooms in Rotherham, coffee shops in Copenhagen, hotel rooms in New York and talked boxing. I listened as he talked about finding and shaping the 'little fella', Naseem Hamed, and gently transforming the career of Johnny Nelson, which was a lost cause at the start. He talked about what was needed to make a fighter. He worked some miracles in that Wincobank gym. Pure magic, to be honest.

There were also ugly splits, disputes and all mixed in with nights of glory in rings all over the world. He upset people with his brutal honesty and his breakdown of the way the business really worked. Often fighters don't like the harsh truth and when that happens, they will listen to others.

'They will pay you 10 per cent of £400, even 10 per cent of £2,000, but once it gets to £40,000 or £4 million, they start listening to everybody telling them the same story. "Why are you paying that much? You do the fighting." Well, I will tell you why: I've just spent 15 years, seven days each week and about eight hours each day. That's why.' It is the sermon I most admire from Brendan.

He said to me in 2006: 'I'll drop dead in the middle of a ring after a fight some night and when that happens youse will all know that Brendan Ingle died happy.' It was not in a ring, but he was happy at the end.

Brendan had been a brilliant journeyman boxer. He had taken short notice fights, met unbeaten men on big nights and also fought prospects behind closed doors at the private clubs. He was learning his trade on both sides of the ropes. He lost to Olympic champion Chris Finnegan in 1969 and finished his career with defeat in Copenhagen in 1973. His record is deceptive, and he was a true fighting man of the road: He won 19 and lost 14 of his 33 fights.

There is a scene in Paddy Considine's *Journeyman* featuring Brendan. It is overwhelming. Brendan plays Paddy's father; there are no words, just smiles and tears. Brendan was fading at the time and that makes it even more poignant. The film is special.

Brendan Ingle: *When Hamed met Manuel Medina in Dublin in 1996, I walked with Brendan one morning. We stopped by the river, he looked at a new housing complex. It had once been the tenement where he had grown up, Dublin's most deprived area. He never needed to say a word; one minute later he was back on Naz's brilliance. It was a nice walk.*

60

DAVID HAYE

— v —

AUDLEY HARRISON

WBA HEAVYWEIGHT TITLE: MANCHESTER, 2010

'We used to be close friends. Now, I'm just going to hurt him.'

It was not much of a fight, but it was a brilliant build-up.

It is not often that two close friends fight each other and during the months, weeks, days and hours before the first bell, they turn into horrible enemies. All the old wounds start to fester and it becomes a bit raw. It is car-crash boxing.

In 1999, at the World Amateur Championships in Houston, David Haye and Audley Harrison were inseparable. They boxed, lost and went out late. The following year, Harrison won a gold medal and Haye was still chasing amateur glory. Haye missed out on the Olympics but won a silver medal at the World Championships in Belfast in 2001. He was the first British finalist and the championships had started in 1974 in Havana. They were an Eastern Bloc plaything.

The pair still seemed to be friends. However, there was a sparring session in Miami in 2006; Haye took liberties according to Harrison. At that time, Harrison's career was difficult, and he was no longer the Golden Boy. He was also fresh from a loss and Haye was in the last weeks of a good camp. It is also something that Haye has denied; Haye was on his way to the cruiserweight world title at the time. Audley seems to have been annoyed that Haye had turned it on in front of Lennox Lewis, a ringside witness to the sparring. It is the type of thing a boxer does not forget.

'When I was the Olympic champion and in Tenerife with big names, he used to fly out and sleep on my floor,' Harrison remembered. 'We were close, I looked after him. He used to lean on me.' It did sound a little bit like Audley was taking credit for throwing the kid a few scraps. Well, he had thrown the kid a few scraps.

This was personal.

And then Haye was arrogant at the press conferences to promote the fight. It was ugly and it seemed to me that Harrsion was surprised by the hate. It was not fake, trust me.

'I used to defend Audley all the time,' claimed Haye. 'When people kept telling me he was fighting bums, I would get in arguments. I was a good friend to him. We used to be close friends. Now, I'm just going to hurt him. Bring a puke bag.' He said some other unpleasant and unprintable things. Harrison was shocked, I could tell. Shocked and perhaps a bit let down.

There was talk of jealousy and I guess there was. That is human nature; Audley had been a king, now Haye was on his way to being the king and they each interpreted their friendship in a different way. They both blamed the other for the current mood. There was no humour in the fight.

David Haye: *It finished in the third. Haye kept his WBA heavyweight title, but it was a hitless flop. It was strange. In the weeks before the fight, Haye had said something about the plan Harrison had from the start of his career and it stuck in my mind. 'The plan was to cream as much money fighting the worst possible guys.' I still have no idea what happened in the ring that night. Harrisons's gold medal changed boxing in Britain. It created the funding.*

61

PHIL MARTIN:
CREATING CHAMPIONS

CHAMPS CAMP · MOSS SIDE, MANCHESTER, 1993

'If a lad has talent and he doesn't use it – that makes him weak, and I tell him.'

In January 1993 there was a face-off in a Moss Side boxing gym that was surely one of the greatest in this boxing business.

Chris Eubank was on the streets of Moss Side, walking in rallies against the gun violence and holding court in front of any crowd that would stop for him. He also went to Champs Camp, the gym built from the ruins of the 1981 riots.

Phil Martin had made the Champs Camp gym. He took over a ruined Co-op and ten years later he had four British champions at the same time. The guns were outside; inside that gym there was a sanctuary, but there were some thin lines, and they could be crossed.

Martin never bowed down, never said what people wanted to hear. He was his own man. And that meant that he, especially in his tower, never had to listen to anything he didn't want to. As a fighter, he had lost a British title fight over the 15-round distance back in 1976. His real genius was making champions.

Eubank arrived at Martin's Moss Side gym. 'Words don't mean a lot down here,' warned Martin. Still, Eubank was in full flow. Then Martin had heard enough and there was silence in the gym

– everybody sensed it. Martin was Moss Side boxing, and this was his domain – he had done it brick-by-brick.

'I listened to him for a while and then I thought, "I built this gym with my own hands, I put years into it and now he is telling me what I'm doing wrong." So, I said, "Chris, just fuck off." I had been here 20 years; he'd been here 20 minutes.' Eubank did leave, no fuss.

Martin had a room right at the top of the gym and in that room, he had hundreds of videos of his boys boxing and some of the greats from the ring. An old-fashioned VHS collection with names of fights and fighters scribbled on the labels: some crossed out and a new fight entered. Everybody in boxing had that same collection. He also had a big leather recliner. That was his retreat, that was where the thoughts and feelings of Phil Martin were shared. Martin was not bothered by what you thought about his views.

'If a lad has talent and he doesn't use it – that makes him weak, and I tell him. I'm not here to please anybody,' he said. The door was open, but you had to follow Martin's rules.

He was direct and brutal with some of his ideas. 'Boxing is all about cash,' he told me once. 'And hungry fighters don't make the best fighters because they are too busy getting something to eat.' Martin knew about hard times – I knew he had boys in there who had not been fed. Martin had been a union organiser, he was dedicated to change.

There was often a bullet-proof vest in the changing room and that is not surprising with the amount of gun carnage just down the steps and through Phil's door. One of his good fighters was solidly involved with that outside life. Most of the boxers lived close to the damage and the danger. I remember that when the buzzer on the door sounded, and even if it was a familiar voice, somebody would go over and look down the stairs to make sure it was just the owner of the voice. Then the release button would be hit.

In 1993, Martin put all four of his British champions on a bill in Oldham and he had another one of his boxers challenging for the British title. The owner of the bullet-proof vest was also on the bill. That would be impossible in modern boxing. It is a great story anytime, for any promoter and at any venue. Martin had found some of those men, saved those men, shaped those men and made those men. He was a black promoter with a gym in Moss Side. He had not sold his soul to a bigger promoter and every penny made was paid to the boxers. It was a tight budget. On that Sunday afternoon, just two national newspapers bothered to show up. That was a scandal, I was angry. Martin shrugged it off when I tried to apologise.

There is a story that Maurice Core tells, and he was a special fighter inside Martin's boxing history. In 1993, when Martin knew that he was dying, there was a steady stream of people ringing that buzzer and coming up the stairs to see the great man. Mums, grandmas, policemen, gangsters, dealers, good guys, bad guys, wounded guys, men with one eye and mums with toddlers – they all knew what they had to do. They were there to see the man before the end. He died in 1994.

When he died there was decent coverage, but in the years since his death at 44 from cancer, his status and legend has grown. Core and Joe Gallagher have pushed Martin's legacy. Core was one of Martin's British champions, Gallagher an amateur with Martin and now one of British boxing's most successful trainers. Core was once held at Strangeways on nine attempted murder charges. 'Nine, can you believe it?' He was acquitted of all charges. He had first walked into the gym with a cigarette in his mouth. 'Phil put us in a position where anything was possible,' he said. Core was there from the start, one of the boys collecting clothing and other items from the nicer parts of Manchester for the jumble sales; there were 18 jumble sales in nine months. The building was a ruin when Martin got it and once he had rebuilt it, he still had to build the gym and kit it out. I wrote that Martin 'developed his own science of decency,' and I think that captures what it meant to be part of his Moss Side story.

Yeah, once upon a time, in Moss Side when men and boys were being shot every week, there was a boxing gym with a 20-foot mural of Muhammad Ali on the outside wall. In 1993, there were over 100 documented shooting incidents on those streets. That is why boxers wore and then left their bullet-proof jackets in the changing room. Inside that safe zone there was magic.

Phil Martin: *The documentary, made by boxing producer Jim Bentley, was called* M14: A Moss Side Story *and it was good. However, it's a film, a movie, Hollywood stuff that is needed.*

62

CHRIS EUBANK:
TWO HOURS LATER

MOSS SIDE, MANCHESTER, 1993

'I'm here to educate and try and tell people that they have to help themselves.'

Chris Eubank's peace mission to Moss Side took place over six days.

The world champion was thrown out of Phil Martin's gym and went to the leisure centre across the street. It was dark and it was cold, and he was not welcome: those are the facts. But Eubank, like Martin, was never bothered by what other people thought. He went there a couple of times, and I was there with him. I was working for the *Daily Telegraph* at the time.

Eubank had defended his WBO super-middleweight title twice in Manchester in 1992 and his next defence was a month away and it was in London at Earl's Court. His Moss Side mission was not about raising publicity for that fight. He would have his rematch with Nigel Benn at the Theatre of Dreams, as Old Trafford is known, in October; the mission was not about shifting tickets.

'He's only here to publicise his fights,' one man in the crowd said.

'Get real, man. Nobody in Moss Side pays to see him fight. He brings a spotlight, he's committed himself. There are a lot of sports stars in Manchester, both black and white, and I don't see any of them coming down here,' as another man in the crowd said.

It was tense from the moment that Eubank, flanked by his trainers Ronnie Davies and Walter Smith, walked in. I wrote that as many as 30 locals were there. Mostly men and mostly under the age of 30. Eubank asked my photographer not to shoot any of the men. 'No faces, please. This is a private meeting, and you are privileged to be here, but no faces.'

Eubank listened. 'There is only so much that I can do. If I had a billion, it wouldn't help – I'm here to educate and try and tell people that they have to help themselves. I'm here to listen.'

There was a lively exchange about rules; Eubank is big on rules.

'The rules are the rules that you mustn't break,' Eubank told a man who had asked him what rules he was talking about. 'What rules will you teach your son? My rules or your rules?'

The answer silenced the hall. 'I will teach him to be smart, not to trust the police or white people.'

Eubank looked hard at the man, held his hand up to his chin and replied: 'Surely you would not teach your son these things.' They agreed to meet and talk in private the next day.

'And your message,' another man asked. 'Isn't there a danger that nobody will listen and that when it is reported you will be misquoted?'

'It was good for you to come out and meet me,' said Eubank. 'I will do what I can, I will speak to business leaders and the street community. I will listen.' He tried, that is for sure, and he met behind closed doors with all sorts of people; the angry, the grieving, the fat and the thin. And probably some liars. They talked, they cried, they each had a story and Eubank listened. Eubank had not had an easy life – people often confused the monocle, the elocution and the jodhpurs with somebody else. Eubank had once been, by his own admission, the best Burberry coat thief in Peckham. And that, my friend, was a coveted title.

Chris Eubank: *The fighter still divides people now. I have known him for 35 years and consider him a friend. On the Saturday of his mission to Moss Side, he joined Phil Martin's British champion, Maurice Core, in a march for peace through the streets. A 14-year-old boy had been shot outside a takeaway. He was shot a few doors down from the door to Martin's Champs Camp gym. The kid never had the chance to ring the buzzer.*

63

NIGEL BENN

— v —

GERALD McCLELLAN

WBC SUPER-MIDDLEWEIGHT TITLE: LONDON, 1995

'There was a horrifyingly blank look on his face and his eyes twitched.'

The hours, days, weeks and months after the Nigel Benn and Gerald McClellan fight were ugly. A man nearly died after that fight.

The savage fight and outcome are now firmly part of British boxing history. Nobody in the London Arena on that cold February night will ever forget what they watched. Both boxers were taken to hospital and only one walked out unassisted. Both were damaged, make no mistake.

That was the night, but the week was equally stunning. And before the two boxers came together there were a lot of stories, and most were bad. There was an ugliness to the week and a lot of what was said and claimed was lost once the fight to keep McClellan breathing started.

McClellan arrived in London after a series of comments about shooting his fighting dogs. There was no misunderstanding, nothing was lost in translation. It was all very bloody and cold. He had fighting dogs, savage pit bulls and when they were beaten or weak, he shot them. The language was graphic and unforgiving. It added to McClellan's proven menace inside the ropes. I have never had a problem with boxers being unpleasant humans – it happens, that is life. There are some in boxing who are horrible but smile and pretend; McClellan was just nasty. I loved him as a fighter, but we were never going to bond over the shooting of dogs in the head.

He had split two fights earlier from his long-time trainer and mentor, Manny Steward. It had been money, let's tell the truth. His new corner team of Stanley Johnson and Donnie Penelt were making a measly $7,500 combined for their work. That is a bargain-basement team for such a big fight.

There is no record of what he was paying his personal and frightening security man, Hyacinthus Turnipseed. That was the man's name, honest.

Benn had also parted ways with his trainer, Jimmy Tibbs, and would be using Kevin Sanders for the fight. Sanders had been on the circuit and had spent some time in Las Vegas. There was nothing wrong with him, but this was a big fight. It is funny, but we never questioned Johnson's credentials and, in the two fights that he had been in the corner, he had not even had to wash out McClellan's gumshield – McClellan had stopped both men in the first round. The truth is that the corners were a concern.

Benn was being chased by a previous trainer, Dynamite Brian Lynch, in a dispute over money. Steward, incidentally, had a large claim in with McClellan. There were a lot of tales swirling before the fight.

'I had a plan worked out for the fight,' said Jimmy Tibbs. 'I'd watched tapes, but then I was just pushed aside.'

The fight had been forced on Benn by the WBC. McClellan had been the WBC's middleweight champion and then he decided to move up in weight and Benn was ordered to fight him. McClellan was Don King's man and King had fantastic powers at the WBC. Benn was the underdog, defending his title at home.

It was an uneasy week in many ways. It was tense, there was violence in the air and the exchanges were vicious. They each talked about hurting the other man, they stood nose-to-nose, and it was chilling. Benn was not backing down – he had been face-to-face with good American fighters before, and he was not bothered. Not in the slightest. In 1990, in Las Vegas, he had dropped, stopped and hurt Iran Barkley in one sensational round. Benn had fought dirty, fought mean and beaten one of the best at his own game. The American fight public was put on notice – Nigel Benn had no fear.

'I fucking hate these yanks,' he said. He had said similar things before.

Their fighting numbers were incredible: Benn had stopped or knocked out 31 men and McClellan 29. They had finished 33 men in the opening round. McClellan was on a winning streak of 14 consecutive knockouts. The bookies had started the week offering 16–1 on a McClellan win in the first and that was reduced to 6–1 or less by the Friday. The London Arena was sold out, 8,000 were there for the war. The promoters Frank Warren and Don King had negotiated their way through a long week. The fight looked set to deliver, and that night, as 8,000 screamed for Benn, I swear it felt like something monumental was going to happen. There was a feeling – and I'm not sure all these years later that it was a good feeling. They had both promised so much and that crowd was there to make sure they delivered. It was not a normal night.

Benn never took his eyes off McClellan when they entered the ring. McClellan seemed distracted. I was positioned right in the American's corner, six feet from Johnson's back. It felt like I was part of the team. The same thing happened at the third Tyson Fury and Deontay Wilder fight in Las Vegas. I was so close to the corner that Malik Scott, Wilder's trainer, had his right elbow on my left knee during the rounds. If that happens, there is no way you can avoid being sucked deep into the fight. It also offers a unique view of what happens in the ring.

Benn was caught, hurt and sent through the ropes in the very first round. He was badly hurt and tangled in the ropes; he was pushed back into the ring and beat the count. 'The damn fight should have been over there and then,' screamed Johnson a day later. 'The referee couldn't referee a dog fight in my town.' Not a person was sitting – everybody was standing and that included the press and officials at ringside. It was one of those knockdowns that takes place in slow motion. It was all drama.

It went on like that until a final sickening right uppercut landed and down went McClellan. He fell slowly, took a knee and blinked furiously. It was the tenth round; the fight was over and the fight to save his life was just a minute or so away. 'There was a horrifyingly blank look on his face and his eyes twitched.' Live copy spares nobody. His eyes had been twitching in a lot of the rounds; we had missed the signs. McClellan had also complained about his head hurting to the men in his corner. There is no blame, but it is important to not overlook the facts.

The fight was over at 9.59 p.m. McClellan walked back to his corner, Benn celebrated with his corner and a couple of friends in the ring, then McClellan slumped forward into the arms of Stanley Johnson, who was still wearing his distinctive sailor's cap. It was the start of the most feared race in sport: the race to get an injured boxer to hospital. At 10.03 he was unconscious. Ringside ghouls clashed violently with Turnipseed and the rest of McClellan's entourage. I was moved in a huddle of emotional people ten feet along the ring. He was carried from the ring at about 10.19.

At the Royal London Hospital, the neurosurgeon, John Sutcliffe, was alerted. He was ready. McClellan was in and out of consciousness. He had a scan; he was then prepared for surgery. Benn, at one point, was in the tented cubicle next to him. He had felt weak when he got back to his dressing room and had followed McClellan in a second ambulance. He spoke to McClellan before he was released. He spent the night being lifted in and out of hot and cold baths.

McClellan went under the knife. Sutcliffe was finished by

1 a.m. He had removed a large blood clot from the surface of the right side of McClellan's brain. 'It came out with a vengeance,' Sutcliffe told Don King, who with Warren, was on a silent vigil at the hospital. In the morning, Sutcliffe added: 'There is a good chance that he will survive, but his boxing career is over.'

His boxing career was over.

However, the story of McClellan's survival only gets nastier. A lot of people have made a lot of baseless claims and there are so many versions. In short, McClellan was well enough to travel, but was advised not to. His people took him and then his condition worsened significantly. It is probably best if we leave it there.

Gerald McClellan: *The boxer was still alive in early 2024 and still required full-time care. And people are still throwing around the blame for his condition.*

64

WOMEN'S WORLD AMATEUR CHAMPIONSHIPS

ANTALYA, TURKEY, 2002

She [Natalia] was 'forced to drop out before the first fight when her boyfriend, who was one of her coaches, slugged her.'

On Turkey's Mediterranean coast, the Cold War allies did their business at the second edition of the Women's World Amateur Championships.

A Romanian was sacrificed, a French woman was going to be stitched up, and Turkey managed to get one female into the final as part of some clandestine deal. It was the type of deal that took the men's game to the very brink of collapse after decades of corruption and some murderous bloodshed. In the Eighties and Nineties, amateur boxing was no laughing matter. Men were killed: one Russian judge was shot, tortured and electrocuted in his bath in Moscow.

The Turkish fighter, Yasemin Ustalar, could really fight but the French woman, Myrian Lamare, was a just a bit special. It's possible that their final was the best female fight to have ever taken place. That's just my opinion. The big professional showdowns had not happened; Christy Martin against Lucia Rijker and Ann Wolf against Laila Ali had melted away. The four had been in good fights but not great fights, and not the two fights that women's boxing needed.

'I'm not stupid,' Lamare told me on the morning of the fight. 'I know I have to beat the fighter and the officials.'

Gloria Peek, a prison officer, was in charge of the green American team and she knew what her women and girls faced. 'Our girls have history outside the ring, but inside the ring we are still learning.' And losing; the Chinese and North Korean women all looked like babies but fought like demons. They were brilliant.

The British nations never even bothered sending. It was considered a waste of resources and also cruel to send the women to get butchered in Turkey. Back at GB boxing's crumbling headquarters in Crystal Palace, there was not even an open day to assess the talent. A few women were on the distant horizon.

This is the championship that changed modern women's boxing; it made it the business that we have now. That is not too grand a statement, trust me. It was where we caught a glimpse of the future.

There were no Africans and no Cubans: the Africans could not get the funding and the Cubans were reluctant to let women box. They are still reluctant. There was a woman from Lebanon – she drove up. The North Koreans appeared, their fighters exceptional, their security brutal.

And then there were the Indians. Well, Mary Kom to be precise. She won gold at 45 kilos. She is a national treasure and by the end of 2023 she had won six world amateur titles, the last in Delhi in 2018. I interviewed her in Antalya, in the duty free at the airport. 'I'm a Christian,' she told me. The Indian team manager, Santosh Dahiya, added: 'She comes from a very backward area. Very backward. It is three days on a train from Delhi.' Mary Kom was a one-woman boxing revolution. At the next championships, India won five medals. Mary Kom finally retired in January 2024.

But it was the Russians, those 'fuckings Russians,' as my Turkish hosts kept calling them, who made the most impression. The women could fight and so could the men and, on a few occasions, they had a mix-up – the women lost every time. There were no gloves or rules in those fights.

The Russian's best hope of gold was Natalia Kalpakova at light-middleweight. She was 'forced to drop out before the first fight when her boyfriend, who was one of her coaches, slugged her'. Natalia went down but got up and people saw it – it was not in private. I was still at the weigh-in, I think. The coach from Lebanon got involved and he got a slap. There was blood and mayhem. Natalia went to her room, stayed there for two days and had to fly back to Moscow where she had some plastic surgery on her cut brow. It created quite an atmosphere.

Gloria Peek kept pointing at the coach, who was not removed, and telling me: 'That's the motherfucker.' He had been questioned about the incident by Sandy Martinez-Pino, chair of the women's International Amateur Boxing Association. 'Do you know what the sonofabitch said when we asked him about the incident?' Martinez-Pino asked me. "In Russia it is no big deal, in Russia the women expect it." What an arsehole.'

In the end, I had to make my own enquiries. He looked familiar, a face from previous Russian teams I had seen at international events. On the Friday, the day of the semi-finals, I set off for the Gridacity Hotel. The Russian KO artist had taken up position by the bar. He refused me an interview and a minute later, another Russian came over and delivered a deathless message. It was, I wrote, straight from the pages of Ian Fleming.

'You are a big man but not too big. Go fuck off and stop asking so many questions.' That was that then.

On finals night, the Turkish special forces with their low-slung machine pistols were in the hall. The French girl, Lamare, worked in a popular pizza place in Marseille. It took me a few minutes to make the French connection. Lamare's fans had drums and Playboy tattoos. The battle lines were clear.

'Nobody heard the bell at the end of round one,' I wrote. I

was reminded of Ustalar's words to me the night before. She had told me that winning was important, but there was more. 'If other women follow that will be good.' She was a Muslim pioneer in the boxing game.

Lamare dominated both rounds and left Ustalar, whose nickname was the Bulldozer, smeared in blood. There was disbelief in Lamare's face before the bell to start the last round. I realised why: she knew that, somehow, she was trailing. The score was 21–20. Lamare boxed like a dream in the last round. It should have been clear. The tension was heightened by the police. The score was 26–26 and that meant something called countback would have to take place. Somehow, and I have no idea how, the fix was not in. The final countback score was 88–86 in Lamare's favour. Justice in Turkey.

It had been some week in Antalya. A few years later, the Russians built a luxury five-star resort there and it was a replica of the Kremlin. Those fucking Russians.

Myrian Lamare: *She turned pro, she was the WBA's first female world champion, and she met the best. She is a huge part of female boxing history. The link, if you like. Simona Galassi was also one of the crucial early links. She won gold in Antalya and then a world professional title. As a final footnote, I wrote in the* Observer Sports Magazine, *in March 2003, that boxing for women would be part of the London 2012 Olympic calendar. That is called an exclusive, thanks. People kept talking about Athens in 2004 and Beijing in 2008, but my Cold War buddies gave me the nod. 'London,' the boys in the caviar circle told me. And they were right.*

65

FLOYD MAYWEATHER
— v —
CONOR McGREGOR

THE MONEY BELT: LAS VEGAS, 2017

'I will send auditors in there like fucking sharks to count up every single dollar.'

The fight between the UFC giant and the King of Boxing was entertaining.

The numbers were overwhelming, and they remain the real story from the week in Las Vegas in the unbearable heat of August.

Floyd Mayweather had not fought for two years and Conor McGregor had not had a fight in a boxing ring since he was a small boy and amateur at the Crumlin club in Dublin.

It finished at 1:05 of the tenth. McGregor was still on his feet, with hardly a mark on him, but he was exhausted. After a slow start, he had taken control. Mayweather had been countered – hit by McGregor in response to something that Mayweather had thrown or done – more by the novice than any of the great boxers he had met. McGregor never hit him more, he just countered him more, and that is something that no gambler in the city could have found odds on. Mayweather at 40 was no longer the ring genius he had been; Mayweather four or five years earlier would have taken care of McGregor with ease.

This is what I wrote: 'Mayweather had looked older, slower and more desperate at times than at any point in his 21 years as a boxer.' That is being kind.

If McGregor had won, he would have broken Las Vegas, the gambling capital of the world. It seems that 90 per cent of the bets placed in the city during the week were for the Irishman. They were not insignificant amounts: some punters had placed $500,000 and $600,000 bets on him winning. The men in charge of the sports book (betting shops) at the casinos were worried.

The true whales, the betting cognoscenti, had stumped up large sums on a Mayweather win. A punter at the Mirage went with $1.2 million and one at the Bellagio went with $1 million. Their returns were $240,000 and $182,000 respectively. It's not romantic, but that is how true gamblers in Las Vegas do their business.

It was Mayweather's 50th win, his last official boxing match. The cash-cow tour started after, and it is hard to keep up with his ridiculous global outings. He met a wonderkid from the karate world and a slugger with roots in the old, old Italian mafia. He made money from the novelty fights, lots of money and there is no end in sight. The appetite for stupidity and silly fights is growing.

In some ways, I guess, Mayweather and McGregor set a high standard for crossover fights. The Tyson Fury and Francis Ngannou fight – the boxing world heavyweight champion against the UFC world heavyweight champion – in late 2023 was the natural successor. It became a legitimate event after Big Francis dropped Fury and pushed him close over ten rounds. It was officially the first boxing contest of Ngannou's life. It was also salvation for the mixed-martial-arts crowd who had prayed for one of their idols to not get a beating in the ring against a boxer. Mayweather beating McGregor was one thing, but Jake Paul, himself operating in a boxing twilight zone, had knocked out and embarrassed a few fallen UFC idols. Ngannou restored pride, Fury was bad on the night. And, so was

Mayweather, but thankfully McGregor's tank, as expected, blew. Ngannou's tank never dipped.

On the day of the fight, it was announced that 1,362 private jets had landed and were parked at the airport. I could see the plane park from my high window at the MGM. It never looked real. It was a record for any weekend in Las Vegas.

I had flown in on the Monday night and the city was gripped. All the oldest and craziest grifters were out and selling and making money. And losing money. On the bridge between New York New York and the MGM, the man with the 'kick-me-in-the-nuts' gag had a long queue on every hour, seemingly round the clock. The trick is simple. He takes ten bucks from you, you queue, he spiels for about ten minutes, the queue grows, his wad of cash grows and then there is the big reveal. He has a massive necklace of hardened nuts, walnut cases and other nuts. They hang down and protect his nuts. Everybody laughs and still tries as hard as they can to kick him in his real nuts. His protective shell holds and a new queue forms – people are close to fisticuffs to get in the queue and part with their ten bucks. Las Vegas was built by people kicking each other in the nuts. Endless mirth, my son.

'I'm the new king of boxing,' declared McGregor on Tuesday. 'I might just dust this fool and then start a new sport. I might mix the octagon with a boxing ring and create a hybrid. I will be the king of that.'

When it was over, the party started in many ways.

McGregor told us on the night and not 30 minutes after the referee had stopped it: 'It's now the counting phase – I will send auditors in there like fucking sharks to count up every single dollar.' And he did.

At 2 a.m. after the fight, McGregor, having eaten at Andrea's, went to the Encore's Beach Club at Night and hosted his post-fight party. The poolside cabanas were selling for five grand – the usual price was a grand. McGregor, with just a slight mouse under his left eye, was a great host.

At 2.30 a.m., Mayweather arrived at his strip club, Girl Collection, and took up residency. The club had increased its entrance cover fee from $50 to $500. That is just to get in, by the way. This is not a tiny bar; this is a giant cavern packed with over 1,000 celebrating people. Mayweather had invited my partner at the time in the podcast caper, Mike Costello, down for a hamburger. He did say and I heard it: 'Our meat is the best.' We had to decline the invitation, BBC rules. There is no record of how much of his $350 million purse Mayweather spent celebrating. I'm not sure that celebrating and Mayweather go in the same sentence; a man pictured sitting next to a million-dollar pile of $100 bills and on his own, at 4 a.m. in a strip club, stretches, in my humble opinion, the notion of celebrating.

McGregor was guaranteed $75 million. There was a side agreement that he would lose as much as 90 per cent if he fouled Mayweather and was disqualified. The fear was real. There was no chance of that, McGregor understands winning and losing on both sides of the ropes. Just four years before the Mayweather fight, McGregor was surviving back in Dublin on social security cheques. His weekly total was €188. That is not hype, that is the truth.

After the loss, he was asked how he would deal with it. He laughed, 'I've been strangled on live TV and come back – I'll be fine.' He was and he did. In 2023, McGregor sponsored the two fights between Katie Taylor and Chantelle Cameron.

Floyd Mayweather: *He is still posing with his piles of money. Asked about McGregor in Saudi Arabia in late 2023, he said: 'He's a lot better than I thought.' McGregor wants $300 million for a rematch. Please, don't rule it out.*

66

GENE KILROY:
THE FACILITATOR

LAS VEGAS, 2014

'Ali burnt me out. There is nothing left to see.'

Gene Kilroy drives a convertible Mercedes, a gift from Tom Jones, up and down the Strip he calls home. His home is Las Vegas.

Kilroy is the last man standing from the inner circle of Muhammad Ali's tight group of family and friends. He is the man that made sure the best doctors were on alert and that the road to the airport was clear. He was the man who made sure his beloved friend survived.

He carried the coffins when Ali's parents died, and he is still supporting people from the Ali days. He has paid for burials, he pays for homes, he is the fixer, Gene Kilroy.

Kilroy is the greatest fixer in the sport of fixers and facilitators. And he was the king of all the Las Vegas executive hosts for a long, long time.

I have been sitting with Gene for over 25 years. I have heard the stories, thousands of stories. Some are known, some are fresh, and some will never be retold. It is the tiny details, the special little touches that only Gene can add.

There was the story about George Foreman and Muhammad Ali meeting by chance in Jack Dempsey's New York restaurant. Foreman arrived, there was a scuffle and Foreman's coat was ripped.

Ali sat down next to Dempsey and Kilroy and leaned in close. 'I just took the first round,' he said. 'You did,' replied Dempsey.

At the end of the Rumble in the Jungle, after Kilroy had been the first to jump in the ring, Ali is on the floor. 'Gene, Gene, let the crazy people celebrate. I'm tired, Gene.' You can still see the fear on Kilroy's face as he embraces Ali and tries to protect him at the end. An hour earlier, Kilroy had been the delegated witness to Foreman putting his bandages on and had returned to Ali's dressing room. Gene tells this story with drama and voices and smells. He is back in the stadium. Foreman's dressing room was rocking, Ali's was silent. There was no joy, everybody was worried; the real story of the Rumble is the fear in Ali's team. Gene swears he walked back to the dressing room in silence. He was frightened and what he had heard had shaken him. The great light-heavyweight, Archie Moore, who was part of Foreman's team, had been pacing and saying: 'I smell death in the air.' The truth is a lot of people did.

Gene pauses at about this point, often to check if anybody else is listening. This is one of boxing's greatest stories being told by the only living man who was there on that night. If you are listening, you shut up.

'I got back, and the mood had not changed, it was worse,' Kilroy said. 'Ali turned to me: "What that n****r say?" I had to tell him, I loved him and couldn't lie: "He said that he is going to make orphans of your children." There was just a second of silence and then Ali jumped up. He was throwing punches and hollering, and Brown (Bundini Brown, assistant trainer) got to hollering and I thought then that he had a chance. I hoped, more than thought.'

It's Kilroy's story, man. The stomach ulcers eased; the fight was torture. Kilroy is in the corner, holding a rope most of the time, his big hair and safari jacket are unforgettable markers. He was not Ali's business manager at that point, he was Ali's friend. He is a man at the very centre of the Rumble in the Jungle. He's not a witness, he was one of the main players.

Gene then tells the final Rumble tale. Who cares if it is true? Gene Kilroy sitting and talking in the shadows of a booth at the legendary Brown Derby inside the MGM is part of the delicious story.

The fight is over. Ali is hurting, Foreman is broken. Ali and his team are on the flight to Paris for a connection to Chicago. The facilitator strikes again – Gene gets a film of the fight, and it is played on the plane. Can you even begin to imagine the hysteria on that plane when Ali leaves his seat at the start of round eight and knocks out Big George again. That is what Gene Kilroy can do.

I once dined with Gene and Tony Curtis. He seemed like a lovely man. I think my last meal with Gene was in 2021 and he had a friend with him in a wheelchair. The guy had been shot and was known as Getdown. He was a close friend of Floyd Mayweather. Getdown's nurse wore a daytime swimming costume, a thong thing. They were the rage in 2021 in Las Vegas. Gene never batted an eyelid – the steak place ran to about 150 bucks for a filet. It was an extreme night. 'Hey, the guy needs a nurse,' mused Kilroy as he dropped me back to my hotel. Gene can still do that type of crazy stuff. The last coffee we had was interrupted by Andre Agassi's father on the phone. 'Hey, Steve, say hello to Mike.' That stuff always happens with Gene. We were served coffee by Robert Wangila's widow one day. We all ended up in tears and Gene tipped her a grand in cash. We had two coffees; she had a hard life.

'I will tell you this, Ali burnt me out. There is nothing left to see,' Kilroy told me in 2014. He had, at that point, dominated the executive host business in Las Vegas for nearly three decades. He had bounced from casino to casino. His office at the MGM in 2021, when he had retired in many ways, was still packed with wall-to-wall pictures of Gene with giants. The walls in his home are the same.

Gene Kilroy: *The man in the safari suit, the facilitator still has power. He once took me to an underground house. It belonged to the Avon cosmetics family. There was an ancient man there, husband to the heiress. He showed me a necklace that Elizabeth Taylor had given him. It was in a frame. 'She wore it in Cleopatra; I funded that film,' the old man told me. Only with Gene could a meeting like that happen.*

67

VITALI KLITSCHKO
— v —
DERECK 'DEL BOY' CHISORA

WBC HEAVYWEIGHT TITLE. OLYMPIAHALLE, MUNICH, 2012

'How's your toe? How's your toe?'

Olga Korbut changed Olympic gymnastics in the same ancient hall in Munich where total boxing anarchy ruled 40 years later.

It was the story of three fights that never happened, three fights that did happen and one that would happen. It was a busy day and night and dark morning in Munich.

I'm not sure where to begin.

So, Dereck 'Del Boy' Chisora was in Munich to fight Vitali Klitschko for the WBC heavyweight title. Vitali had been untouchable since losing on cuts to Lennox Lewis in 2003. Chisora had bad history with the Klitschko clan, and it was unlikely to improve.

In December 2010, Wladimir Klitschko had pulled out of a world title fight with Chisora at just 48 hours' notice. In April of 2011, back in Mannheim, Wlad did it again. Del was furious. On the Thursday before the first planned fight, Chisora had been a phone guest on my BBC Radio London show. 'I looked in his eyes, Steve,' he told me. 'He's going to bottle it; he's going to pull out. I mean it, he's going to pull out.' The next day, Wladimir pulled out.

David Haye was in Munich on double duty: he was working with me on BoxNation, and he was also considering an offer to end his temporary retirement and agree to a fight with Vitali. The previous year in the summer, Haye had lost a world title fight to Wladimir in Hamburg. It was a poor fight and after 12 rounds, Haye blamed a broken toe. It was not a great excuse.

There was a perfect storm brewing, and it was obvious to nobody.

At the weigh-in, Del Boy slapped Vitali and it was a real slap. Vitali took it. 'That was not meant to happen,' said Don Charles, who was Chisora's friend and trainer. 'This is a sport and that was not good.'

On fight night, the temperature increased.

Vitali sent his brother, Wladimir, to Chisora's dressing room to witness the bandages being wrapped. It was a provocative but legal move. It was a great move, and it was no shock when Wladimir asked for the bandages to be removed and Chisora's fists to be wrapped again. There was a flash point, Del threatened to walk out. 'He was going, trust me,' said Steve Lillis, who was on BoxNation duty on the night. It was resolved with a lot of diplomacy.

In the ring, as they all came together in a giant huddle in the centre, Chisora took a gulp of water and spat it all in Wladimir's face. There was chaos.

The fight was terrific. Chisora was smart from the start and Vitali looked a bit rattled. It was clean and the hardest fight Vitali had been in since losing to Lennox Lewis nine years earlier. Chisora had his moments and had done his homework.

'I know the Klitschkos, I know their style,' Chisora had said the day before the fight. 'It's jab, jab, jab, jab and then a big right and then rest. I have to work and keep working.' He also had to make sure he was not hit on the chin; Vitali had knocked out eight of his last ten victims in WBC title fights.

At the end, the three scores were harsh and far too wide. There was no way that Chisora only won one or two rounds. The scores were 118–110 twice and one of 119–111. The final score means

Vitali won 11 and lost just one round. That is ludicrous, but it quickly became old news.

An hour or so later, the crowd of 13,000 had filed away in the bitter cold and the boxers were gathered for the press conference.

It started out with a lot of compliments and love. And then David Haye arrived.

From the back, perhaps ten rows back, Haye shouted out to Vitali, asking him if he wanted to fight.

'You had an offer, you didn't want to fight,' said Bernd Bonte, the business manager and promoter of both Klitschko brothers. 'Chisora showed heart, contrary to you. You showed your toe.' Ouch, that hurt.

'Let's fight,' countered Chisora.

'I've got a great idea,' said Chisora's promoter, Frank Warren. 'If Dereck fights David, the winner fights Vitali.'

Haye ignored that and went back at Bonte. The tension was mounting.

'Can security get him out of here?' asked Charles.

'How's your toe? How's your toe?' said Chisora.

'You're a loser,' replied Haye.

'Tell that to my face. I'm coming down. Tell that to my face,' said Chisora and he got up, walked through the crowd, came nose-to-nose with Haye and that was it. That was enough – it went off.

This is what happened in the next 30 or so seconds. Street fights never last as long as you think, but a lot happened. Haye used an elbow to drop and knock out Chisora. There was a rush of people – some to the trouble, others away from it. Haye broke Charles' jaw with a right cross. Haye swung a camera tripod that caught his trainer, Adam Booth, on the head. There was blood all over the place. The members of the media were falling over seats, over each other, over fallen tripods. Nobody wanted to be anywhere near Haye's arc of combat. Chisora got up, complained that Haye had 'glassed' him and Booth wanted to know who had 'glassed' him. It all happened in a flash and then it was the inquest. What happened? It seemed to be the only question people asked. Haye was drinking from a plastic bottle. He never glassed Chisora. It was confusing, Chisora acknowledges that now.

Haye and Booth escaped in a van driven by Jim Rosenthal, the presenter and nice guy. Jim, the getaway driver, parked in the shadows outside the hotel, the sirens were blaring. It seemed like the police were everywhere. I dressed Booth's head in my room and sent him back to the van. The sensible move was to get to the airport and get on the first flight and escape under the cover of darkness. They did, leaving without a problem at 7 a.m.

A few hours later, Chisora and Charles were detained at the airport by the police. They were released without charge.

At 4 a.m., there was a pounding on my hotel door. I looked through the spyhole. It's not funny, but it looked like the rejects from a Village People tribute band had rolled up for a private gig. One guy had on a full-length leather coat and sunglasses, another a motorbike helmet and a third, a baseball cap and a tight, short-sleeve t-shirt. The woman was just straight-out S&M, a dungeon babe. I opened the door; they checked my shower for Haye. I nudged the blood-stained tissues under the sink as they searched.

It was hard to kip after that. 'So, what happened?' I was asked on 5 Live at about seven in the morning. 'I'm not sure,' was my honest reply.

Vitali Klitschko: *The big lad had one more fight, won and then retired. He became the Mayor of Kiev and a different type of fighter. As for Haye and Chisora, don't ask. They fought outdoors at Upton Park in July. It was brilliant. The British Boxing Board of Control was not involved, instead the legendary Luxembourg Boxing Federation were in control. Haye won again, this time by stoppage in round five. There was a lot of love after in the ring. A few years later, Haye took over as Chisora's manager. What a business.*

68

MUHAMMAD ALI:
THE FINAL MAGIC TRICK

FREEDOM HALL, LOUISVILLE, 1997

**'It was a great shuffle, not an uneasy stumble, but fluid
and clean and beautiful.'**

There is always space and time for one last magic trick in the life
of any boxer.

In September 1997, in Louisville, Kentucky, at the Freedom
Hall on an unforgettable night, Muhammad Ali appeared like a
vision in the boxing ring. It was the same ring, the same hall, the
same city where the kid had made his professional debut in 1960.
That kid was back. Ali's debut against Tunney Hunsaker at the
Freedom Hall is such a massive part of my boxing life. I have no
idea who Sugar Ray Leonard, Mike Tyson or Joe Calzaghe fought in
their debuts – we all know Hunsaker, who was a policeman, went
the full six rounds with a teenage Ali.

In 1997, the St Stephen's Baptist choir, all 300 of them, had
belted out their songs, the crowd of 12,000 had grown louder
and louder. 'Ali! Ali! Ali!' they chanted. Evander Holyfield was at
ringside; the great Ken Norton was next to him. The boxing photographer, Mick Brennan, was bustling on one side of the ropes.
'Wait for it, just wait for it, Stevie. It's going to be unbelievable,' he
told me at one point. There was something special in the air; Ali
had been in town all week.

Mike Tyson was not there and had instead sent a crisis-management spin doctor called Sig Rogich to tell a story. Nobody was listening and Rogich's speech was booed. Tyson's plane, you see, had broken down. Rogich explained and then offered – he was working for Don King in Louisville that night – a donation to keep the Ali Cup, an amateur boxing tournament, going. The tournament had been on all week with 200 boxers from 20 countries. The tournament never ran again. Nobody cared about Tyson and Rogich and bags of cash. This night was about love. 'Muhammad knows Mike respects him. We believe there was a mechanical fault with his plane,' said Ali's wife, Lonnie. Nobody else did, sorry.

The night at the Freedom Hall was just ten weeks after Tyson had taken a lump out of Holyfield's ear and spat it out onto the canvas at the MGM. Holyfield still had crusty, black blood on his ear. The heavyweight royalty in attendance was introduced. And still they chanted: 'Ali! Ali! Ali!'

The lights dimmed, but it was not darkness. Not yet.

In the ring, in a chair in the middle, was James Earl Jones. He had a book in his hands; it was Ali's autobiography. He started to read and nobody on earth reads like James Earl Jones. There was instant silence in the Louisville night. If you know boxing and you know Ali, then you know all the stories. It's close to a religious thing with us nutcases. The stolen bike, the tears, the anger and the beauty of finding an outlet in the boxing ring. The boy, the teenager and the man. The gold medal in 1960, the first world title, the great wins, the refusal to go to war and then the return and sport's most memorable nights. That is our history. That is our Greatest. This was Louisville, this was Muhammad Ali's home. And 12,000 people were hushed by the words and the rich voice of James Earl Jones. Mick Brennan was smiling, then he winked over at me. And then it got real dark. Jones was illuminated by a single beam of light in the ring. That was it, 12,000 people vanished and just one man was left to hold that moment. He continued to read. Man, that voice.

I felt something in the dark. There was a sense of movement in the ring. A 'gentle disturbance' I wrote. There was a feeling that something truly incredible was going to happen. Jones had not moved, but there was movement and then the lights slowly came up. The ring was lit, the Freedom Hall exploded. In the ring and floating like a butterfly was Muhammad Ali. And he was dancing. He was moving and flicking out his jab, his body suddenly free. No shackles. The year before at the opening ceremony for the Atlanta Olympics he had stumbled, and his hands had shaken with effort. At the Freedom Hall he was free to move. New medication for his Parkinson's had helped.

Ali was back, the Greatest had visited for one last dance.

Jones read, the crowd roared, howling and chanting and hugging each other. Brennan had a tear in his eye. He was just standing and watching, not shooting the man he adored. Brennan had done that all over the world – it was time to watch. It was a moment to enjoy. Ali was moving and smiling and then it happened. It was 15 feet in front of me, it was in his ring.

Muhammad Ali performed his finest and last public Ali shuffle. The shuffle that a million kids had done in front of mirrors and in their bedrooms. He did it and it was a thing of beauty. I wrote: 'It was a great shuffle, not an uneasy stumble, but fluid and clean and beautiful.' And it was. 'Ali! Ali! Ali!' they howled. That was a tear on Brennan's cheek.

A kid called Christopher Jordan, just 13 and kitted out in blue with headguard and gloves, got in the ring. Ali danced and flicked out jabs two feet above Jordan's head. Jordan hustled and bustled, trying to get close to the old man. Then Ali picked him up and placed him gently on the canvas. The crowd loved it. Ali then raised his hands high above his head and hovered over Jordan. That was the pose, the famous pose from the night he beat Sonny Liston for the second time. That picture, taken by Neil Leifer, is one of our holy documents. Ali gave us a version of that immortal portrait in that Freedom Hall ring.

'Ali! Ali! Ali!' It had to be heard to be believed.

It was the end to a good week for Ali. It felt like a late, late homecoming for the gold medal he had won 37 years earlier at the Olympics in Rome. He visited his old high school, attended civic events and went to see old neighbours.

Everywhere he went, Norton his great rival and Ernie Terrell stood as his permanent guards. Terrell is the man from the famous 'what's my name?' fight. Terrell had known Ali when he was Cassius Clay and made the mistake of calling him Clay before their fight in 1967. I had a long, long buffet lunch with Terrell at the MGM one day in 1995 and he told me the whole story. 'It was not planned, it was a slip,' Big Ernie insisted. 'Ali went on and on. I just kept doing it. It meant nothing, it was not an insult. I always respected him.' Ali was savage in their fight. In Louisville, the two old bruisers never left their friend's side.

Brennan, in his book, *They Must Fall: Muhammad Ali And The Men He Fought*, has glorious pictures of Ali and Norton that week and they are beautiful. Ali had turned back all the clocks in Louisville. Sure, he was 55, and we had seen his shuffling for too many years, but he was back for one night only.

Muhammad Ali: *There were very few great days or nights after Louisville. It is a cherished memory.*

69

THE LIVERPOOL FESTIVAL OF BOXING

1998

It changed the way the British were viewed by all the traditional amateur boxing powerhouses.

The handwritten sign in the bar was simple and to the point: 'Moet $50'.

The bar was not in New York, it was in the grand old Adelphi, one of the most notorious hotels in Liverpool. The Russians, you see, were back in the city for the Festival of Boxing. It was 1998, the fifth year, and the Russian women sold their furs and the men had after-hours sessions in jewelry stores to buy Rolex watches. They loved dollars, those boys. They loved life, it seemed.

I had seen Cuban coaches at the world championships in Budapest, Houston and Belfast sell cigars direct from their team adidas bags. A box of the best Cuban cigars for $100 – had to be American dollars. A box of Cohiba Esplendidos for peanuts; a box of 25 cigars would have set you back about £400 back then. In Liverpool, the officials with boxing teams from any of the old Soviet Republics sold caviar. They had the same adidas bags.

Olympic champions Wladimir Klitschko, Alexander Povetkin, Audley Harrison and Somluck Kamsing won gold at the Festival before winning gold medals at the Olympics. David Haye and Carl Froch and dozens of other top professionals also fought at the Festival. It ran from 1994 until 2001 and it changed the way the

British were viewed by all the traditional amateur boxing power-houses. It was run by Paul King, a proper boxing man.

There was an Early Day motion in Parliament to congratulate King and Liverpool City Council for their international efforts. There was no mention of the 16-year-old junior champion from Rotunda who sold a kilo of felt-pen-coated blue Smint to a Russian and told him they were Viagra. Odd that. In all fairness, they were a fair copy of the original.

In 2005, King delivered a 50-page document to amateur boxing's rulers and secured the right to stage the European championships in the city in 2008. His bid won, beating three other cities. At the European Championships in Liverpool that year, Oleksandr Usyk and Vasyl Lomachenko won titles. Luke Campbell, from Hull, also won; it was the first time an English boxer had won the European title since 1961. King's gamble had worked, and he was a player. In 2011, he went for the big seat in amateur boxing, the presidency of AIBA, but the old Cold War warriors handled him with ease, and he ended up on a trumped-up charge and banned from boxing for two years. Kingy got it overturned, but the fur coat and Rolex brigade were gone for good in his life.

They killed people, those old bastards. One senior Russian official was famously tortured and shot in his bath in Moscow after a scandal at the World Junior championships in Havana in 1996. I was banned by the *Daily Telegraph* sports desk from going out to cover the death. Ricky Hatton, then a kid from Manchester, was caught up in the killing. 'Too dangerous,' the editor told me. It turned out judges at the event in Havana had been handed envelopes stuffed with cash; Ricky lost in a suspicious fight. A British judge was given an envelope but handed it back and reported it. It set in motion the deadly repercussions.

At the Festival, King knew what was needed. He knew the language of the amateur boxing bosses and he gave them whatever they desired. He was a class act.

Paul King: *I was there in 1997 when five Ugandan boxers arrived. There was no record of them applying and they had no money. Kingy put them all up and fed them for a week. I like to think there is a small shrine to him at a gym in Kampala. Word spread and the Kenyans arrived the following year – same circumstance, same result.*

70

WLADIMIR KLITSCHKO
— v —
TYSON FURY

WBA, WBO, IBF WORLD HEAVYWEIGHT TITLE: DUSSELDORF, 2015

Fury was brilliant, fast, sharp and clever.

Big Wladimir Klitschko had been a giant in the boxing business for a long, long time.

Wlad had fought 28 world heavyweight title fights, he was making the 19th defence of his second reign, he had knocked out 53 of his 64 victims. He had 50,000 tickets sold for the Esprit Arena in Dusseldorf. He was a one-man boom for any German city. He got what he wanted on both sides of the ropes.

And then the Fury Clan came to town.

'I have heard all of this before,' Klitschko explained. 'Fury is another big-mouthed talker. I will teach him.'

Nobody was brave enough to talk about just how old and weary Klitschko might be. It was mentioned, but it was not the main thing about the fight. Once the fight was over, his age and old body were the main part of the midnight inquest. He was 39, he had been carrying injuries for decades, but he had also been knocking out or handling his challengers. The fight was pushed back from October because of a niggle.

Fury was slowly getting to him. There was no fear in Fury during the week in Dusseldorf. He was surrounded by the big men in his family: his father, his uncle, his brothers and cousins. All big lumps. It looked like Wlad was having to think a bit more; he knew Fury from his training camp a few years earlier. It was clear that Fury made Wlad feel uneasy and Klitschko didn't like that feeling.

'What you have to do with him,' Fury said. 'You have to make him uncomfortable at all times – in the ring and out of it. That is the plan, and I can tell it's working.' Fury was right and then it was the weigh-in and Wlad hit back.

Fights can be won, and they can certainly be lost in the days and hours before the first bell. Fighters look for a weakness and that is because it is a cruel business. At the weigh-in, it was Wlad's show. It was private, there were no fans and that meant hundreds of travelling British supporters were denied the chance to shout and scream. Fury loved the fans.

Fury found himself on the stage, alone at one point. Wlad arrived and exchanged a fist-pump with Michael Buffer, the legendary announcer: they were old, old friends. It was the Klitschko show, a way to let Fury know that this was not his circus any longer. The insults and predictions and claims were over – it was time to fight. Wlad, standing next to his brother, Vitali, suddenly looked in control again.

Fury left the stage and claimed he had seen fear in Klitschko's eyes. Maybe, I'm not convinced. However, I was happy with what I saw in Fury's eyes, and I wrote that 'the fun sparkle that has been there since this fight was announced has certainly dimmed. That is not a bad thing.' The fight had turned serious. The Klitschko brothers have often been accused of fear, but the reality is that they are calculated, consummate professionals and like to be in total control of the whole situation. Some might say they were bullies.

An oddly reflective Gypsy John remained near the weigh-in stage. In 2015, he was a different beast, a calmer human back then. I went over to speak to him. 'You see all this,' he said to me. 'I feel like I've lived a hundred lives – this is just boxing. I want them both to leave the ring healthy. I still think about Tyson as a six-year-old.' That Gypsy John is preferable to the raging, too-often shirtless loose cannon from 2023. I honestly believe that Gypsy John could have become a national treasure had he not wanted to strip and fight any man with a bit of celebrity and a pulse.

I was in the same hotel as the fighter and all of his people. The Friday night was quieter. It was a big deal; it was a massive fight.

The next day, a party of Fury people went over to the football stadium – there was a roof – to check on the dressing rooms and take a look at the other facilities. A man called Asif Vali, who had worked closely with Amir Khan, went to the ring with Peter Fury, the boxer's uncle and trainer, and Gypsy John. Mick Hennessy, the promoter, who had taken Fury on the mad journey from obscurity to the world heavyweight title, was also there. They had a problem.

They felt the canvas and it was soft and deep. It would take a fighter's legs, it would drain a mobile fighter and Fury was always going to be mobile. The quartet ripped the canvas back, pulled away layers and found that there was a 2-inch-thick layer of foam padding. It was additional padding. They ripped lumps of it away as proof. Then, there was a lively debate at ringside with some of Klitschko's people. The fight would be off if that foam remained, was the simple message. 'I told them that it had to go, or we were going,' said Vali.

The foam party returned to the hotel and handed out the fat pieces of padding. It was hefty. The phones were ringing; Fury won, the padding came out. That was a rare, rare victory against the Klitschko brothers. A few hours later, Vali would strike again at the very heart of the Klitschko fighting empire.

The Germans know how to do a big fight.

Rod Stewart was booked to sing his new song. It never worked, the murmur at that point from 50,000 fans – perhaps an hour before the fight – was too great and the sound was bad. Rod was fuming and left the ring in a cream puff.

There was a rumour about Wlad's bandages. It turns out that Vali had been sent as the witness to watch Klitschko have his bandages and the legal amount of tape applied. It's one of our rituals. The hands were done and only then did Vali complain and ask for the whole process to be repeated. Wlad was screaming. 'No fighter likes that,' Lennox Lewis told me at ringside. It was a trick that Wlad had played when his brother, Vitali, had fought Dereck Chisora in 2012. It was, to my mind, two-nil to Fury, and the first round was still 30 minutes away.

Buffer gave it full welly when he introduced them. The Germans loved him. It had that special fight feeling. A big crowd, the heavyweight title, a boxing icon and a man who had promised so much.

In the first round, Klitschko went for the knockout. He dug his huge white boots deep into the canvas to get the grip to let the big right cross go. He was not interested in anything but a quick win. Fury had got to him. Klitschko had developed a great deaf ear, but Fury was inside Wlad's head. He puzzled the champion, and I wrote: 'Trust me, that is an odd indicator.' At the start of the fight, I kept hearing Fury telling me that Klitschko hates being uncomfortable, he hates the unpredictable. 'I will make him uncomfortable,' he told me. And he was – Big Wladimir Klitschko, a man devoted to his craft, was lost at sea in that bright ring.

Wlad was being beaten, not bashed up, not hurt and reeling, but beaten. Fury was brilliant, fast, sharp and clever. He turned Wlad, he showed Wlad shots and landed something different and he never once lost his concentration. Klitschko would need stitches to close a cut on his left cheek and a cut by his right eye, but they were superficial blood wounds – the damage was inside his head. Wladimir Klitschko was getting the type of beating that nobody could have imagined. He was getting a boxing lesson. For Klitschko it was hard being that good, that big and that old. It was still not a massacre; it was close enough. I was not convinced at the end that Fury would get what he deserved. But he did and what scenes of joy.

Buffer took the same microphone that he had used for the introductions 50 minutes earlier and this time, his voice was not so strong and lacked any conviction. Fury had won a unanimous decision and three of the four recognised belts. The scores were 115–112 twice and 116–111 for Fury. Klitschko was beaten and furious.

It was obvious that critics would put victory down to an old man fading, but that neglects the beauty of Fury's bold dancing plan. I had listened to a lot of good heavyweights tell me for a decade how easy it was to beat the robotic, slow and predictable Klitschko. It's easier said than done. I remember something that Manny Steward had said, and it was ignored again and again and again. 'Wladimir is faster than they all think – that is their mistake.' I also knew how highly regarded Klitschko was by the Fury Clan – they were fighting men, not foolish men. Sure, Wlad was not at his peak, but equally he was not an old, faded, injured and wounded soldier. Fury was sensational, punch perfect, it is that simple.

By ten the next morning, the dark days had been launched. It really was this quick – I was at breakfast with Hennessy on the Sunday morning. The eggs were ordered when it all started to go wrong. 'We have the choices now,' Hennessy told me. 'There will be no slip ups.' The problem was the IBF and their mandatory challenger, Vyacheslav Glazkov. The IBF wanted an immediate fight between Glazkov and Fury. The man had not been world champion for 12 hours. Glazkov's people wanted the fight signed-off that morning. It made no sense. Klitschko could also ask for a rematch and that would make sense on every level. It was scrambled at breakfast and then Fury limped down in a pair of flipflops. He had giant blisters on both feet. Fight? He could barely walk.

And then it got ugly, and a bit crazy. Fury and Klitschko agreed to do it all again. The IBF matched Glazkov against Charles Martin for the vacant IBF heavyweight title. I believe Fury lost that belt at breakfast; I really do. Martin ruined Glazkov in three rounds in a fight that took place less than 50 days after Fury beat Klitschko. Glazkov never fought again. Martin was then lured to London and knocked out by Anthony Joshua for the title that Fury had won less than four months earlier and never lost in the ring. The heavyweight division was moving fast. Fury was matched with Klitschko twice in Britain in 2016 and twice had to withdraw. His body was not great, his mental health was in bits. Fury vanished from boxing until the summer of 2018. He gained about six stones and lost his way. He admitted that from his darkest hole, suicide was an option. Hand on heart, I thought we had lost him for good.

Wladimir Klitschko: *Big Wlad lost a thriller to Anthony Joshua outdoors at Wembley Stadium in 2017 and then walked away from boxing. He has been busy with the war in his Ukrainian homeland since then. I have one lasting memory of Wladimir, and it is from the post-fight conference back in Dusseldorf. He is sitting with his newly stitched face and there is a look of pure hate in his eyes. Fury had just walked in. That was a nasty look.*

71

GRENFELL: A BOXING TOWER

LONDON, 2017

**'Men like Mick Delaney can train fighters on wasteland
– they don't need fancy bags and new rings.'**

'Tell my boys that I love them,' said Tony Disson. He was on the
22nd floor at Grenfell Tower and he died in the fire.

A few hours before the desperate and final phone call from
Disson, a man called Mick Delaney had locked the doors at the
Dale Youth amateur boxing club. The club had a new home inside
Grenfell Tower, on a different floor from the ground floor gym they
had occupied for about 17 years. It was all so new: the pictures and
trophies were still on the floor. Delaney locked the door at about
10 p.m. The fire started soon after. Dale Youth was about to lose its
home.

All three Disson boys had boxed for Dale Youth: Harry, Alfie
and Charlie. They had lived high above the gym when the door to
Dale Youth was round the side of the Tower on the ground floor.
They had trained and sparred in that space. Club boys, locals,
normal young boxers. Not every kid who walks through the doors
of an amateur boxing club has to be a world champion: it might be
their dream, but it is rare.

At Dale Youth, Delaney had two and he had them at the same
time. James 'Chunky' DeGale and George Groves.

'In 2002 they were kids in the same gym, in the 2007 Amateur
Boxing Association Championships they fought, in 2008 one won

a gold medal at the Olympics and on Saturday James DeGale and George Groves will fight in front of 18,000 people at the O2 Arena in Docklands.' That is what I wrote in the week of their fight in May 2011. Delaney's old boys were still babies in the professional game. It was an odd event – DeGale had fought just ten times, Groves just 12. On the night, Groves won a narrow majority decision to take the British super-middleweight title. The rivalry has never faded. In 2015, DeGale won a world title and in 2017 Groves won his world title.

When they were children under Delaney's command at Dale Youth, they had travelled together all over London for fights. 'I made sure that everybody supported everybody,' Delaney said. 'It was no different for them. James had to support George and George had to support James. All boys in here have to get on.' At 3 a.m., after long journeys back from distant places, the trainer would shake the pair awake in the middle of the night. They would then get bundled into waiting cars, all in the Grenfell Tower car park. The fights, the gym, the tower – it was their boxing life.

They became men inside the gym at Grenfell but never friends.

'We were never close, to tell the truth,' said DeGale, once again back at the gym to do some publicity for their fight at the O2. 'We existed, we were both members of Dale Youth – I never really liked him and he never really liked me. What's the point of lying?'

DeGale retained his chunky nickname but lost the pounds. The rivalry was intense. They started to train at different times; it had to happen. It's interesting that they never left the club. DeGale would go down a bit earlier and work with Steve Newland, who trained the junior boxers.

'It was obvious that we would have to fight,' said Groves, on the same day at the publicity shoot for the O2 fight. 'We had been kept apart and only bumped into each other on the odd night. We never really spoke.'

In 2007, they met at Brent Town Hall in the North West London divisional championships of the ABAs. Groves won a tight, majority decision. It was the last fight of the night; the tickets were probably a tenner and a devoted flock had stayed for the Championship of Dale Youth. Groves was 18, DeGale 20 and they fought over four two-minute rounds. They touched gloves at the end of each round and when it was finished, they embraced twice. DeGale thought he had done enough to win and refused the hand that Groves extended when the verdict was announced.

In theory, that was their last exchange before their professional fight four years later. There was one tiny moment, an incident that both deny, but an incident I know happened. At Brent Town Hall on the stage where the boxers changed, DeGale walked over to Groves, who was just in his underpants, and they embraced one more time. 'Now, go on and win it,' he said. Groves did go on and win the national title.

'You have to understand that in an amateur boxing club no boy is bigger than the club – George and James both knew that,' said Newland.

A year later, DeGale got the nod for the GB spot at the Olympics in Beijing, and he won gold. Groves had dreamed of that slot. 'All I wanted was a box-off,' he said. There was an unofficial box off where the men met the same people and DeGale came out in front. His Olympic selection was not a travesty, please, never believe that.

They both turned professional, and Delaney kept making fighters at Dale Youth.

Delaney and the boxers had only been back in Grenfell for about six months when the fire happened. They had been moved out to allow the building to get a new look and that included the cladding. It was tarted up at a price. The club had been temporarily placed in a converted car park. It was damp and exposed and local dossers used it to stay warm. Delaney still had every inch of the place packed with boxers of all ages, size and sex.

'Men like Mick Delaney can train fighters on wasteland – they don't need fancy bags and new rings,' Groves told me in 2016.

In 2018, I went with Groves to do an emotional podcast from behind Grenfell. He talked of walking through the doors at the old gym, talked of the steamed-up windows, the smell, the tiny ring, the long car journeys to fights and of the big broom he bought Delaney. 'Every night, Mick stays at the end and sweeps up. So, I got him a big broom,' Groves said. We recorded the podcast, with the blessing of the community. Standing at the back, in the burnt shadow of Grenfell, the random journey of the fire was clear. Some windows were gone and all that remained was a gaping black hole, the fire having consumed every single item in the room. In the next window, eight feet across, mugs were still hanging from a rack and a kitchen towel stood untouched on the windowsill. Groves took a moment to look back at the place where he had spent many years, a place that made him the fighter he was. Anybody trying to take a picture was moved on.

Delaney was allowed back in after the fire, and he collected the honours boards. That was all that was salvageable from the wet. The club moved back into the car park on Ladbroke Grove again. The dossers had come back, Gary McGuinness, one of the trainers, had to throw them out.

Dale Youth finally left the damp and dirty converted car park and moved into a purpose-built gym in 2018. It was part of a BBC SOS show: celebrities, royals, the mayor and footballers were all involved. It is under the Westway, close enough to still see and get a sense of Grenfell.

Dale Youth: *Every Sunday, Groves goes down to the gym and works with the juniors. Delaney is still there, still has a big broom and he still sweeps up every night. There is one image that haunts me. In the* *publicity photographs for the DeGale and Groves fight, the boxers pose outside Grenfell. The tower is in the background and there is no cladding. It was added to make the place look less like the council block it was.*

72

KATIE TAYLOR
— V —
AMANDA SERRANO

FOUR LIGHTWEIGHT WORLD TITLES / MILLION-DOLLAR WOMEN:

MADISON SQAURE GARDEN, 2022

'Where stood a wall, now stands a way.'

Jackie Tonawanda was known as the Female Ali, and she was the first woman to ever enter a ring and fight at Madison Square Garden.

It was 1975 and Tonawanda knocked out Larry Rodania with a phantom left hook in round two. Rodania was topless and he was a big lump, Tonawanda wore a white t-shirt. It was a wonderful circus event during something called the All-Martial Arts Tournament. Larry was definitely a man, by the way.

In 2022, Katie Taylor and Amanda Serrano made history in the sacred venue when they each cleared $1 million and 19,187 devoted fans paid to witness their fight. This fight was not a circus – they belong in two very different worlds, baby.

The Taylor and Serrano fight was the first time two women had headlined the Garden, the first sell-out for women and the first time two women had been paid $1 million anywhere in the world. It was history and it had its own history.

It had been talked about in early 2019, shelved, announced for May in 2020 in Manchester, then Covid came and then it was going in Eddie Hearn's childhood garden in Essex in the summer of 2020. It would have been behind locked doors, a Covid fight watched by under 90 people and the four or five wandering llamas in that sprawling green space. That fight fell through, and Taylor v Serrano looked lost. It would have been a boxing tragedy had the fight gone ahead in the garden. The deals and counter deals were long and complicated. At one point, Serrano took to social media to tell all the men running her boxing life and making plans for her fights that she was 'not a toy'. She wanted her worth.

'You just keep making the offers and eventually you get to a number they cannot turn down,' Hearn told me in New York in April 2022. The fight was days away. The city was in fever, the Empire State Building was lit in the colours of the Irish and the Puerto Rican flags.

In 2018, Taylor had beaten Amanda's sister, Cindy, and beaten her with ease. It had been a shut-out, 100–90 for Taylor. At the end of the fight, Cindy's husband and trainer, Jordan Maldonado, had ignored his wife in the ring to confront and tell Taylor and her trainer, Ross Enamit: 'You never beat the best sister.' That was cold and true.

On the night of the fight at the Garden, Serrano had lost just once in 44 fights, she was 32 and she had won world titles at seven different weights. She was extraordinary and felt like a link with New York's ancient and sketchy female boxing roots. She was not that far removed from the Female Ali. She had been paid as little as $2,000 for world title fights and cleared as little as $200 for other fights. 'I have been everywhere and done everything to get here,' she said. She had fought on the MMA circuit and had an offer from the Diva brand in the wrestling world. And then Katie came along.

'When Katie turned pro, I was so excited. I knew she would change things for us,' Serrano said.

When Taylor did turn professional in 2016, Serrano had fought 31 times and had won world titles at four different weights. She really did whatever she could and that included jumping up and down in weights. In September 2018, Serrano weighed 138 lbs in a WBO light-welterweight title fight and in her next fight, just four months later, she weighed just 114 lbs when she won the WBO's super-flyweight title. That is a ridiculous achievement. Men have made similar transitions, but they have done it over years and not weeks.

Serrano, by the time she met Taylor, had Jake Paul with her. He had transformed her life and had promised a year earlier to get her a seven-figure purse. Hearn praised Paul's role in the fight. It felt big that week in New York, it felt special and then on the night, in a classic Garden tradition, all the best fighters came out. I remember Jake LaMotta being ringside to watch Bernard Hopkins in his middleweight title fight with Felix Trinidad. The Garden loves its history, it loves its warriors.

At ringside in a theatre of hugs, Laila Ali, Ann Wolfe, Christy Martin, and Claressa Shields took their bows. Somebody even told me that 'Kojak', as Marian Trimiar was known, was there. Trimiar had been, alongside the Female Ali, one of the first three women that were given licences to box by the New York State Athletic Commission in 1978. She had shaved her head when she was a fighter, and she was striking.

Kojak had fought at a time of some confusion. The simple truth is that the female business then was a shambles. It was not helped by the creepy tiny girls boxing league in Texas. Imagine a scary beauty pageant for under-tens, but with the little girls wearing gloves and swinging away at each other in the ring. It was called the Missy Junior Gloves. Pictures of the tiny girls with massive gloves appeared in a magazine called *Amazons in Action*. The main features in the edition that was sent to me at the *Daily Telegraph* were about mud wrestling and topless boxing. If you liked women fighting, then *Amazons* was your reading. The list of cheap videos on offer was truly startling. There was a lot going through my head as I sat down in a heaving Garden and took a breath or two.

And then it was finally fight time.

Serrano came in with Paul on her shoulder, happy, smiling and under a shattering noise. It seemed that everybody was standing and howling. I wondered, live on 5 Live, how Taylor's entry could be louder. Idiot, how did I doubt it?

As some point in the hour before the fight, Taylor put down her bible in the calm of her room and put on her gloves. Brian Peters, the enigmatic and mysterious Irishman and manager was there, Enamit was there, Hearn popped in close to the time she was due to walk. They ran a tight and closed shop. Nobody from the boxing world had ever been to Taylor's house in Connecticut. She was private, her boxing was her communication. She walked out the door and through the corridors where the pictures of the greatest sports and performing artists in history were hanging. They were the men and women who ruled the Garden on the greatest nights: Kiss, Muhammad Ali, Elvis, Billie Jean-King, Barbra Streisand. There was a look of tranquility on Katie Taylor's face as she paused near the start of the last tunnel before the Garden. This was it, this was her history.

She had a face of calm, but there was a towering intensity in her stare. Behind, at a safe distance was Enamit, Peters holding all the belts and Hearn in a dickie bow. A bad boy band reunion, if you like. It was a frightening walk to witness. It was pure theatre. On the giant screens, a short history of Taylor's journey was playing. The noise made broadcasting close to impossible and then she appeared, and it *was* impossible.

'Awake My Soul', her spiritual song for the night, started. She mouthed a word or two and moved an inch or two. She took a pause, closed her eyes and you could see her breathing it in. Calm, serene, dangerous and ready. The Queen of boxing was the main event in the sport's fabulous spiritual home. She was in no rush, she wanted to enjoy every second of that walk and of that night. That's entertainment to me. I stood and I could see her as she edged slowly towards her destiny. 'Where stood a wall, now stands a way.' That is one of the lines in the song and I like to think that Taylor mouthed those words. She was on her way very slowly. I knew what she was doing. She had talked about enjoying the moment. Told me she would. She was. It was overwhelming.

She looked off into the vast sloping walls of the ancient Garden. She saw the mix of flags, she saw the green glow sticks in every row, people threw Irish flags at her, she had a small smile at times. She must have also seen the young girls in that crowd. She did that Katie Taylor, she put those girls in those seats. Her eyes a mix of awe and concentration, she nodded slightly a few times, mouthed the words of the song. She heard the roars and sucked in every single little bit of it. Not a word from me was broadcast, just the noise of history being made in the Garden.

She entered the ring. The fight started and it was better than anybody ever expected. Round five will live forever in the Garden archives as one of the greatest rounds to ever take place under that roof.

Serrano held the four belts at featherweight and Taylor's four lightweight belts were the official prize. That was the glittering part of the fight. It was close from the first bell, hard from the start.

Taylor could not intimidate Serrano. The history between them was real. In round five, the fight changed. I wrote: 'It looked over for Taylor; trapped in Serrano's corner, cut over the right eye, her nose bleeding and the punches just kept coming.' Taylor's hair had worked loose and there was a manic look in her eyes, her soaking hair flicking all over her face. Not a soul in the Garden was sitting. Was it over for Taylor, had the years and the fight taken a final toll? She was 35 and it looked like she was on the very dark edge of defeat.

Taylor's left arm was tangled in the ropes for three long, long seconds; Serrano just kept hitting away. Her career was stuck in that moment, stuck as Serrano let her fists go. Serrano had stopped or knocked out 12 of her last 18 opponents. It was a blur, and it was, I swear, also in slow motion.

It changed again. What was I watching?

'And then, with her flock standing and throwing punches with her, Taylor fought her way to the centre of the ring, and they stood toe-to-toe. It looked like a choreographed dance of savagery. It was breathless craft.' If you know the *Rocky* music, if you know those moments in those absurd fights when the music lifts and Rocky fights back after taking 311 left hooks to the eye socket, then you will know the music in my head as Taylor pushed Serrano back. It was more than a moment of Rocky insanity. It was from a dream.

The rounds continued. At the very end, as they matched each other punch for punch, the bell sounded, and it was over. The noise never dropped; they were both hugged by their people. They were both exhausted.

The scores came: For Katie 96–93 and a booming noise. For Amanda 96–94 and an even louder roar. The pause and then the final score of 97–93 and it was for Katie Taylor. It was that close.

I left my table and climbed the steps to the ring and took up a position on the apron against the ropes. The Garden was still full, the flags still being waved, the chants still loud. I was in the ring at the Garden about to interview Katie Taylor. A record 19,187 had been inside to watch, but for a few minutes I would be the closest person to her on earth.

'Let's do it again at Croke Park,' she told me. She never had to tell me how exhausted she was. It was obvious in every pained word she spoke and gentle step she took. She was helped down the steps and was lost in a moving crowd. The broadcast finished and people started to leave.

I remembered something that Arthur Mercante had said after refereeing the Fight of the Century at the Garden in 1971 between Muhammad Ali and Joe Frazier. He said he had 'the best seat in the house.' I had this in mind when I went to find the referee, Michael Griffin. I found him in a nondescript room, in his kecks and on his own. He seemed lost in thought as he dressed. 'What was it like?' he said. 'Well, it was just a great fight. A privilege to be involved with.' I felt the same way.

We went to the Tick Tock diner, out the back and across the street from the venue, to record the post-fight pod. We were all stunned. I remember being up late that night, very late, perhaps close to dawn. We had coffee at 1 a.m., beers before 3 a.m. and got it done. I wrote: 'On Saturday night at the Garden, Katie Taylor and Amanda Serrano owned the ring, the boxing business and the chaotic surrounds. It was Saturday night boxing fever in New York City and nobody will ever forget it.'

Katie Taylor: *In 2023, Katie Taylor in an emotional homecoming in Ireland, lost a tight decision to Chantelle Cameron in Dublin. One judge returned a draw. It was her first loss. There was shock and six months later, there was sweet revenge. The journey was not quite over – it never is.*

73

BOXNATION:
GAMECHANGER

**It was a revolving door of talent and often we would have
ten guests in one hour.**

A sofa for kings and queens, a thousand guests, thousands of fights,
snowballs at 3 a.m. and hundreds of hours of boxing each week.

Welcome to the world of BoxNation. It changed the boxing
landscape forever.

It all started on a Friday night at York Hall in London's boxing
heartland. Where else could the first bell be? The last bell is not
so clear. Between first and last, the finest fighters of a generation
fought on a BoxNation live show.

We once went from midnight to dawn on 13 consecutive Saturdays. I think that there were live British fights on five of the same
Saturday nights before the nocturnal chaos. And it was chaos.

On one winter broadcast, we had a snowball the size of a
football gently melting on the table, and on another night, Tim
Witherspoon had to bring in his little girl. She was about two and
she slept from 2 a.m. through to 7 a.m., her tiny feet in vision
every time the camera was on Tim. On other nights, the person in
charge of the camera fell asleep and at 6 a.m., when the broadcast
from Las Vegas had finished, the studio in London would be back

in vision and there might be three inches of my head. The gentle snoring could be heard.

The schedule was relentless and BoxNation, because there were no time constraints, could broadcast for as long or short as they liked. It is normal now, back then it was unique. The first show had six live fights, but we regularly broadcast ten or more. Our record was just under 25 finals from the Haringey Box Cup in 2012. We also had Floyd Mayweather in some massive fights, and they were all included in your monthly tenner.

Roy Jones Jr came on the sofa a few days after meeting with Vladimir Putin in Russia. He had his new Russian passport and a jacket that Putin had given him. I think it was a Russian Olympic jacket. Somebody nicked the jacket, stole it from a tiny room we liked to call the Green Room. He was not impressed.

The sofa and chair combinations that we used for the Boxing Hour had some of the best bums in boxing. We had live, dozens and dozens of champions. It was a revolving door of talent and often we would have ten guests in one hour. We once did a live show in Amir Khan's gym in Bolton for one hour and we had 13 live guests: Amir Khan, Virgil Hunter, Audley Harrison, Deontay Wilder, Arnie Farnell, Paul Butler, Jack Catterall, Jon Kays, Terry Flanagan, Nate Campbell, Shah Khan, Haroon Khan and I finished walking off set arm-in-arm with fight fixer, Asif Vali.

The producer, Jim Bentley, went with me for a coffee an hour before the show and he scribbled the running order on a napkin and then got it photocopied. That is a list: five world champions and three Olympic medal winners. And another thing about that ridiculous night: Steve Lillis, who did a couple of interviews, took a bus back to Manchester. We had few taxis or any of the luxuries associated with a televised event.

Two days after losing in the World Amateur Championship finals in Azerbaijan in 2011, Anthony Johsua was back on the sofa with his medal. He shared the sofa with James DeGale and Frankie

Gavin on that night; DeGale and Joshua both won Olympic gold medals and Gavin remains the only English male amateur boxer to ever win a world amateur title. That was a great show. The following year, when Joshua won gold at the London Olympics, I had a wanted poster for Joshua made and we showed it each week with the words: 'Have you seen this man?' Hey, he never came back, but a lot of other heavyweight world champions did sit on the sofa.

Lennox Lewis had a turn, David Haye had a cameo, Tyson Fury was in a dozen times before he beat Wladimir Klitschko and in June 2013, Riddick 'Big Daddy' Bowe limped in. On the night Bowe appeared, Barry Jones was bouncing off the walls – Barry loved him.

Bowe was 45, weighed about 23 stone and had just had the shit kicked out of him at a venue on a beach in Thailand by an unknown Ukrainian Muay Thai fighter called Levgen Golovin. He was meant to have been paid $150,000 for his misadventure in the Muay Thai business. I doubt that; we found something like £300 to make the great man happy. Bowe delivered his own sense of anarchy and when we went live, I think him and Barry were shaping up for pictures and talking bollocks. It was a delight having him on.

I think that either live in the studio or on the phone, I spoke to over 30 world heavyweight champions. We had men like Mike Weaver on for fun. Sugar Ray Leonard did most of an hour, a heavyweight called James 'Quick' Tillis less than a minute. Tillis, a cowboy, was suffering from his ring exploits. We also did whole shows with fake beards, Viking helmets and fabulous, glowing ten-inch toy cigars. Whole shows, interviews with greats and Barry Jones and I would be wearing a three-quid Viking helmet. It's fine for Mikkel Kessler, harder for Adrien Broner.

We once did a phone-in live and the only person free to take the calls, take the notes and give me the details was a runner from Spain on her first night. She came to make hot chocolate at 3 a.m. and order taxis at 6 a.m., but instead she spoke to a man from his hospital bed who was close to death and wanted to come on and talk about Jim Watt. He was in tears after we had spoken. She was traumatised at dawn. Hundreds called.

We did a live night of fights from Newport once using kit from the Fifties – the microphone weighed five kilos and was connected by wire as thick as a seabed gas pipe; our main guest got too drunk to broadcast and we had to take him off air. In Glasgow one night, it was me on my own for four hours. The same happened with Sergey Kovalev against Nathan Cleverly in Cardiff. The guest list just fell apart: Ricky Hatton went home, somebody failed to show. It was mayhem. But what a fight that was.

There was a golden period between 2012 and 2018 when every single major American fight was live for no extra cost on Box-Nation; the domestic front belonged to Eddie Hearn, Sky and his Olympians, but nobody could touch our American nights.

And then the lights dimmed ever so slowly. It was a brutal death in many ways. I found out one day that the show was being cut and it was gone two days later. I was gone sooner. Hard days for me, Barry Jones, Steve Lillis. Jim Bentley, the producer, had already jumped ship to BT. It limped on until late 2022, showing repeats of the many nights. It was an odd reminder of the great days.

At the end, we had a celebratory fish and chips by the Thames. No management, just some of the 20 people who lost a substantial part of their income with the passing of BoxNation. Cameramen and women, producers, directors, engineers and others from behind the scenes and in the trucks at fights. I was surprised people rejoiced at its demise; it's no fun losing your income. Cruel bastards.

BoxNation: *It was about the tenth thing that had gone down with me losing my income. I sank sofas, my son. The ancient and brilliant Sporting Life had no chance as soon as they planned a relaunch with me, Setanta Sports was just too good to be true and a couple* *of other newspapers also went. A few online outlets folded. I take it personally, trust me. Most vanished owing me a few quid and they still do. In the media business it is odd how many people actually enjoy other people suffering. I think it's shit.*

When Setanta folded, I had to sue a major columnist and media darling at one national newspaper. She was out of order – she hated me; I won, I got a massive settlement and a High Court apology. I have never met the woman! My great pal, from the Black Country, Dean Powell, the matchmaker, trainer and manager, called me when he read the column and said: 'Fuck me, who pissed on her chips?' I like that.

Dean, sadly, carried too many demons and walked in front of a train near New Cross in 2013. Two weeks earlier, at a fish restaurant in Cardiff, he had asked me if I could just walk away. I was not sure. 'You?' I asked in reply. 'Absolutely.' It was just an innocent word at 1 a.m. in August. Dean was a BoxNation regular. The woman still writes a column, and it is probably best to not say what I think of her. I have still never met her. I'm still not sure if I could walk away from the business of boxing.

74

DREW DOCHERTY
— v —
JIMMY MURRAY

BRITISH BANTAMWEIGHT TITLE: GLASGOW, 1995

'Jimmy, get up. Get up, Jimmy.'

The blood on my notepad pages was from Jimmy Murray. The blood on my hands was from a lifetime of devotion to the mad sport of boxing.

Once upon a time in a Glasgow hotel's converted conference room, two wee boxers fought an unforgettable and tragic fight. A fight to the death. Drew Docherty against Jimmy Murray finished with just 34 seconds left in the last round. Murray lost, nobody won and there was the sickening race to save his young life.

While he was being carried away, two fingers were placed deep in Murray's mouth to assist his breathing. I saw this from two feet away. This was when his body left the ring on the stretcher, this was when the riot was still going on and this was when his mother, Margaret, touched his leg. She was crying: 'Jimmy, get up. Get up, Jimmy.' The body was taken from under her hand and from her sight. He was taken to Southern General Hospital in the Govan part of the great city. The end race was on. He would be declared dead about 34 hours later. Murray was in a bed on Ward 61, the Intensive Therapy Unit. 'All signs of neurological activity were extinct,' said Garth Cruikshank, the neurosurgeon.

It was Sunday morning. As he spoke, and I had heard this before, people sobbed.

The British bantamweight title was the prize on the night.

In the ring, Docherty was in tears, protected by a circle of his friends from the 'evil scum' fighting in the ruined banquet suite at the hotel. He would visit the Murray house. 'They treated me like a son,' he told me. It was saddest of black nights for the old sport. The Nigel Benn and Gerald McClellan fight had been eight months earlier and 13 million had watched that. Bradley Stone had died after a British title fight the year before. It was a tough time to be in the British boxing business. Docherty would have six more fights, all for either a world, the British or the European title, and would lose five of them.

Before the fight, on the night in one of the temporary dressing rooms, I spoke to Dave Douglas, Murray's trainer, and he told me. 'Docherty can't hurt Jim, but Jim can hurt Docherty.' That was the feeling. I had made the journey to cover the British title fight because I knew it would be good, I knew pride would be a factor, I knew Murray was the slight underdog, I knew it would be noisy and I knew I would get good copy. They had met six years earlier as amateurs and Docherty had stopped Murray in the third. Docherty was the British champion; Murray held the Scottish belt. Nobody travelled with me from the national newspaper south. Inside the Hospitality Inn, 400 had paid £50 for a meal and a ticket and another 300 had paid £20 to stand; a month later standing tickets were outlawed. Murray's fans had travelled from his home in Newmains and they had come out in big numbers; there was a great atmosphere.

And it was a brilliant fight. Docherty was dropped in the first. Murray had a bad cut above his left eye from the third. By the end, Docherty's nose was bleeding, Murray had a cut across his nose and a nick by his right eye. There was a lot of blood. The referee, John Keane, was covered. I was right on the apron at ringside; blood was on my clothes and notepad. That notepad lives, wrapped in tissue, in a box with my son's first Arsenal shirt and my little girl's first shoes. It deserves that resting place. You want an example of just how involved you can get at a fight? A bad example, by the way.

In the ninth round, the fight's direction changed as Murray tired. Docherty caught him with a big left hook. Murray was badly hurt. I wrote at the end of the ninth: 'Murray dead from the shot.' It was an expression I used, an expression I never used after Friday 13 October 1995. Murray's nose was also bleeding and the white on his shorts was stained. It finished with just 34 seconds left in the 12th and last round. The damage had been done before the last few punches of Murray's boxing life – perhaps that left hook in the ninth. That is what the experts told me.

Before the start of the 12th, on a page dotted with their blood, I scribbled. 'Both fucked. Docherty needs knockout but doesn't have enough left.'

Murray was hit with a light jab on his chest and with 44 seconds left in the round, he fell to his knees and folded his body over his legs. His gloves were resting on the canvas. He was three feet in front of my eyes. I could hear Keane's count. At ten, Murray's body went limp. My pad tells me that it was 10.43 p.m. when it was waved off. Docherty did have enough left.

I have one random and very cruel note in my pad. I must have written this in the debris of the room after the police had regained control. It is 11.19 p.m. and I wrote: 'Just dehydrated. Coming round and asking for his mother. He is OK.' To this day, I have no idea what bastard told me that. It was not true, never true. It was a shameful fucking lie. By midnight, I had been warned he would die.

The first bottles started to fly just seconds after Murray was stopped. It escalated quickly. It was a riot in seconds. Men took their tops off. Some men, having been cut by flying bottles, smeared blood across their chests. It was a *Braveheart* scene. In the ring, under this pressure, the paramedics were desperately trying to stabilise Murray. If you can control the breathing, you can help the survival. It's a race against time and the paramedics need calm.

He was officially pronounced dead at 8.50 a.m. on the Sunday. Just over 34 hours after he slumped to his knees. I lived every second of that death, writing, chasing details and crying in a shit hotel room.

One year and two months later:

'If you look from here, right there, that is Jimmy,' said Alex Morrison, his manager and the promoter on the night. 'That is perfect, just look at the lips above the glove. I couldn't believe it when I first saw it.' Morrison had taken me to Newmains and there was a statue. Wee Jimmy had a statue. It was December 1996.

In Newmains, the ordinary people stood and looked at the statue and remembered fondly the fighter known as the wee boxer. The Craig Nuick Estate is at the centre of Buckfast Valley, which was in 1995 an alternative name for Newmains. It was in honour of the potent tonic wine. Also, at that time the place was infamous for tombstone raiders. It is a brutal landscape, ideal to celebrate the dead.

The sculptress, Alison Bell, had sat and watched tapes of Jimmy's fights in the house with Margaret and Murray's father, Kenneth. She had then gone to her studio with pictures of Jimmy as a child. It must have been a hellish assignment. Margaret had traipsed the streets of the town collecting cash to fund the statue, and in Glasgow, the Calton Club had donated £1,000. The Calton was famous then for its tough-love treatment of heroin addicts and it's football team of recovering drug abusers.

The statue moved Big Alex and very little moved that giant of a man. He was the original bare-knuckle Glaswegian hardman. He told stories never to be retold and they were true. He loved Jimmy Murray.

Jimmy Murray: *A week or so after he died, I went to Ibrox with Alex to watch Rangers. We had an empty seat between us and that belonged to the wee boxer. The weekend of the fight and the death and being isolated in my hotel room on my own, had been brutal. None of my national newspaper colleagues had made the trip. On that Monday night after the fight, my wife picked me up at the airport and we drove home. She was concerned about my state of mind; she knew I had been awake for two nights and days. On 5 Live, which was relatively new, John Inverdale told listeners to stop driving and buy a copy of the* Daily Telegraph *and read about Murray's death. I heard this in the car, it was weird. As we got out of the car, a woman of about 70 came over; I think she was waiting on my doorstep. 'Thank you for this,' she said and held out the paper. That has not happened since. Sadly, there have been more deaths. This was how the report finished: 'I never again want to hear a boxer's mother wailing like Margaret Murray did on Friday night, as her son's life faded in front of her eyes.'*

75

THE TOUR

SALFORD, SUNDERLAND, SOUTH LONDON, BETHNAL GREEN, BELFAST, NOTTINGHAM, BIRMINGHAM, SWANSEA, LOUGHTON, LEEDS AND DUBLIN, 2009

'Nah, darling, Buncey said it would be alright.'

Five days after the last *Boxing Hour* on Setanta, the channel went dark, and I was in trouble. It was June 2009 and times were tough: the Setanta gig had lasted about two years, and it was popular and lucrative. I made an advert for the channel where I served hot dogs from a stall inside Fulham's ground on matchday.

I let things get the better of me and decided to take the show on the road. The plan was 12 cities. That was ambitious. The original plan was a 50-city tour. That was always stupid; my ego was out of control. I was an idiot, and nobody told me.

I pulled in favours, asked people in different cities and I got some great venues – all for free. Why not? I was going to deliver 500 people on a Tuesday or a Thursday night. Made sense to me. I also got a group of people who gave up their time to help set things up.

The 2009 Tour was pulled together and run by my wife, Jacqueline. She never said a word when she knew a month before the first gig that it was going to be a total disaster. She had faith in me – she always did. And what a disaster it was. It was also very, very funny. And a bit sad. Nostalgia in the boxing game is a big business. My mistake at the start was taking it seriously, taking myself seriously. Delusional bollocks at its best.

I had 12 cities, but I had to cancel Cork when I found out the pub was derelict. I was sent a picture by a punter. I called the fella I was dealing with, the man who told me he owned the pub. He told me that it was not a problem. His plan was to get a generator, get a Portaloo or two, get the boards off the windows, get the squatters out and it would be 'as good as new, so it will'. I had to kibosh Cork and that was when I had an idea that perhaps the tour was not going to be a sell-out. I was using a ticket company and they paid me, and I made a promise to repay everybody who had booked for Cork. I had to pay 17 people. The geezer in Cork had told me 350 would be there. He also told me it was a pub and not a derelict building. He's a nice fella, a good friend and I don't doubt his generator story, but I was not playing a boarded-up building. Cork was off the list; I was down to 11 and I started at the Lower Kersal Social Club in Salford in September.

What a venue.

We drove up in the afternoon and stayed in a soulless apartment near Media City. We went over to the venue early to do some local television. On Granada I talked of a big, big crowd, perhaps 500 or more. Tony, who ran the famous club, came over after the interview and I told him that we needed more chairs, more space, more bar staff and more security. One of the people helping me had a lively Facebook page dedicated to the tour, and he warned me that hundreds were coming. I thought for a second that we might have to cancel – that is how deluded I was. I feared 700 people on the streets, with 200 not being able to get in.

Fuck me, what a fool.

On the night, I stayed in the dressing room and boxers came in to see me: Matthew Hatton, Carl Thompson, Matt Macklin and Steve Foster. The boxers never let me down. My wife came in an hour before the curtain was going up. I was still locked away in the dressing room at this point. 'How many?' I asked. She hesitated and it was then that I knew. 'Don't tell me,' I quickly said. I never wanted to see her hurt. That was the last time I set foot anywhere near a dressing room on the remaining ten nights.

The show was great. Ninety minutes of tales and interviews and questions. Brilliant. The details are not so good: One person paid. I had sold 40 tickets and 20 never showed. I was in a boxing heartland, I was doomed. I sold about ten T-shirts; I gave away more than ten and that left me with about 1,978. Ten cities later that number had shrunk to about 1,910 and most of those were freebies. They are still out there somewhere in a garage.

That night, in that sterile apartment, we were speechless. Stunned. I was embarrassed. The ego had landed, make no mistake; it had crash landed. Six months earlier, the Setanta *Boxing Hour* was up for big television awards at fancy hotels in Park Lane, I served hot dogs in promos and now I felt like I was sleeping in an IKEA warehouse. And I knew my wife was hurting; she took it personally. It was my fault.

And then, we had some laughs. The Cork caper came to light. I then went to Sunderland and hit a comic low. A local boxing promoter had offered to buy all 250 tickets – they were priced ridiculously at £17.50, plus a booking fee. And that was my fault, I had listened to people telling me to make it expensive. I wanted to charge a tenner. I refused his offer. I was even told that I would need a bigger venue. In the end, six paid and came. What type of bigger venue? Like a kitchen? I tried to auction a signed Ricky Hatton T-shirt and was offered five quid. And the local boxing promoter, who had offered to pay me £4,375, arrived with about six people and not one of them paid. He would have paid me for all the tickets, he is a good man. He is also a lucky man.

My wife swerved Sunderland, thankfully. I was staying above a pub. A bad pub.

In Birmingham, I was playing the Dubliner, a famous boozer in Digbeth. The fighters came out; Macklin came with his European title belt in a bag and Joe Egan, who sparred a million rounds with

Mike Tyson, added a bit of glamour. It was packed, but it was just the bar, and we shared the space with the guvnor's special homeless night. One night each week, he fed the homeless. He covered a pool table and put out plates of food and the homeless came, carrying their life in plastic bags and their sleeping bags for survival. I had a captive audience, they loved me. Where were they going to go? It was pissing down. My people mingled with the homeless. I missed a trick; I could have got my T-shirts out on the streets. I did about three hours live, and then we had a very, very good drink. I think about 12 paid for tickets.

In Swansea, once again the fighters came with their belts: Enzo Maccarinelli, Nathan Cleverly and Jason Cook. Big names. I was in a nightclub, and I had been promised two coach-loads of people from the other side of Cardiff. The man making the promises never stopped calling to check that 90 tickets would still be available. I had about 30 people inside the place. I kept delaying the start because of the two coaches. Suddenly, he was no longer calling. Finally, at about 8.30, I called him. It was our last conversation.

Apparently a woman had fallen over walking a dog and that started a series of events that led to the inevitable cancellation of the two coaches. Obviously.

And finally at some point in November after ten consecutive weeks of shows, the Tour finished in Loughton, Essex. The logistics are impressive. It was my third show in London or the London area and there was a loyal following for the show. Old boxers, old friends, some young fighters, felons, boxing people, faces, broken faces and a lot of truly lovely people came to that last gig. Nobody paid a penny on the door. 'They all told me: "Nah, darling, Buncey said it would be alright," so I just let them all in,' my wife said to me. It was a bit late to get picky. She was laughing non-stop; she loved the lunacy of that last night. We had done a show in Bethnal Green where David Haye came on stage, just ten days before he beat Nikolai Valuev; in Belfast I packed out the Dockers: in south

London people I had not seen for 30 years came over and had a cuddle. We had not made a penny, but it had its moments. That shit night in Salford was history.

It was the final night, and it was a leisure centre bar in Loughton, and you could not move. Swinging off the chandeliers; I think we sold ten tickets. There must have been 120 people in there. It was a reunion of long-lost friends and former opponents. It was wonderful.

It was an adult night and often the language was a bit choice. In Loughton, because it was so packed, they were standing on the stage. They were about three feet from me. I recognised one particular fella, an amateur boxer from the Repton boxing club. He was about 40, a well-known character and he had with him his 13-year-old daughter. That is good, but I felt very uneasy with the swearing. It put me on edge. I kept apologising to her. I soldiered on, I'm a trooper.

The night was chaos – the faithful just talked to each other the whole time, they were loud, happy and telling each other stories they had heard a hundred times. Boxers love that comfort, sharing those old fight tales. I would be halfway through a Joe Bugner tale of my own, and somebody from a group of about six men would shout out: 'Buncey, who did Sylvie (Sylvester Mittee) beat at the Royal Albert Hall when he came back from the Olympics?' I would think and reply: 'Sid Smith, caught him cold.' And then I would go back to the Bugner story. After 30 minutes of this, I took a break. My wife had not stopped laughing. I told her about the girl, and she said, 'What girl?' It turns out that she was 38, a yoga instructor. I gave her a T-shirt.

I tried a second half but gave in to the love in the room. Former British and European champion, Jimmy McDonnell was there – it was the place where he trained James DeGale. I had been in Benidorm at the same time as Jimmy Mac when I was just 16; there were dozens and dozens of stories like that in that room. Tales like this from different little huddles: 'I remember boxing for London in Rotterdam, it must have been about 1979, and Silly Bollocks (it could have been any one of the men in that room) whacked a geezer who was trying to nick his bird, and it turns out, the bird was married to the geezer.' That is a sample of the talk; it was hardcore boxing people taking connected detours down memory lane. It was perfect and about the only way to end the Tour.

The Tour: *I'm doing another one and might even go to the same venues and sell the same T-shirts. Well, not the pub in Cork, that is a Thai now. This time it will be free.*

76

REG PARKER'S
UNDERGROUND BOXING

A WAREHOUSE IN SOUTH LONDON, 1992

'I'm making more for these fights than I made for winning the British title at the Royal Albert Hall.'

The meeting was in a pub in Orpington, and it was the only way to find out where the boxing was going to take place. The fights were underground, off the sanctioned grid.

The venue for the night was still unknown. It would be, so the organiser claimed, on the border of south London and Kent. That is one helluva border. It kept the police on their toes.

The main event attraction was Jimmy Cable, and he was due to meet us at the pub and be part of the convoy to the venue. He was a real local hero, faded for sure, but still an attraction was Gentleman Jim. And he was a gentleman.

Cable was still only 34 that night, but his best fighting days were long gone, and I had been witness to those up close and personal. When I had last seen him, which was probably in 1988, his face had been changed from the punches and his voice had started to slur. I had first met Jimmy in about 1977 when he boxed for the Fitzroy Lodge amateur boxing club in Lambeth, south London. The kid was a star, a rock star in that smelly railway arch gym.

Cable had been the British and European light-middleweight champion in 1984. He had bounced far too quickly between fights, hiding cuts and taking fights he could have delayed. Money was the problem: Jimmy never had any and promoters kept offering it to him. He won the British title just 22 days after a fight; six weeks later he was stopped by Buster Drayton in just one round and six weeks after that he went to France and, against the odds, won the European title in the 11th round. The cheque for the fight in France bounced; Jimmy was back painting and decorating. The win in France against Said Skouma was thrilling, a lost classic. Cable was dropped three times, rocked, hurt, given a standing count and then he rallied. Skouma was dropped in the tenth and again in the 11th. 'That was some fight – I was not meant to win,' said Cable. He is right.

He had won the British title, won the European, topped the bill on the BBC at the Royal Albert Hall and painted a three-bedroom maisonette in Beckenham all in about 100 days. In September, he went to Germany and lost the European title. His ridiculous schedule took place under the careful and calculating eye of the British Boxing Board of Control. 'I just kept taking the fights that were being offered,' he told me in 1992. 'It was the money – how could I say no?' It was Cable's great boxing year, but there was no plan; he was offered fights and he accepted. In 1985, when he was still only 27, he lost his British title and lost his way. He was not in a great place. It was no shock that Jimmy Cable emerged as a star on the underground boxing circuit less than a decade later.

I waited in the pub for my old friend to arrive, and not sure what he was going to be like.

It was a Tuesday night and Cable arrived at about six. It was dark and cold. The venue was Unit 6 of the Thames Industrial Estate. The fans started to leave; there was a queue for the phone in the pub. Word spread. We were in the convoy – I was travelling with Steve Lillis, of the *Daily* and *Sunday Sport*.

'I remember that night,' said Lillis in early 2024, speaking from his house in Spain. 'The one thing I remember most?' I knew the answer and told him: 'It was how much clearer Cable sounded.' I was right. It had shocked me and Lillis. Cable's eyes were sharp and clean, and his voice was crisp, not the slow version I had last heard one night at York Hall in 1988.

The underground fights were run by Reg Parker and his office was above a World of Leather shop in Eltham. His business was called the Independent Boxing Association. He operated outside the governing body, but inside the law.

'The British board refused to hear my request for a licence,' Parker told me that night. 'They have not given me a reason and all I want is for one of their officers to attend my shows.'

On the approach to the venue, it was clear that the police had been tipped off. They were everywhere in the surrounding streets. Some of the streets had been sealed off. The venue was just an empty warehouse with a ring in the middle.

'The police arrived and threatened to shut the place down, they didn't realise that I had permission from the owners to run the show,' said Parker. 'It was my sixth choice of venue; every time I find a place, I get told it is suddenly unavailable after false claims that I'm running a bare-knuckle fight.' He was certainly not: he was giving retired or banned boxers a second or third chance. Cable was his champion, and he had a belt to show for it. He won that night, comfortably and without a cut or mark or any damage. Gentleman Jim was too slick for Parker's hardmen.

Everybody entering walked through a long line of police and Parker's own hired security. No booze was allowed. 'The officer in charge watched three fights and fucked off and took the old bill with him,' added Parker, just before midnight. Reg was happy, over 1,200 had paid their £25 to stand and watch and there had been no trouble. That is a lot of cash, a big, big bag of cash.

Cable had an alarming take on his new fighting gang: 'I'm making more for these fights than I made for winning the British title at the Royal Albert Hall.' That was the damning takeaway from the night and not the lack of facilities at Unit 6, the heavy police presence or the quality of some of the undercard.

At the time in the *Daily Telegraph,* I wrote that the British Boxing Board of Control should talk to Parker and not ignore him. My fear was that his unregulated shows might just attract a young fighter and that we would lose the kid to the underground fight club. They ignored him and he eventually vanished. Cable defended his title a few times. Looking back, it is safe to say that Parker's edgy, warehouse fights were wonderful compared to the growing trend in bare-knuckle dust ups and terrible so-called 'white-collar' boxing, which is pirate boxing with a fancy tag.

Jimmy Cable: *This is not pleasant, sorry. In 1996, Jimmy's life was ruined and it had nothing to do with boxing. His daughter was an innocent witness to a brutal stabbing death. The dead man was her fiancée. The killer was a known and notorious London gangster called Kenneth Noye and he had form: he had previously stabbed to death an undercover policeman and had got away with it. The man had been in Noye's garden and Noye had proved that he felt like his life was in danger.*

After the second killing, Noye fled to Spain and was arrested in 1998; Cable's daughter went out to identify him. Noye stood trial in 2000 and Cable's daughter was a brave witness. He was found guilty of the murder and sentenced to life. He was released in the summer of 2019. Another witness to the stabbing was shot to death in late 2000 after the trial. 'A life sentence should mean a life sentence,' Cable said in 2017. 'Her life has been destroyed.' Cable's daughter had been given a new identity and placed in a witness protection scheme. She was as fearless as her father. Jimmy was broken. He died in 2020, another old boxing friend gone too soon.

77

AGOSTINO CARDAMONE
— v —
NEVILLE BROWN

EUROPEAN MIDDLEWEIGHT TITLE. SOLOFRA, ITALY, 1994

'Gelato?'

At midnight in the heart of Solofra there is suddenly not a soul to be found.

The boxing in the town square had finished an hour or so earlier. The lights had gone out, the people had vanished. My usual post-fight ritual, before mobiles worked, was to find a phone, use the free number, dictate my copy to a woman somewhere in Yorkshire, and then get a drink. I had found a public phone to file my 450 words to the desk. It was not poetry, but it captured the failed mood of Neville Brown's attempt to win the European middleweight title. It was always going to be a hard night for Neville.

I had flown to Naples, which is about 80 kilometres from Solofra, two days and nights earlier. It was July and hot and I had to keep a low profile, very low to tell the truth. I was not wanted in that part of Italy and was not officially there.

At the time, I was in dispute with Mickey Duff, the promoter and manager of Brown. Our dispute had nothing to do with Neville, but Duff had banned me from all his shows and any shows that his boxers were on. A year earlier, in Berlin, I had to buy two tickets when Duff had seen me at a fight – I was about

30 rows back – and he sent security to eject me. I was not going to make the same mistake in Italy: I stayed away from the fight hotel, avoided the weigh-in and wore a hat. I figured shades were a piece of spy legend too far. Duff was not mucking about – he hated me – and he eventually got a few quid in a settlement with the *Sunday Telegraph*. Our dispute was simple: A fighter had lied to me, I wrote the lie, Duff proved it was a lie and he won. It was, obviously, not a lie, but it was proved it was. It happens in the newspaper business. 'What do you want, a fucking Pulitzer Prize?' Duff had screamed at me when he evicted me from the first conference after the article appeared.

I made my way on two buses from Naples to Solofra. I think it was about 5,000 lire, something like two quid. I was deep cover, I wanted to see this fight. Brown was the underdog, but he could bang. I was determined not to let Duff see me. I knew that I could not apply for a press pass because the promoter, Elio Cotena, worked with Duff and had once defended his European title at York Hall in 1976 on a Duff bill. That route to ringside was a non-starter.

The square in Solofra is dominated by the baroque church, Collegiata di San Michele Arcangelo, and right in the middle of the square is a fountain. The lion in the fountain has a permanent stream of water gushing from its mouth. The ring was built right up to the fountain. The dusk settled, the light was fantastic – a golden hour to never forget – and I finally broke my cover, took my cheap seat and waited. What a day and night that was, perfect. My vision was not obscured by the lion, but the fountain at ringside was odd.

It was proper dark when Brendan Ingle led Neville Brown to the ring. He seemed relaxed. Cardamone's entrance was a lot louder, and I felt isolated in my seat. I have no idea what I paid, but it was cheap. I'm sure that Duff saw me a couple of times, especially when he climbed up on the canvas as Brown entered the ring. Mind you, he did squint and glare a lot even when he was happy, and he was not happy very often. I was not evicted.

I wrote that Brown was knocked out in the seventh 'of a brilliant attempt'; the real story is that Brown let the fight slip away. Cardamone was close to going over twice in the opening round; in round two, Brown touched down. By the end of the fourth round, Brown was in front and then he just fell to pieces, under pressure and under attack from the crowd. Cardamone was an aggressive fighter, not dangerous, but relentless. In the seventh, Brown was dropped by a 'perfect southpaw left cross'; he beat the count, looked finished, boxed on and was sent down again – the crowd loved it and I had to stand to watch the end of the fight. It was not pleasant: 'Brown collapsed in a heap, his head hitting the canvas, and the referee did not even bother to count.' It was over for him; my fight was about to start.

The buses had stopped and there was not a taxi or a car anywhere. It was late and dark, and I was flying early the next morning. I had seen the boxer's mini-bus leave about an hour after the fight. I had filed my copy and was desperate to get back to Naples; desperate to find anybody in Solofra still awake. And that was when I saw the light inside a pizza restaurant. There were a couple of waiters hovering and just two men at a table; the place was empty. It fell silent when I walked in.

I asked if anybody spoke English and the men at the table both said 'yes.' I asked if there was a taxi firm or a late, late bus to get me back to Naples. They shook their heads, invited me to sit and have a beer. 'We take you, no problem.'

The big red Mercedes outside was their car. They took me and I was impressed at how fast a Mercedes can go on the, as I know now, A30 from the dark hills to Naples. I would like to lie and say that we talked about football or Primo Carnera, but the truth is the pair in the front just babbled on in Italian. I was the silent passenger and was feeling just a bit uneasy by the time we entered the streets of Naples.

'Gelato?' one of them finally asked me. It was about 2 a.m. Why not? We stopped in front of the busiest ice cream parlour I have ever seen. There must have been 200 outside in the heat and the neon glow. The car stopped in the middle of the street. They got out and the crowd opened, parted. And fell silent. I was not shocked; I had a feeling I was not in the company of two ordinary pizza-loving Italian men.

I had coffee and pistachio in a cup; a grown man can't have a cone at 3 a.m. Men and women approached their table, their heads bowed, they said a few words – my drivers said even less, often they just shrugged. 'Is nice, yeah?' they asked. 'Lovely, fellas, thanks.' An hour later, they dropped me at my hotel. I made the plane the next day. I guess they were top boys.

A few months later, I was back in Italy at the iconic Ariston Theatre in San Remo. It was Cardamone again and the British challenger was Leicester's Shaun 'The Guvnor' Cummins. They both ended up in hospital after a savage brawl; Cardamone benefited from the Austrian ref, Walther Schall, who gave him hours and hours to recover from a heavy knockdown in the eighth – it was close to 30 seconds in the end. Cardamone got the decision, kept his title.

Cummins had very little luck in his life. In 2004, he was injured in a bike crash. After that, he was stuck in bed, troubled, damaged and angry. He had a carer and that never worked very well.

Shaun Cummins spoke to me in 2010; he was morbidly obese, bed bound and in a very bad place. We struggled to play the interview; it was too dark. 'I look back and I have a lot of regrets. I did stupid things when I was young.'

In 2012, Cummins' carer bought two freezers, a chainsaw, goggles and a mask with a credit card that belonged to Cummins. At some point in early September, Cummins was chopped into ten pieces and stored in three freezers. The Guvnor was gone. The carer had some serious issues and was sentenced to 34 years in prison.

Neville Brown: *In 1995, Brown defended his British title against Shaun Cummins. It was the Guvnor's last fight. Brown fought for a world title in 1996 and left boxing in 2000. I guess Cardamone still drinks espressos on the seafront in San Remo; I looked for him in late 2023. I still mix pistachio and coffee when I go for a gelato, and I have never seen the two boys from Solofra again.*

78

PETER BUCKLEY AND
KRISTIAN LAIGHT:
600 FIGHTS – THE PROFESSIONALS

EVERY VENUE IN BRITAIN, 2021

They were artists, they knew their trade better than just about everybody who beat them.

Peter Buckley and Kristian Laight had 300 fights each during their careers. Two men and 600 fights.

It is unlikely that boxers will ever have that many fights again in British boxing. They were the last of the breed, the last of the sport's greatest losers, throwbacks to the days in the Twenties and Thirties when parts of East London had two or three shows each night. They are dinosaurs in the modern game.

Buckley lost 256 times and Laight lost 279 times. In many ways the numbers are distorted and must never be used against either of the two boxers as a measure of their ability. They would, if the price was right, accept fights on the day.

In 2018, when Laight boxed for the very last time, Buckley walked him to the ring wearing a Team Laight t-shirt. Laight lost; it was only July, and yet it was his 18th loss of the year. The venue was the Alan Higgs Centre in Coventry, and his opponent was Luke Beasley, who won for the second time and promptly retired. It is the forgotten side of the boxing business, the underbelly: a place of anonymous fights and anonymous fighters. Laight met enough quality and ambitious boxers to show up on radars, but he mostly made his money on obscure shows in rare venues like Derby University and Fit City in Broughton. And he also had a few cameos far down the bill on a big night when a boy was making his debut. Laight met 68 men making their debut. In his penultimate fight, Laight, having his 299th professional outing, lost to debutant Simon Corcoran over four rounds at York Hall. Laight would have been back in Nuneaton before the last fight.

When Buckley fought for the 300th and last time, he won on points over four rounds. It was 2008 at the Aston Villa Leisure Centre and his first fight had been in 1989. Buckley beat Matin Mohammed, whose only other fight had been a draw a few weeks earlier; Buckley had been the opponent then. In that month, Buckley fought four times. These guys are supermen, trust me. Gone forever from our business.

Laight and Buckley were the designated losers on hundreds and hundreds of nights, sharing a dressing room with a big, useless Latvian heavyweight and a hopeless lightweight from Hungary. Often, in the travelling pack of losers, there would also be one Estonian or Polish trainer who is often the universal translator. The boxing language is not complicated, in all fairness. Those rooms are not good for the soul. They are the losers' rooms, tiny and smelly. No shower, no lockers; they all had a job to do, they all knew they had been booked to lose. It was strictly business, and they also knew that they had to try and win. The Board can withhold money if they think a kid has jumped on the floor. What a series of mixed messages. 'I would look over and see the kid and I knew that he wanted to kill me – I also knew there was no chance of that,' said Buckley.

I can remember looking up Buckley's record online and often noticing that he was booked out again and again. He told me that he once had six fights scheduled. Both Laight and Buckley were, on occasion, pulled over and asked a quiet word about a kid they had just lost to. They were asked – this might sound brutal – if the kid could fight. Their answers were private, and they stayed private. It's no good being known as a big mouth.

Laight, especially, never took risks or liberties. He was known as Mr Reliable. He knew exactly why he was travelling from Nuneaton to Norwich on a Tuesday night; it was not to expose a kid making his debut, a kid who had sold 200 tickets, who had his nan at ringside and his pregnant girlfriend throwing up in the toilet. Laight drew nine times and a careful look at his 279 losses – he was only stopped five times – suggests to me that he would have easily won 80 or more fights. However, if he kept winning, he would not keep fighting. Promoters making a match for a kid who was, say, seven and zero, would rather take Laight with 83 defeats, than an unbeaten kid from the same gym with three or four fights. This is fact, not fantasy. How mad is that?

Laight took far fewer hard fights and no big-money fights – which is code for meeting an unbeaten prospect, possibly even a champion, at short notice on a televised show – compared to Buckley. It's called 'saving the show' and Buckley saved a lot of shows. Laight knew and understood the dangers of bad beatings. He would often have three or more fights lined up – a stoppage loss ruined the schedule and cost him money. It's a business, not a hobby and it's certainly not fun. Bad defeats attract attention and that is no good for a kid with a massive losing record.

Jon Pegg, the trainer, promoter, matchmaker, manager and former professional fighter, worked with Laight.

'There is probably a grand more on offer for a television fight against a dangerous prospect, but it's not worth it,' Pegg told me in 2021 when I interviewed Buckley at Bar Sport in Cannock. 'Kristian never took those fights and that gave him extra rounds. I have no doubt about that.'

Buckley did take fights like that and met something like 20 world champions, 161 unbeaten fighters and had about 70 fights with champions of some type. He fought giants. Buckley was only stopped ten times and that is one of British boxing's most amazing achievements. 'Not one regret,' he told me.

I remember when he was stopped by Naseem Hamed in Cardiff, and he complained to the referee, pleaded his case. 'I was not hurt, and I had a lot of fights lined up; the loss cost me money,' he told me. Buckley fought Hamed, who had knocked out eight of his nine opponents, and it was just seven days after losing to Barry Jones; both Hamed and Jones won world titles. A few months after the Hamed loss, Buckley lost to two other future world champions. Buckley was the one man in nine fights to go the distance with Hamed before their second meeting, the one in Cardiff. Hamed finished his career with 31 stoppages in 36 fights; Buckley was in rare company.

'You know,' Buckley told me that day. 'Some refs would say to me, just before the last round, "Good round here, Pete, and it's a draw." That means I had pissed it.' Buckley drew 12 times and so many of his other losses have odd scores. He would never even bother to look at the referee at the end of four or six rounds against a local ticket seller. I wrote something about Buckley once and it remains true: 'The nights when he did just enough to lose should always be balanced against the nights when he had to do everything possible not to get hurt.'

Laight did his best to avoid the most dangerous fighters and it worked. Buckley once fought an unbeaten man called Acelino Freitas and the Brazilian's record before their fight at the Everton Park Sports Centre was 18 wins, 18 by knockout. It improved to 19 in round three. That was not Laight's style, and it was certainly not the way Pegg operated.

'I started working with Kristian after 90 fights,' Pegg told me. 'He was only stopped once in the 210 fights he had with me. And that was his fault; the fight was too easy, he got stopped, got caught and got dropped.'

After his 300th fight, Laight was told to retire: it was a firm message. He listened and called it a day. The job offers for fights kept coming in.

Buckley had to save his career on one occasion. It was in 1996 and he had lost 58 times and had mixed in recent months with Colin McMillan, a former WBO featherweight champion, brilliant Irishman Paul Griffin and future British champion, Patrick Mullings. The word came down that Buckley needed a win; another loss would end in some type of suspension. Buckley was matched in south London with a south Londoner, Matt Brown, who was unbeaten in seven fights. Buckley stopped Brown in one round; the win was not good for business but kept him in business. It was three months before Buckley got another fight. His trainer, Nobby Nobbs, knew it would happen. 'The phone went dead – Peter was a ghost.' Nobbs ran a gym in Birmingham called Losers Unlimited. He was a funny man in the business. He once told Buckley to warm up and then pointed at a radiator.

There is an argument that the modern British Boxing Board of Control would limit a fighter like Buckley to far fewer defeats, and certainly stop him fighting the type of men that he fearlessly met. He is never getting permission to fight Freitas now.

Kristian Laight and Peter Buckley: *We don't fix fights in boxing – we don't need to. We have matchmakers and men like Laight and Buckley to make sure the business runs smoothly. A newspaper once tried to call Laight and Buckley Britain's 'worst' boxers. That is so far from the truth. They are artists, they know their trade better than just about everybody who beat them.*

79

SUE ATKINS AND THE BRITISH LADIES BOXING ASSOCIATION

A PUB IN TOOTING, SOUTH LONDON, 1993

'It's sport, not a freak show.'

Sue Atkins started the modern British boxing revolution. It's really that simple.

She founded the British Ladies Boxing Association, and she headlined the first show under the new banner at the Foresters Arms in Tooting in April 1993. The event was hijacked by the dirty-mac brigade. It was nothing new to Sue.

She had fought in France and Germany, toured in America, and on a filthy sofa at a freezing farm near Bristol in March 1993, she shared her boxing vision with me. She was having a steaming mug of tea with her opponent, Jane Johnson. They had just fought a four-round exhibition. The pair also sparred with each other and a few weeks after the tea on the farm, they fought each other at the pub. Atkins was a gardener and Johnson had a market stall in Brighton.

'I don't want women boxers to compete before or after mud wrestlers or anything like that,' Atkins told me. 'We train hard, we love the sport, and we deserve to be recognised. We need to get rid of the image of two dykes with shaved heads slugging it out top-less.' They were hard times, and some brutal things were said and printed. And, by the way, that is an image.

Atkins had once gone to a hotel in Watford to fight a German woman. The woman was called Karen Hech. When Atkins got there, she realised that all the German women on the bill were fighting topless. The show was being filmed by a German company. It was part of a freak show, a soft-porn circuit of fighting women. Atkins fought with her top in place. There were already protective breast shields for boxers. At that time, one of the main fears about women boxing was the supposed increased risk of breast cancer. Studies of martial artists in France had disproved the fear. Atkins was big on the fake reasons women were being denied the right to fight.

'We have a problem with our boxing at the moment,' continued Atkins. 'It is either a sleaze thing or the tattooed crew-cut woman thing. It upsets me to think that people think I'm queer because I box; the sport needs an image change and that is why I formed the BLBA.'

By about 2016, boxing had led the way with openly gay female fighters. There is no subterfuge like there still exists in football. We just get on with it; you can either fight or not, the other stuff – religion, sexual preference, colour, country, politics – all comes second.

Some of the comments by Atkins might seem harsh now, but the most famous female fighter of the Nineties and one of the wealthiest, Christy Martin, also said some damning things at about this time. She was stabbed and shot and left for dead by her husband, who was also her trainer. He's gone, she moved on. She now lives with a woman.

Atkins had been boxing for over a decade when I sat with her on the sofa at the farm. The experience at the hotel near Watford was not unique. Deidre Gogarty, who fought on the first BLBA show, also had to fight a topless woman in either 1986 or 1987. 'It's sport, not a freak show,' she argued. That was certainly a debate.

Gogarty was told, as late as 1991, that fighting topless would get her exposure. Gogarty was struggling to get fights, but she would simply not take no for an answer and eventually would have 23 recorded and legitimate fights in a boxing ring. All with her top on; she also won a version of the world title. She had other fights, just like Atkins, and they are not recorded. Atkins, disgracefully, does not exist on the main boxing record site.

Atkins had once been stranded in France after a European title fight. She was stopped on her feet, but that was the easy part. It was 1989 and the promoters left her alone and vanished with the £150 she was promised – the £150 she needed to get home. She laughed at the memory and then she told me about a fight in Germany. I love this crazy stuff.

'The opponent was switched,' continued Atkins. 'I had to box a former Taekwondo champion called Iron Doris; she was over 12 stone and six-feet tall (Atkins is five-four and was nine stone). I ran for six rounds to survive.' The organisers had also given her a coach for the corner who only spoke Italian. It has to be said that a lot of British men had similar nightmares on the road in Europe in the Seventies and Eighties.

She also, in the early Eighties, went to America to pursue her boxing dream. She met a group of women called the Foxy Boxing Chicks. They used big gloves, pink things like pillows. 'They used other things to attract punters to their shows,' Atkins said. 'The sport suffers. It's more than just bimbos with busts.' Atkins was right there in the middle of the storm, and it would take decades to get where we are now. It is an unrecognisable business to the one that Atkins knew back then.

The Foresters Arms was filling up nicely. There would be four fights. Atkins would beat Johnson. My piece in the *Daily Telegraph* a few weeks earlier had alerted some proper sports photographers, but it had not deterred the dirty-mac gang. The boxing was not great, but it was a fearless attempt to do things the right way. After the show I was sent copies of magazines with names like *Aggressive Women* and *Amazons in Action*. The eight women from the BLBA

fights above the pub, all ended up sharing the pages of those magazines with topless or nude scrappers.

The show at the pub in Tooting was filmed by a company called
Festelle Video; the show was FV103 in their catalogue. The star of
FV101 was Sabine and she was 'a mean wrestler from Austria clad
only in a tiny thong'. One alternative was FV102 and that was a
five-fight card called Topless Tournament. There were, according
to the blurb, some 'superb close-ups'. The ads ran in the mags.
That is where Atkins and Gogarty ended up that April, lost deep in
a world of Sabine, thongs and nipple close-ups. Atkins confirmed
that nobody on the bill had signed and agreed to having their legitimate night of boxing exploited. However, one of the BLBA boxers
was elsewhere in the magazine in topless fights. What a sleazy
business.

Right there, right then, women's boxing was on the very edge.
Jane Couch was on the horizon and would have her first registered
fight in Wigan in October 1994. She stopped somebody called
Kalpna Shah in two rounds. Shah then vanished. I would love to
talk to Hech and Shah – they were truly invisible cogs in the female
boxing revolution. Couch was never going to let anybody put her
on the pages of a soft-porn fighting magazine. Couch came with
her attitude, her pints and her determination to raise the women's
game. She did, make no mistake.

In May 2003, ten years after the dirty-mac brigade invaded the
Foresters Arms, the first female national championships took place
at the Metropolitan Police College in Hendon. Atkins should have
been the guest of honour. This is really ground zero for what we
have now in Britain; there had already been two editions at world
level. No British boxers were good enough to send.

At Hendon, 19 women, all registered amateur boxers, arrived
for the championship. They were care workers, an armed response
policewoman, an amusement arcade cashier from Paignton pier
and a nursery teacher. Some were mums.

The crowd was about the same size as it had been ten years earlier in the banqueting suite at the Foresters. They were not quite as eager. And, like Atkins and her pioneers, the women from the first national championship had their stories, their reasons for being in that ring. Tamasin Mallia lost for the fourth time in four fights. She was beaten in the bantamweight semi-final by Jenny Dowell. 'I have to call my five-year-old son, Tommy, and tell him that I've lost again. I would never let him see me fight and it's hard enough making the call.' That is a nice tale. I know male boxers who watch hours of their children sleeping when they are in camp. Sacrifice is not a game, it's not a competition in the boxing business and it comes in all shapes and sizes.

That is our history. In 2023 I gave a copy of the Sue Atkins column to two-weight world champion, Terri Harper, and she couldn't believe the struggle. Harper's story from peeling spuds at the chippie to a world title in two years is the type of story that Sue Atkins would love: it's the type of story that Sue Atkins was fighting for.

Sue Atkins and Deidre Gogarty: *In 1996, I saw Gogarty lose to Christy Martin on a Mike Tyson bill in Las Vegas. In 2023, as I was walking into a comedy club in Cardiff for a night with Joe Calzaghe, I was stopped by a woman. There was something familiar about her face. I had not seen her for 30 years. It was Sue Atkins and she looked great. I was moved near to tears. She was the pioneer.*

80

THE LONGEST DAY

RIYADH, SUNDAY 29 OCTOBER 2023

'Don't cry, you a man.'

Part One: 2 a.m. Tyson Fury v Francis Ngannou

It was our very special carnival. Muhammad Ali had fought a wrestler for 15 rounds in a boxing ring, Rocky had fought Hulk Hogan and Tyson Fury was fighting Francis Ngannou in another freak fight.

That was the mood during the week in Riyadh. There would be 26,000 people and the ring would rise, like magic, from a 26-foot-deep pit in the middle of the indoor stadium. That trick had cost $5 million for the Italian lift. Michael Buffer would take the microphone and smoothly introduce the gladiators. It was theatre, wonderful stuff. And then it so nearly went wrong.

Ngannou was picked for his size and his history of bludgeoning people in the UFC. He had a brilliant backstory, a tale of immense hardship, suffering and then redemption through fighting. He was a classy guy, but he had never had a single boxing match as an amateur or as a professional. Sure, he was a danger in the UFC octagon with his fists, but that is another business. He had other tools in that other sport including his flying elbows, flying feet, chokeholds and using just about every part of his body. He was a weapon, but against Fury he would just have his fists. His tools would be withdrawn. Fury was taller, heavier and unbeaten in 34 fights as a professional boxer. He was also the heavyweight champion of the world. As I said, it was our circus.

'Ngannou has no chance of winning and that is fine, but this is still a real fight, it's just not a competitive one.' I wrote that and it made tremendous sense. It was one of the kinder preview lines.

In Riyadh that week, I heard just one voice of dissent – the people directly in the employ of Ngannou don't count. Scott Welch, former British heavyweight champion, warned me that Ngannou was so much better than what we had seen. And what we had seen was bad; Ngannou looked slow, predictable and vulnerable. 'Stevie, stick with me; he's not here for the money,' Welch had warned.

The heavyweight undercard had taken place before midnight in the smaller outdoor arena. It had been carnage out there under a full moon. The five fights had been scheduled to go 48 rounds, instead they went just 11 completed rounds. The real prospects, some hyped men, the overlooked, the savage, the woeful, the ruined and the ignored fought like men trying to avoid the gallows. It was breathless stuff.

The real fight was the Battle of the Baddest in the main arena, just a 50-metre walk away. They were the two best men from their own fighting codes, they were the kings of their codes. Make no mistake, Fury in the MMA arena against Ngannou would be a horrible, horrible mismatch. He would have been toppled quickly, kicked in the shins and then choked out in about a minute. Surely, we all reasoned, the reverse would be true. Ngannou would get jabbed to oblivion and his face broken by Fury landing big right crosses from a safe distance. Surely, Ngannou would get stopped on his feet after seven rounds of bravery. The fight was still a major attraction. I wrote: 'It's a genius, simple and lunatic event.' However, nobody could have predicted the mayhem that started when the first bell tolled after 2 a.m.

Fury went for Ngannou from that first bell. He let a few big right crosses go and they landed somewhere above Ngannou's shoulders.

They bounced off. They never rattled the big man, there was not even a grimace in acknowledgement. And that there, in about ten seconds, was the fight. Fury could not hurt Ngannou. It would be a long, long night.

Ngannou had entered the ring as the 1,358th ranked heavyweight from a global list of 1,358 registered heavyweights. Fury was number one.

After about two minutes of round three the unthinkable happened. Fury let a lazy shot or two go, Ngannou read the punches, bent his knees and let fly a looping left hook. It caught Fury somewhere on the neck and head and down he went in a heap. Ngannou danced at the fallen champion's feet. There was bedlam.

In the TNT presentation area, there were mixed emotions: Dan Hardy, the former UFC fighter, was jumping up and down and Carl Frampton, a two-weight world champion, was just shaking his head. Lennox Lewis arrived and told me: 'That shouldn't happen. That should never happen.' I think Big Lennox took it personally: he was a custodian of that heavyweight chalice, a man of greatness in our sport.

In that moment, with Fury in a tangle on the canvas, there was a lot going on. It's a moment when you see more in a few seconds than is normal. I have it all the time in dramatic fights.

Oleksandr Usyk in a ringside seat froze at first and then laughed. He then started to shout and tell Fury to move. The Fury v Usyk fight was going to be officially announced for 23 December at the end of the fight. Frank Warren, the promoter, was up on his feet; Turki Al-Alshikh was getting a harsh lesson about how plans in boxing can fall apart with just one punch. It was a great plan: Fury batters Ngannou, Usyk gets in the ring and the hype starts. The hundreds of millions of dollars involved in that fight had just been placed in jeopardy by a big left hook from a raw novice.

Boxing never fails to deliver the unexpected. Time most definitely stood still on both sides of the ropes. Fury was up, easily beating the count and pulling off a little Fury move by walking away from the referee to gain a few extra seconds. Right then, as Fury struggled to clear his head, boxing's position as the main fighting sport was on the line. Fury had a lot to defend and a lot to answer to. He survived the round, he got his head together and by about round eight, Ngannou started to show signs of exhaustion.

It was a poor performance by Fury and an inspired fight by Big Francis. At the end of ten rounds, Fury won a split decision. Ngannou never complained; ringside opinions were mixed. 'He got away with one tonight,' I said on air from the ring at the end. And he did. Fury was marked on the left side of his face, he had cuts, he was hurting. His pride was dented. There was no major announcement at the end; Usyk reluctantly got in the ring and Fury called him 'brother' and not the 'ugly middleweight sausage'. It was odd up in that ring, the strangest of moods. Fury rushed to his dressing room; the autopsy started immediately. And it ran and ran. 'It is Tyson's night, I'm going,' said Usyk.

In theory, Fury would be back in the same ring just 55 days later for the Usyk superfight. There was no chance. At about 3.30 a.m., Frank Warren told me: 'I have just been in with him, and I have told him to take a long, hard rest. He's not fighting this year.' The Usyk fight was officially pushed back about a week later. It was unofficially pushed back when Ngannou dropped Fury in the third round.

The crowd of 26,00 had appeared like magic after midnight and they left like magic at about 3 a.m. They were gone.

Part Two: 9 a.m. Oleksandr Usyk at the Four Seasons, Riyadh

We got back to our hotel on the edge of town at about 5 a.m. that night and we met at 8 a.m. in the lobby to go and interview Oleksandr Usyk at the Four Seasons. It was meant to be the morning after the night before knockabout stuff. No chance.

Usyk and Alex Krassyuk arrived on time. Both were in a good mood. Krassyuk is Usyk's translator, friend and promoter. He gets things done.

'I told him, "Mate, you need to take a proper rest,"' said Usyk when I asked what had been said when they were in the ring a few hours earlier. 'I'm sitting in his head like a little tractor.' Usyk then demonstrated how a tractor would be constantly reversing and going over old ground.

I suggested that had Usyk been dropped by a man having his first fight, then Fury would keep reminding him. Will you do the same, I asked. Usyk seemed a bit confused. Krassyuk shrugged. 'No, I am a man. I don't work like that. I can't use dirty tricks, I just can't,' he told me. 'I have children and my sons watch me. One cannot be like a pig.'

He talked about the troops on the frontline. 'This victory will be their victory.' And then, he mentioned his father. There was an instant change in the room. The TNT crew stopped; I could sense it from my seat five feet in front of Usyk. This was different. He pulled out his phone and showed me a picture of his father. I knew he was dead. 'Did he get to enjoy your success?' I asked. Craig, Matt, James and Jack were invisible spectators. They listened and filmed. Usyk blew out a breath, looked up, clenched his fists and started to talk.

'When I was standing with Mike Tyson and Lennox Lewis, I thought about my dad,' he paused to blow out another breath. 'He liked those fighters.'

Usyk stopped. I could see his eyes; the tears were there and then he told the story.

'He watched me win the Olympic gold, but I didn't make it in time to show him the gold medal.'

Usyk returned from London in 2012 with the gold medal. He stopped for a couple of days to get a new car. He called it a 'super' car. He wanted to show his father the gold and the 'super' car. 'I wanted to show him what a cool car I had,' he said. He was a boy trying to impress his hero, his dad.

'When I arrived, he was already lying in the coffin. I handed him the medal, put it in his dead hand and then left the room.' Silence, just the noise of Usyk suffering. And the rest of us trying to hold back the tears.

'Sometimes he comes to me the day before the fight. He comes and he smiles.' He then just looked up. Tears and suffering all over his face.

There was a break and then he laughed and said in English, in his brilliant pantomime voice and clenching his fists at the same time: 'Don't cry, you a man.' That broke the silence and every one of us could exhale. 'Men cry sometimes,' Krassyuk said.

A few minutes later, Usyk hugged us all and left. There was, I'm not going to lie, a fair bit of emotion still in that room.

'How did it go?' Charlsey, the producer asked from the airport.

'I think you will like it, son,' I told him.

In that suite, high above the city, sitting opposite Oleksandr Usyk, I shared for a moment, a minute, a second or two the paralysing grief that comes when you lose somebody you love. I imagine Usyk looks at that picture of his father a thousand times a day. He can sense his father's pride and he can feel him staring back at the boy. I know that feeling. Usyk's father had fights with other men when they laughed at suggestions that little Oleksandr, who was about 12 at the time, would win an Olympic medal. He seems to have done it a few times. Usyk really liked that. His father looked like he could handle himself. I told Usyk that and he liked that.

In February, just days before the first bell, Tyson Fury was cut in sparring and the fight was pushed back. 'I knew something would happen,' Usyk said. On the day the fight was postponed,

Usyk sparred ten rounds. It was just another day on boxing's frontline for him.

They fought in May 2024 and Usyk won. It was an unforgettable
night.

Part Three: 11 a.m. Mike Tyson in the hotel lobby

In the lobby, I sat and had a coffee and just tried to get my emotions in check. I was knackered and Usyk had made me cry.

I did ten minutes on BBC 5 Live to talk about Fury and that
knockdown. I went to leave, and Scott Welch called out my name.
Scott had been the British heavyweight champion and I had been
around him a lot over the years. He runs the gym in Hove that is on
the seafront, but below sea level. It is the gym the Eubank family
made famous.

Welch was sitting with Mike Tyson. The pair were just laughing
and talking rubbish. I knew they were close. It seemed like ancient
history, but I had once toured with Tyson, and Welch had been his
security. I think we did about six cities in ten days. It paid well, but
it was a disaster. I was not allowed to ask him about boxing – it was
just pigeons, Birmingham tumblers and Birmingham rollers. If he
talked about boxing, that was fine.

Both Tyson and Welch stood; we shook hands. I congratu-
lated Tyson on the work he had done in the gym with Ngannou.
Welch reminded me that he had told me Ngannou would shock
the world. I had to ask Tyson how a raw novice connected with
the punch and dropped the heavyweight champion of the world.
Tyson never told me, he showed me.

He moved closer. He was wearing the skimpiest shorts, his legs
as big as ever. His movement sharp, fast – he looked ready to go,
but his face is gentle now. He bent his knees; his eyes watched an
imaginary Fury punch miss and then he swivelled and let the left
hook go. He did it several times and it landed about a foot shy of

my chin. The punch finished at the same spot every time. It was uncanny and each time it landed, he dropped Fury. Each time he looked at Fury on the floor. This was a masterclass from a master. 'Francis is a great student,' said Tyson.

And that is how you end a fight day in Saudi. It was not even noon. And it's not a bad way to say goodbye.

THE LAST ROUND

You might need a break after 80 rounds on the road with me. It has been a global adventure to some of boxing's holiest and unholy places.

We have met the men and women from some of the greatest fights in boxing history. We have met the people from inside the sport: the good ones, the bad ones and the despots. We have met far too many dead people from the boxing business, and I apologise if there was too much death. This book covers 40 years and people die in and outside the ring.

Hopefully you have enjoyed the ride. Hopefully you have laughed, had to take a deep breath at some of the twists and enjoyed the savage, tragic and wonderful characters that make boxing the sport it is. They are not all pretty, but they are not all ugly.

I have taken you to cemeteries, intensive care units, palaces, tiny pubs, giant outdoor arenas, ancient gyms and sat you down next to me at the biggest fights in history. That is a privileged place and hopefully you have felt like a special pass has been placed around your neck.

I have always felt it is a privilege to be as close to the action as possible, the boxers and the insiders in the boxing world. Even if I dislike the fighter, I still have respect.

It's probably a bit late to say this now, but there is no hidden message in the sequence of the rings. I wanted to start with York Hall and finish with Mike Tyson in his skimpies throwing punches in Saudi Arabia. The rest, well, they just fell into place. And that is a bit like this book – it just happened.

This book started in a parked car one afternoon in early September 2022. My wife had just shuffled through the door at a cancer treatment clinic in East Sussex. I needed a few quid to send her to Düsseldorf for some more intensive treatment. I sat in that car and watched her close the door. I was about ten grand short. She needed me. I bloody needed her.

I pulled out the phone and typed a 2,000-word pitch about the Heavyweight Championship. I put myself ringside as often as possible. I was ringside for a lot of the fights, a witness to the highs and lows. It was a good pitch. I had sent it to my agent, Maggie Hanbury, by the time Jacqueline emerged three hours later. I had not left the car.

The pitch went out that week and people liked it. Then it was January, and I got a call from Maggie about a request to meet with Jonathan Taylor at Headline. It took a few days and then we met. He liked the pitch, but he said it felt rushed. He felt I could have done better. I told him why it felt rushed. 'I needed the money, and I needed it in a hurry.' He understood and then he suggested a few things. We sat for a couple of hours and this book was born there and then. It was 14 February 2023.

I got up to leave, we shook hands and then Jonathan asked: 'And how is your wife doing?'

'Not so good. She died on 7 December.'

She would have loved this book. I hope you did.

Thank you.

Acknowledgements

Now the important stuff.

Thanks to every editor and producer who ever sent me on the road to a fight or an interview. And those who said 'No'.

Thanks to every person who travelled with me. And those who refused; a good choice, probably.

All these stories appeared somewhere first: newspaper, radio, television, magazine, book, legal statement, podcast, a kitchen floor at 3 a.m., pulpit at a funeral, prison visit.

Somewhere, somebody was talking and fighting. It took thousands of voices to make this possible over a long, long time. Some are still talking, and many are dead. Thanks to all of them.

Thanks to the Fitzroy Lodge Amateur Boxing Club for their hospitality for the front cover photo shoot. It's a sacred place.

Index